MAKING NOTES
Music of the Carolinas

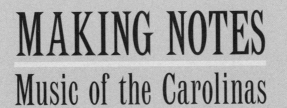

MAKING NOTES
Music of the Carolinas

EDITED BY ANN WICKER

NOVELLO Festival PRESS

CHARLOTTE, NORTH CAROLINA 2008

Making Notes: Music of the Carolinas
Edited by Ann Wicker
Novello Festival Press, Charlotte, North Carolina

Published in the United States by Novello Festival Press, Charlotte, North Carolina
ISBN 0-615-15969-9
ISBN 978-0-615-15969-0
Design and composition by Jacky Woolsey, Paper Moon Graphics, Inc.
Printed in Canada

Library of Congress Cataloging-in-Publication Data

Making notes : music of the Carolinas / edited by Ann Wicker.
     p. cm.
  Includes bibliographical references and index.
  ISBN 978-0-615-15969-0 (pbk.)
  1. Music—North Carolina—History and criticism. 2. Music—South
·Carolina—History and criticism. 3. Musicians—North Carolina. 4. Musicians—
South Carolina. 5. Musical groups—North Carolina. 6. Musical groups—South
Carolina. I. Wicker, Ann.
ML200.7.C3M35 2008
780.9756—dc22
                       2008002059

For my husband, Mark Williams

Contents

Introduction

For most of us, music enriches and permeates our lives. We hear it in our heads; we hear it in the elevator. We hear it in auditoriums; we hear it on street corners. We collect music on tape, vinyl, CDs and other electronic media. We collect musical experiences, hanging on to tickets and T-shirts long after the band has left the building.

In *Making Notes*, we have tried to tap into that collective cultural consciousness and pull out a few touchstones for North and South Carolina. And when it comes to cultural touchstones, few states can boast as many musical connections as the two Carolinas. It's a cliché, but could there be something in the water? A truly astounding number of musicians have called North or South Carolina home. The vision for this collection was to connect to a sincere passion for music and engage writers—both amateurs and pros—to write about music, songs, musicians and events that have genuinely moved them.

Some of the writers here are musicians themselves and some are more like me, fans. I grew up in a household where a radio was tuned to music most of the time and very early on had my own small record player and collection of 45s—some of which I still have. Like many people, I took piano lessons and guitar lessons and sang in choruses. I can probably still read music if pushed, but I think I knew I'd never really be a player. My life changed when I saw that *Ed Sullivan Show* with the four lads from Liverpool, and it changed again one night at the Sandwich Construction Company when I heard the Spongetones for the first time.

I've seen hundreds of other shows and concerts in venues large, medium and small—so many wonderful, memorable moments. Yes, I'm mostly a rock 'n' roll fan, but I think the meaning in any musical experience comes from what touches you in a certain song or piece of music, no matter the genre.

✳ ✳ ✳

Making Notes is divided into four parts. Section I, "Carolina Music Connections," offers a selection of pieces with strong North and South Carolina roots. Woody Mitchell takes us down that "Glory Road"—the highway many a musician will find familiar. Dr. Tom Hanchett explores another kind of glory at the United House of Prayer's Monday night shout band service. Jonathan Singer tells us about Concord native Marshall Sehorn, a pivotal figure in early R&B and rock. Writer Dan Huntley's "Gullah Gospel" shows how music can bring people together when the music speaks to them. John Jeter takes us backstage in his account of running a nightclub in Greenville, S.C. "Chevy Van" is Tommy Tomlinson's love letter of sorts to the song of the same name.

✳ ✳ ✳

Section II focuses on "The Entertainers"—a sampling of the lives of singers, players and leaders of the bands in jazz, rock, soul, bluegrass, country, punk, folk and more. Each and every person included here has been, and really still is, important to the continuing musical heritage of this region.

We begin with Frye Gaillard's wonderful look at the careers of Arthur Smith and Don Reno and the story behind "Duelin' Banjos." Other anchor pieces include Jerry Shinn's story on pianist Loonis McGlohon and his longtime partner in songwriting, Alec Wilder; and stories on Coltrane, Dizzy and Monk as well as Billy Taylor, a Greenville, N.C, native. Steve Crump connects all these jazz greats in "The Carolina Bebop Kings." Along the musical road through the Carolinas, stop and meet Doc Watson, Peg Leg Jackson, Charlie Daniels, Ben E. King, Etta Baker, Earl Scruggs, Hope Nicholls, Randy Travis, Shrimp City Slim, Sam Moss, Gina Stewart, Maurice Williams, Carlisle Floyd and others. Closing out this section, we focus on Manning, S.C,

resident Fred Wesley Jr. who served as James Brown's music director among the many other things he's done; a life-changing James Brown concert; and a profile of another famous James (Taylor).

✳ ✳ ✳

Section III rounds up "The Bands." The best bands in any genre are more than the sum of their parts. We'll see how Hootie and the Blowfish made their leap to the national spotlight in an excerpt from Michael Leon Miller's book about the band. Before basketball took over, Duke University and the University of North Carolina in Chapel Hill proved to be fertile ground for growing some of the biggest names during the "Big Band" era of the 1920s through the 1940s and beyond. Lynn Farris introduces the Carolina Chocolate Drops, and Baker Maultsby remembers The Accelerators, some of whom are still riding that "Dream Train." Courtney Devores profiles The Avett Brothers, who are working to conquer the musical world. Follow Steve Stoeckel onstage in his first-person account of playing at Charlotte's Double Door Inn with his longtime bandmates, the Spongetones. Grant Britt explains why Southern Culture on the Skids loves chicken and banana pudding. We'll also see how those musical ambassadors from North Carolina, the Red Clay Ramblers, fare on their adventures out west. This section closes with Don Dixon's memoir about the recordings R.E.M. made in Charlotte and Winston-Salem—music that changed the course of pop music in the 1980s.

✳ ✳ ✳

Which brings us to "The Experiences" shared in Section IV. Kevin Winchester's essay "Catching Smoke" is a wonderful, heartfelt look at the performing life. Bluesman Bob Margolin continues that story with his behind-the-scenes memoir of The Band's Last Waltz concert and the blues jam that followed. Lori Tate introduces Roger Burt, a Gaston County disc jockey and Big Band music historian. Folksinger-activist Si Kahn and Marjorie Hudson both write about the power of music and single songs. *New York Times* bestselling author Sharyn McCrumb takes us to the mountains of North Carolina to revisit an old murder case immortalized in a famous folk song. A visit to the Heavy Rebel Weekender in Winston-Salem shows the heart of a musical gathering that draws folks from all walks of life. Stop by the Hotel Charlotte and learn from Lew Herman about historic recordings made there. Fred Mills remembers Johnny Cash, The Man in Black, surprising the guests at a party that turns into a very special night of music. Rick Cornell explores how MerleFest keeps folks coming back year after year. Learn how the Charlotte Symphony Orchestra was born. Kent Priestley's visit to the Mount Airy Fiddler's Convention may get your toes tapping but you'll also need your waders.

Then head down to the Carolina shore with Rev. Billy C. Wirtz for an account of the early development of what we now call "beach music." Mark Kemp explores how the influence of Latino music is transforming Southern culture once again. David Childers' essay about the integration of a formerly all-white movie theater in Gaston County highlights the power of a shared musical experience that speaks to the hope that music of any genre can bring to us all.

*** *** ***

In the introduction to the *DaCapo Best Music Writing 2006*, guest editor Mary Gaitskill writes, "All day songs fly past; some get lost in traffic noise, some enter your imagination and take strange dream-shapes that get inside your thoughts and feelings and make them different."

Whether songs "fly past" or, as Kevin Winchester's grandmother would say, the melodies "come bubbling up," music comforts, hurts, teaches, teases and calls to us. And, as with anything genuine and passionate, we can't ignore that call.

—ANN WICKER, SPRING 2008

1

CAROLINA MUSIC CONNECTIONS

The Glory Road

BY WOODY MITCHELL

Of all life's mysteries that have crossed my screen so far, the most elusive has been this: Why was the one-legged man hopping across the tobacco field at gray dawn trying to bash the mad cello player with his artificial leg?

Maybe it's just one of those insidious pranks youth plays on the aging mind. Boomer angst takes on many forms as we wrestle to reconcile who we were then with who we are now. We fancied ourselves so clever, so bulletproof, so immune . . . only to find age laughing in our faces.

The '60s were shouting their last hurrah in the mid-'70s in parts of the Carolinas, but cowboy hats had replaced Nehru jackets as the uniform of the day. Journeyman rockers who refused to succumb to the Disco Virus took to the outlaw-music trail, infusing country roots into barroom rock and generating an under-the-radar culture that slips through the cracks when that era is chronicled.

In North Carolina, this ferment spawned a band called Loafer's Glory. Based in mountainous Yancey County, the band started as a weekend lark for musically inclined back-to-the-landers. Dick Webb (now known as Iron John), from the Tennessee Plateau, fronted, picked rhythm and sang lead vocals. John Dalbeck (guitar) and Pete Stevens (drums) migrated from the L.A. area, where they'd played together for years.

When they offered me a job in 1975, they'd been building their act for a year or more and had recently recruited Ron Cheek, a superb bassman from Boone. They were ready to take the band on the road and were looking for another lead guitarist to punch up the sound.

It was a no-brainer for me. The burning desire to master electric guitar had fueled my will to live during a year prowling the jungles in Vietnam. I wound up in San Francisco, playing in garage bands and occasionally cracking the bill at Fillmore West jam night. But as the psychedelic scene degenerated into cocaine, heroin and other destructive trends, I bailed for Carolina, looking for the roots I'd glossed over in my cosmic fervor.

Joining the Loafers was like getting picked up hitchhiking in the Mojave Desert by a vanload of hippies with a full cooler. Their ragtag, hell-bent delivery appealed to me, and they were a goodhearted bunch. Plus, they introduced me to western swing, throwing some jazzy seasoning into the country-rock stew.

Music was the lifeline that kept me off the dark path so many of my fellow vets wandered down, and road life provided the adrenalized postwar lifestyle I craved—a warrior in a less deadly sort of war. I unleashed my country inner beast and signed on for the extended trip that led to that morning in the tobacco field out in the sticks of eastern North Carolina.

As we developed a twangy twin-guitar attack, a sound began to jell—the blend of Bob Wills, Willie & Waylon, Jerry Jeff shit-kickers, good ol' "Rocky Top" and a growing body of originals generated a following who showed up expecting an experience. No stars or virtuosos, just five guys driving one mind and having a real good time at it. Wherever we landed, it was party time.

Younger musicians often give me the fish-eye when I regale them with tales of a time when you were surprised if the house wasn't packed, when people showed up early to get a good table and were still hollering for more at last call. Some urgency was afoot in the zeitgeist then. Live music was more than an entertainment option—it was a community experience, like a Dionysian town hall meeting in a pagan church.

Along with SuperGrit, Laryat Sam, Tumbleweeds, Sutter's Gold Streak and other Carolina bands, we developed a circuit from D.C. to Atlanta, East Tennessee to the Outer Banks, traveling in an old church bus we gutted to install bunks, Greyhound seats and a card table. We left the CHRIST IS THE ANSWER sticker on it as protective camouflage.

And man, did we need it. That old rustbucket was a rolling bust. We warded off road anomie with herbs we grew and plenty of beer. The need for rest stops was alleviated by cracking the bus door and peeing out the slipstream, and we could change drivers in-flight—one guy climbs over the aluminum rail and slips into the driver's seat while the other guy slides out past the gearshift, holding the wheel steady and keeping the pedal to the metal until the new driver's ensconced. Gotta keep truckin' on.

But we were no longer footloose young men. The median age was pushing thirty, and we had families, keeping up homesteads in the mountains. Several of us heated and cooked with wood, so an inordinate proportion of our home-time was spent with a chain saw, ax and go-devil.

We thought we'd arrived when we hit the fifty-dollar-a-man-per-night pay level (never dreaming that in 2007, fifty dollars would still be the wage floor for many bar gigs). The Loafers' mojo felt so strong that prosperity seemed all but inevitable—the muse willing. But in the meantime, we had to make ends meet.

Isolated in a rural setting, we didn't have a hometown where we could hunker down and do local gigs for a week or two—Asheville was the nearest city, forty miles away, and at the time, it had no clubs that welcomed our kind of music. We had to get creative about augmenting our income.

Now and then, we'd wire up an old tobacco barn on Jack's Creek and throw a barn dance that lasted all night—five bucks a head, no hassles, no law, just a good throwdown, then roll out your sleeping bag and bunk in the barn.

About this time we hooked up with audio maven Mark Williams and recorded our only album, *Hotel Carolina*, amid dense clouds of smoke and stacks of beer cans. Thanks to Mark, it came out pretty well, so we had product. But our backer insisted we release it on eight-track cartridge tape, rather than the emerging cassette technology. Our run of 200 sold at a trickle, and we used the proceeds to print up some T-shirts. But it still wasn't nearly enough to shore up our revenue shortfall. After two years on the road, we were barely breaking even, and some of us were under domestic pressure to bring home a little more bacon.

Making a living at any art is cruel, and electric music may be the worst due to the travel. All that time away from home in unsavory environments runs up costs that don't come due till years later. As an artist, you never quite feel alive unless you're playing. But if you're not the artist—a spouse, or a child—that may not mean much. Unless, of course, the artist is bringing in six figures.

We weren't, and a lot of money went into keeping the bus roadworthy. Once when we had it in the shop, our mechanic's daddy pulled out a jug of liquor about the color of Cuervo Gold and had us taste it. He wondered if, in our travels, we might know anybody who'd be interested in such traditional mountain products.

He fixed us up with twenty one-gallon jugs, which we stashed under the bus bunks, charging us ten bucks a jug. We passed it on for twenty. Only much later did we realize that if anything had gone awry, we were looking at a federal rap. It's crazy what folks will do with the wolf breathing down their necks.

Folks think of moonshine as liquor, but in reality it's far beyond that. Firewater is what it is, burning open crazed recesses in the brain to unleash a howling storm. With exceptions, it's a guy thing . . . few women are inclined to burn their guts out while turning into a wild beast, and many hate it for doing that to their men. But there it was, under the bunks, and we were rolling down the road.

It was a devilishly smooth concoction, smooth and cool as 120-proof blends go, almost too easy to glug down. We nicknamed it the Amber Current, after the line in the Willie Nelson song "Whiskey River." Folks liked it and it kept us in running money so we could take our pay home.

It worked so well, we restocked before our next three-week trip. Typically, if we were traveling far afield, we'd book the weekends at places we were established, try to grab a new venue on a weeknight or two along the way, and barnstorm between stops on off-nights. Quite a few times we'd walk into a joint cold, ask them if they wanted a band that night for tips and free beer—if they did, we'd set up and play. That way, we could afford a motel room and everybody could get a shower . . . one of the road's tender mercies.

The second Amber Current run culminated in Greenville, N.C., where we played a double bill with a band called Plank Road. Their manic bassman actually played a cello, strapped over his shoulder like a giant *guitarrón*. We hit it off with those guys, and the one-legged man seemed to just sort of materialize backstage. An affable guy in a planter's hat, he invited both bands to party after the gig out at his place, deep in the grid of Pitt County farm roads.

After buying up all the Amber Current we had left, he opened his big old farmhouse to us for an all-hands jam. Moonshine-stoked, we raved on for two or three hours, the crazed cello player thumping himself into a lather, his Greenwich Village cabbie cap flopping like Jell-O, and I don't recall a cross word. Eventually, deep night descended on me and I went out to crash on the bus.

Probably not much over an hour later, I'm hearing this ruckus, cuss-fighting . . . cracking my inflamed eyes through a blinding hangover out the bus window, thinking this bizarre chase can't possibly be happening . . . the one-legged man hopping like a madman, brandishing his prosthetic leg, actually gaining on the cello player, who's stumbling over every tobacco row with his ungainly instrument strapped to his back. Curiously, both still had their headgear on. Obviously some sort of flashback, I figured, much more than I could process right then, so I collapsed back into stupor.

Afterward, half-awake and mobilizing for travel, I asked Iron John if that had really happened, and he said yes. Why, I asked? He looked at me flatly in stark morning daylight and said, "Cause he pissed 'im off."

I suspect the Amber Current was a factor. But that vivid flash has haunted my memory as the mile-marker where our freewheeling way of life began to Go Wrong. Iron John was the first to leave, and we recruited my old pal John Wicker to take his spot, keeping the band alive for another year. But the Glory Road was petering out, a victim of changing times.

At this point, it's evident that the counterculture died of self-inflicted wounds. The world didn't change as expected, and everybody was scrambling to catch up with real life, which was leaving us and our families in the dust.

Nowadays, at this balancing-the-books point in life, I'm looking back and wondering what we have to show for the costs we incurred. The lore, of course—enough tales to keep the old-folks home entertained even if we live to see eighty. Some firm friendships that have lasted through the years. Stage savvy that enabled us to make extra dough playing after being forced to pursue other occupations.

And, oh yeah, the music. Around 2002, Mark conjured up an eight-track copy of *Hotel Carolina* and jacklegged some gear to miraculously produce a digital remaster we re-released on CD, with sales skyrocketing into the dozens (mostly to friends, old fans and family).

We celebrated with a reunion mini-tour, rehearsing a week in the mountains for three appearances in Asheville and Charlotte. We still had the mojo, and, as was our legacy, we nearly broke even on the venture.

But the real payoff was realizing that magic never dies—it's just a lot more work to conjure up. As experiences oxidize into memories, a hazy glow suffuses them: it's hard to tell where the bounds of reality stop and start. Resurrecting the band after twenty-five years for that brief glimmer affirmed that the Glory Road, in a world that no longer exists, was as real as the one-legged man and the cello player.

~~~

God's Trombones: The Shout Band Tradition in the United House of Prayer For All People

BY TOM HANCHETT

Praise Him with trumpet sound; . . . praise him with timbrel and dance; praise him with sounding cymbals; . . . . Praise the Lord!
—PSALM 150

It's eight o'clock on a Monday night, at the Mother House of the United House of Prayer for All People in Charlotte, N.C. Opening devotions are already going on as musicians drift in, setting up drums and unpacking trombones. Several church elders in their fifties and sixties, dressed in dark suits, take turns at the microphone. As they exhort the crowd, half a dozen young players, most in their teens and early twenties, arrange themselves at the front of the room in a rough semicircle around the drummer.

At the mike now, a teenaged junior elder, dressed in a sharp, gray, single-breasted suit, takes charge. Two keyboard players echo the ends of his phrases as he drives home his message. "Let us give thanks for this gathering! Let this worship keep our young people away from drugs, away from the street!"

As he speaks, the drummer comes in under his words, setting up an insistent rhythm. As the last syllables ring out, the band leader rears back an opening note, his slide reaching for the ceiling. With a mighty chord, the massed trombones swing into action. The Monday night shout band service at the United House of Prayer is underway.

* * *

. . . my house shall be called a house of prayer for all peoples. Thus says the Lord God, who gathers the outcasts . . . .
—ISAIAH 56:8

Hear it once, and your soul will never forget shout band music. It's a tradition found only in the United House of Prayer for All People, an African-American urban Pentecostal denomination concentrated in the southeastern U.S. The massed trombones, anchored by drums, a sousaphone and often a baritone horn, create a high-energy driving sound that is very different from New Orleans jazz, perhaps its closest cousin. Roots of shout band music stretch back to Africa, with important input from the gospel quartet singing of the mid-twentieth century, all passed down person-to-person without written notes. Shout bands seldom perform outside the House of Prayer, but rather use their music as an integral part of church services, improvising on the spot to catch the emotions of the congregation and bring listeners into the Spirit.

To explore the shout band tradition, perhaps the best place to begin is with the Pentecostal Holiness movement, a powerful religious force starting in the early years of the twentieth century. In 1906, at an inter-racial revival on Azuza Street in Los Angeles, worshippers began speaking in tongues and moving uncontrollably as they felt possessed by the spirit of God. This emotion-charged form of worship swept the nation, catching on especially with African Americans. It recalled spiritual practices brought over from Africa during slavery times, especially the "ring shout."

The United House of Prayer for All People grew out of the Pentecostal Holiness movement during the 1910s and 1920s, led by a charismatic evangelist named Charles Manuel "Sweet Daddy" Grace. Born in the Cape Verde Islands off the coast of Africa, he immigrated to New England, then traveled nationwide spreading his message. On June 26, 1926, Grace launched a revival meeting in a tent pitched on a vacant lot in Charlotte's black Second Ward neighborhood. The revival stretched on for the entire summer. Newspapers estimated that on some of the hot summer evenings "in excess of 20,000 persons . . . not only completely filled every available inch of space on the lot at Third and Caldwell streets, but overflowed into nearby streets and alleys."

Daddy Grace eventually planted his church's headquarters in Washington, D.C., but Charlotte remains the second most active center of the denomination.

Over a dozen Houses are peppered throughout the metro area, and the large complex on Beatties Ford Road serves as the Mother House for all of North Carolina. For its congregants, the United House of Prayer offers activities to fill all waking hours outside of work. For young men in the United House of Prayer, a most exciting form of involvement is the shout band.

✳ ✳ ✳

With trumpets and the sound of the horn make a joyful noise before the King, the Lord!
— PSALM 98

No one seems to know when the trombone shout band tradition began. Instrumental music is a hallmark of Pentecostal Holiness churches, and photos of House of Prayer baptisms in the 1920s show brass bands, but featuring a full range of instruments rather than massed trombones. Brass band music was popular throughout America, among both blacks and whites, in the decades around 1900—the era of the great brass band composer John Philip Sousa. The House of Prayer's unique contribution to that music seems to have evolved around the 1940s. One story suggests that the music started in Houses in the vicinity of Newport News, Virginia. Another says that Daddy Grace's sister originated the style. In any case, the fact that Bishop Grace and his core followers moved from Mother House to Mother House each fall, conducting annual Convocations, quickly spread the new sound. By Daddy Grace's death in 1960, trombone shout bands had become a signature of the United House of Prayer for All People.

The structure of shout band music backs up the claim that it dates from the 1940s—and that structure also marks it as quite distinct from New Orleans Dixieland jazz. In the New Orleans tradition, the instruments join together to play the melody once through, then repeat the basic chord structure while each instrument takes a turn improvising a solo on top of the chords, and finally all come together for a last playing of the melody. A shout band song is structured more like the gospel quartet singing of the 1940s and 1950s. First the band plays the melody, supported by chords in quartet-like four-part harmony. This may be repeated several times with changes in ornamentation. Then the players shift into what quartet singers sometimes call "the drive," a short rhythmic figure that is repeated again and again as the lead singer improvises exhortations. Shout band players call this repeated pattern "back-timing." Over the back-timing, two trombonists called "Run men" improvise call-and-response cries. Once the peak is passed, the band may return to the original melody or move seamlessly into another song.

Young men (and a very few young women) enter the shout band tradition early, often as soon as they can hold an instrument. Cedric Mangum, past leader of Charlotte's Clouds of Heaven band, tells of making his own trombone from a funnel and a length of garden hose when he was less than six. Young players learn from the oldest members of the band, typically in their twenties, or from a "professor" who may offer instruction to several bands. The newest players simply blow the root note of each chord, something that changes seldom during a song. As they become more adept, they move up to playing harmony notes, and may eventually become run men.

The heart of the shout band sound is the emotional power of the slide trombone, with its ability to sing or preach almost like the human voice. "You can hear somebody, when he's playing his trombone, he's trying to sing what he's trying to play," said shout band player Tim Brown in a 1989 interview. "[You've] you heard me lead a song by myself, 'We're Not Ashamed of the Gospel of Jesus Christ'" (sings first line) "... I played it on trombone just like somebody singing it" (hums line, using identical phrasing). "You're trying to make the melody part really touch somebody."

In a United House of Prayer church service, music forms an integral part of the worship in a way that seems extraordinary to listeners raised outside of the Holiness movement. During a three-hour service the band plays almost constantly, never stopping to announce a new piece. At first hearing the music seems less to be discrete tunes than an ever-changing kaleidoscope of musical patterns.

The shout band leader takes the responsibility for assembling the "collage" of segments in performance. "It really takes the leader to know," according to Brown. "Let's say it's a full house, a packed house. It's a big program. Somebody says something about their, umm, their child was sick and they prayed and the child felt better. And a lot of people start speaking in tongues, feeling good, wanting to shout. O.K., now you start off with a song. . . . Nobody starts off with a drive; you always start off with a song."

Sometimes the song alone will reach the audience, but usually it just begins to warm them up. "But you play 'em the shout—all of a sudden you go into that back-timing . . . and pull in those . . . Run men playing that drive—and you clean the house! Everybody's shouting!"

Scholars who study the roots of African-American music point to themes that date back to Africa itself. One is music that tends not to be so much "composed" as "collaged," made up on the spot out of phrases that members of the community know or improvise. Another is the call-and-response pattern, as one member sings or plays a phrase and is answered by other members. Yet another African practice is that music is not set apart, but is "socially integrated" into every sort of event. Song, speech and movement are viewed as interchangeable expressive elements. The instruments most highly prized are those that have the capacity for speech-like communication, and the music must possess a propulsive rhythmic drive. There is little distinction between performer and audience; rather, all are involved in the "co-creation" of an event. Africans who came to the United States as slaves in chains could not bring musical instruments. But they carried these ideas with them and melded them with the new sounds they found in America, creating some of the world's most vibrant music.

✳ ✳ ✳

Clap your hands, all you peoples; shout to God with loud songs of joy . . .
— PSALM 47

The Monday night service begins about 8 P.M. with a half hour of prayer and song. Accompanied by two musicians at electronic keyboards, elders trade places praying and singing at the microphone as the Spirit moves them. The audience adds its part, with amens and comments at the ends of phrases, and particularly inspired members may rush forward for a turn at the microphone. The congregation on this night is fairly small, perhaps fifty or sixty people ranging from adults dressed in suits to teens in sweat suits to grandmothers clad in work clothes. All, except for two white visitors, are black. Some members listen closely, some talk and move about, tuning in only when the proceedings become most emotional. The casual atmosphere makes all feel welcome, encouraging everyone to make the evening service part of their life, no matter what their level of commitment.

Around 8:30 the shout band begins to play. No grandly-robed pastor stands at the front of the room, no printed program outlines the order of worship. Instead, one of the keyboard players walks to the microphone and takes charge as the evening's leading speaker. At around 9 P.M., the band halts while two collections are taken. A second halt comes around 9:30 P.M., as a half dozen "Pentecostal Singers" in their early twenties rise to sing a series of well-rehearsed gospel songs with keyboard accompaniment. Sometime after 10 P.M., three youthful first-time preachers get their chance to try four-minute sermons on the crowd. Soon, though, the band is back. More and more church members spring up, shaking uncontrollably, speaking in tongues, or dancing hypnotically in the aisles and at the front of the room.

Toward 11 P.M., after the leader anoints the foreheads of those who desire it with holy oil, the crowd melts away. Nearly everyone in attendance has spent time in front of the congregation, singing or testifying or simply possessed by the Spirit. The shout band packs up its instruments, tired but glowing from work well done. With their music, the players have helped the worshippers tonight make contact with God.

✳ ✳ ✳

God has gone up with a shout, the Lord has gone up with the sound of trumpets.
— PSALM 47

Helping focus listeners on God, so as to invite visitation by the Spirit, is the guiding purpose of the shout band tradition in the United House of Prayer. This purpose informs every aspect of the band's sound, from the employment of trombones, to the use of harmony and driving rhythm, to the way that music is put together on the spot to catch the congregation's emotions. "It all means one thing," says Clouds of Heaven leader Cedric Mangum. "They're all playing giving God's praise."

～～～

Why Marshall Sehorn Matters

BY JONATHAN SINGER

If Marshall Sehorn remains largely unknown in North Carolina's musical history, it is only because he was destined for a greater ministry: to carry the music of New Orleans to the world.

Without this self-described wheeler-dealer from Concord, the world would never know the joy of hearing the effervescent half-pint, ex-boxer, body-and-fender man Lee Dorsey moaning plaintively, "Lord, I'm so tired. How long can this go on?" in "Working in the Coal Mine." Without Sehorn, his partner Allen Toussaint, and Dorsey's "Yes We Can," the Pointer Sisters would have remained bereft of their debut hit; Robbie Robertson would have been left without the inspiration to write "Life is a Carnival."

Absent Sehorn, the canon of American music would be far less rich without Allen Toussaint's sublime "Southern Nights"; Dr. John's greasy maneuvers; and the Wild Tchoupitoulas—something close to what one might have heard in nineteenth century's Congo Square. Without Sehorn, the world might never have glimpsed the legendary Professor Longhair in Stevenson Palfi's film, *Piano Players Rarely Ever Play Together,* or been *voulez-voused* to death by Patti LaBelle and "Lady Marmalade." Both were filmed and recorded, respectively, at Sehorn and Toussaint's SeaSaint Studio in New Orleans.

Without Sehorn, there's a pretty good chance you wouldn't be so familiar with the Ur-funk rhythm section, the Meters, or New Orleans' "first family of funk," the Neville Brothers.

Had Sehorn not been the only white patron inside Charlotte's Excelsior Club on Beatties Ford Road, listening to Wilbert Harrison one night in 1958, North Carolinians would have one less claim to rock 'n' roll fame.

✳ ✳ ✳

Sehorn was born in Concord in June 1934. A childhood bout with pneumonia and the remedy—a drug too harsh for a young child—burned away half his lungs. The grueling surgeries that saved his life left him with lifelong respiratory problems. But the many trips down to Charlotte's doctors also drew him closer to his father. As a boy, Sehorn accompanied his father to weekend livestock auctions, where he soaked up the patter between skeptical buyer and savvy seller, learning how to read people.

This horse-trader wisdom helped him distinguish between the gentlemen and the con men—and strike favorable deals with both for the rest of his life.

By the time he graduated from Winecoff High School in 1953, he was already caught up in music and the business of music. He played in bands while attending N.C. State. But after graduation he pondered his future. He wasn't a good enough guitarist to pursue a musician's career. Still, he felt there had to be something he could do to make a living with the music he loved.

He made a futile trip to New York, "Just waitin' for somebody to tell me what to do," he told writer Jeff Hannusch. A kindly label executive pointed him home to look for a job in radio. He returned to North Carolina but found little opportunity. He was more savvy for his next foray to Miami for a radio convention.

He passed himself off as a DJ, winning the attention of Bobby Robinson, a black independent label owner from New York. Robinson casually extended an invitation for Sehorn to look him up next time he was in New York. The following week, Sehorn walked into Robinson's Harlem record shop. For fifty dollars a week, and a fifty-dollar expense allowance, Sehorn, twenty-four, became Robinson's promotion man/talent scout. Driving through the South with a car trunk full of Fire and Fury label releases, Sehorn hyped the latest by Tarheel Slim, Elmore James and Lightnin' Hopkins, hoping to get airplay.

During his first trip home in 1958, he heard local singer and pianist Wilbert Harrison singing "Kansas City" at Charlotte's Excelsior Club. From the club's pay phone, he dialed Robinson in New York. "I swear I got a hit record," he yelled over the Excelsior's din.

Sehorn took Harrison to New York, cut "Kansas City" at the tail end of a gospel session and came out with a huge hit. Later that same year, in a promotional swing through New Orleans, he heard a record called "Lottie Mo." Convinced it was Ray Charles playing piano and singing under a pseudonym, he brought the record back to Robinson in New York. After a little detective work, they discovered the singer was Lee Dorsey, and the pianist was twenty-two-year-old Allen Toussaint.

Sehorn and Robinson enlisted Toussaint to play behind Dorsey on a rough demo tape of a hastily composed tune. New Orleans studio musicians then replicated Toussaint's jaunty piano in recording the Fury label's first release by Dorsey, "Ya Ya."

An Army hitch for Toussaint in '63 prevented Sehorn from recording a follow-up to the million-selling "Ya Ya." But as soon as Toussaint was mustered out two years later, Sehorn was on his doorstep with a plan to record Dorsey. He took Toussaint's "Ride Your Pony" to New York, cut a deal with Amy Records, and saw Dorsey's record explode on the pop charts.

During Dorsey's engagement at the Apollo, Sehorn invited Toussaint to New York to back up Dorsey on stage. Toussaint accepted and while there, he and Sehorn sealed their partnership with a handshake.

They were an odd looking pair: Toussaint—soft-spoken, tall, thin, impeccably dressed, looking for all the world like he was descended from a long line of African kings. And Sehorn—a loud-talking, full-bearded combination of Ronnie Hawkins, Al Hirt and Wolfman Jack. Gladys Knight described him simply as "the biggest white man I ever saw."

"[Sehorn] had a nose for talent," said Cosimo Matassa, the dean of rock 'n' roll recording engineers.

Matassa also cited Sehorn's ability to put an artist at ease. His good humor seemed to relax even the flightiest artist. Sehorn also "spoke both languages"—Matassa's euphemism for someone comfortable in both black and white cultures. Sehorn periodically faced criticism for partnering with a black man, though he waved away such prejudice.

For the ease with which he operated in both cultures, Sehorn also took a severe beating in 1968. In August, at a National Association of Television and Radio Announcers convention in Miami, a radical group of blacks within the music business felt it was high time that blacks received a greater share of music business profits. At the convention, just months after Dr. Martin Luther King had been assassinated, tensions and angry rhetoric ran high.

As Sehorn stepped out of his hotel shower, he caught a glimpse of the rest of his room and realized someone had slipped in—and his holstered pistol, which had been draped over a chair, was gone. Sehorn tried to appear unruffled, calling out, "Can I help you fellas with something?"

The four thugs waiting for Sehorn didn't care that he had worked for two black-owned record labels or that he had marched at Selma with Dr. King. He was pistol-whipped, stomped and left unconscious on the floor. He came to in a hospital bed.

✳ ✳ ✳

Sehorn was tenacious when he believed that something—a song, an artist—deserved to see the light of day. Like "Working in the Coal Mine."

"That song wouldn't be on the planet if it wasn't for Marshall," declared Toussaint. The song had lost the groove halfway through the session and Toussaint moved on to the next tune. But Sehorn, under deadline to get the master to New York, commandeered the control room with Matassa, had him copy as much as they had, then spliced the identical pieces of tape together. "Marshall took wishbones and feathers and made a whole chicken out of it," Toussaint laughed.

When Sehorn and Toussaint opened SeaSaint Studio in 1973, artists began flying into New Orleans: Frankie Miller, King Biscuit Boy, Robert Palmer, John Mayall, Elvis Costello, Paul McCartney, Patti LaBelle, Albert King. Sehorn shrewdly negotiated deals with major labels to not only record their artists at SeaSaint, but also to guarantee that their artists would record songs written by Toussaint.

Like the 1950s, when New Orleans flowered as a recording center, artists recording at SeaSaint once again cast the Crescent City sound to the rest of the world. Sehorn dreamed big. But his dream was focused on one solitary individual: Allen Toussaint. It was Sehorn's contention that those who profited from Toussaint's talents before him had purposely constrained Toussaint's growth as an artist—until Toussaint himself considered such a role beyond his abilities. In fact, for most of their partnership, Toussaint avoided the spotlight. But starting in 1975, when Toussaint released his classic solo album, *Southern Nights,* Sehorn nudged his partner center stage while demanding that the music business change its perception of the songwriter/producer. Today, Toussaint is known less as a producer and more as a performing artist.

***

Production at SeaSaint slowed in the 1980s as other recording studios were established in New Orleans, forcing Sehorn to meet studio overhead by licensing old masters. The respiratory problems that began when he was a child continued to wear him down. Hospital stays to keep him breathing became more frequent. He eventually underwent an emergency laryngotomy leaving him confined to his home under the care of his wife, Barbara, a nurse.

When Katrina struck, Sehorn was moved safely to a hospital in Baton Rouge. He stayed there a few weeks, then moved back home—miraculously, his Lakeview house was unscathed. After Katrina, Sehorn made a few trips back to Concord for the holidays, always returning to New Orleans with a package of contraband from his favorite restaurant, Troutman's Barbecue. Old friends who saw him in the hospital in 2006 said it looked like all the "fight" in him had gone. On December 6, 2006, Sehorn died.

SeaSaint Studio was one of Katrina's casualties. The hurricane destroyed the studio that Marshall Sehorn built. But his partner of nearly forty years was standing strong at Sehorn's memorial service in Concord on December 30, 2006. Speaking warmly before a church packed with friends and relatives, Toussaint said, "I'm very glad that God gave us the opportunity to have crossed paths—not just to pass like ships in the night but to stop and spend a whole hunk of life together. The best part of my life was spent with Marshall . . . I loved him then, I love him now . . . whatever he gave is still here and will live here for people who never even met him."

Gullah Gospel:
Preserving Spirituals of Another Race, Time

BY DAN HUNTLEY

Eighty-five-year-old Tigger Smythe doesn't need a hymnal to sing praise to her Lord.

Nearly blind, she closes her eyes and the words gently come:

Oh Norah, hice duh winduh, Norah
Hice duh winduh let the duh dub come een.

The spiritual, sung in *Gullah,* is about Noah waiting by the ark's window for a turtledove to return after the flood.

Smythe is part of an all-white group that for nearly a century has sung these songs in black dialect and is dedicated to preserving this slice of musical Americana. Beneath a moss-draped live oak in her formal garden, Smythe's high, airish voice is joined a capella by her son David's barroom baritone. Their Gullah lullaby is linked to the Carolina Lowcountry as surely as sweet grass and the pluff mud of Charleston harbor.

Smythe's father-in-law, husband and now her son have been presidents of the Society for the Preservation of Spirituals. The society, which made a series of historic Gullah recordings in the 1930s, has started to shift focus by discontinuing public concerts and getting more of the music to the public by producing two CDs and a book.

The changes were prompted, according to society vice-president Tommy Thornhill, by a renewed interest within the black community in singing the old-style spirituals. "We decided as a group that we weren't going to 'compete' with blacks singing their own music. The music has always belonged to them; it's not ours. We were simply the caretakers," said Thornhill, who joined the group in 1957. "One of our goals all along has been to keep it alive long enough to return the music from whence it came."

THE FIRST TIME

Tigger Smythe was born in Britain, raised in Bermuda and married in Charleston, S.C.

It was here she first heard Gullah, a Creole language spoken by some slave descendants along the Atlantic Seaboard.

"It was like nothing I'd ever heard," she said. "The song is about the flood, but it's also one of hope."

The society was founded in 1922 by twenty-two Charlestonians. The group, part of the Charleston Renaissance movement of the 1920s, came together through its members' love of the spirituals they had learned as children from their black maids and their parents. The private group functions more like an aristocratic book club than a community chorus—members socialize over cocktails in a nineteenth-century home near the Battery before practice; most can trace their lineage to a founding member of the society.

The spirituals were not printed in hymnals but existed mostly in the former slaves' collective memory. The spirituals were often sung without musical accompaniment, such as pianos or organs, because the congregations could not afford such luxuries. Singers kept the beat with hand clapping and foot stomping. The same song often changed tempo and sometimes, even the lyrics, depending on the lead singer.

In the 1920s, the society began performing. The performances, which benefitted Lowcountry African-American charities, were so well received that the singers took their act on the road and performed at the White House for President Franklin Roosevelt and at Harvard College.

One of their members, Dubose Heyward, penned the Charleston-based novel *Porgy*. Composer George Gershwin later came to Charleston, where Heyward brought him to a society rehearsal and then to hear black congregations. Gershwin later wrote the folk opera *Porgy and Bess*, which gave birth to classic songs such as "Summertime (and the livin' is easy)."

But perhaps the most important accomplishment of this group came in the mid-'30s when members real-ized the purity of these original spirituals was being influenced by jazz, blues and gospel. They decided to capture the authentic spirituals by using cutting-edge technology, at the time, that enabled them to record in rural churches without electricity.

They bought the iPod of their day—a recorder that used a metal lathe device to cut songs onto aluminum discs. They powered the contraption with a Model T by removing a tire to run a belt to a generator that powered an amplifier and recorder.

Harry Hughes helped in the recordings as a boy. In 1982, he described the sessions to society members: "The equipment we're talking about was portable like a casket. Six good men could move it."

The recordings caught the attention of folklorist John Lomax, who had made similar field recordings with blues legends such as Leadbelly. As curator of the Library of Congress' Archive of American Folk Songs, Lomax asked the society to donate its discs and eventually got more than fifty.

Linda Kershaw heads the S.C. Spirituals Project and directs the Concert Choir at Benedict College in Columbia. She has extensively studied the origins of spirituals among slaves who worked Lowcountry rice plantations.

As an African American, Kershaw understands how some people could be resentful of an all-white group performing black songs—citing numerous instances in which music originated by blacks was later commercialized by whites.

But she says it's different with the society.

"What spirituals represent is a tragic part of our nation's past," she said. "But you can't really hold this group to that same standard. They never profited from this music. They simply fell in love with it and have spent a lifetime celebrating it. They recorded this music in the 1920s and '30s when no one else was. And for that, they should be applauded, not criticized."

On a quiet weeknight in early September 2005, about thirty society members—mostly descendants of original members—gathered in the parlor of the Smythe home. It was a rehearsal and a song sheet was distributed, but no one bothered to read the words.

Some members close their eyes when singing; others leap to their feet in exaltation.

"The songs can not be ignored; they wash over you and take you to another place," said Edward Hart, society member and associate professor of music theory/composition at the College of Charleston. "You can feel the African rhythms—the purity and simplicity of the music is almost overpowering."

From the sidewalk on LeGare (pronounced *LeGree*) Street, it sounded like an old-time African-American church singing.

The repertoire bridged a waterfront of emotions—from slow, plaintive contemplations on death, *"En I'll meet chu een duh Primus Land,"* to work dirges, *"Draw lebel, de ainjel am comin' down,"* to righteous celebration, *"Who yuh got een Heben? Lawd, I cyan stan' still."*

Society members are the first to admit they are amateurs.

"We argue all the time about pronunciations. It would be impossible to re-create that original sound," said David Smythe.

The society rarely sings publicly anymore, and even then, it's usually at small gatherings. However, concerts in 2005 saw the society perform for larger black and white audiences, steps perhaps toward the goal of returning the music "to the source from whence it came."

"We recognize the historical legacy that these songs represent," said Park Dougherty, chair of the Society's recording committee. "These spirituals are part of the collective history of both blacks and whites."

At one of those 2005 performances, more than a dozen African Americans attended. Joyce Coakley of Mount Pleasant, S.C., was surprised by the authenticity of the music.

"This is the music I grew up with," she said. "I congratulate them for doing what they have. You could feel it tonight in this room: These spirituals are anything but dead."

~~~

MORE ON GULLAH

Gullah is the name given to the 250,000 descendants of former slaves who live mostly among the sea islands between Wilmington, N.C., and Jacksonville, Florida.

Gullah and *Geechee* are interchangeable terms. Gullah (believed to be derived from Angola where many slaves originated) is the name used in the Carolinas; Geechee is used in Georgia and Florida.

An estimated 80 percent of all African slaves brought to the U.S. first stepped ashore in America at Sullivan's Island near Charleston.

Several books and films have focused on the Gullah-Geechee experience. The documentary *The Language You Cry In* explores the African origins of the Gullah-Geechee.

Many African words have been passed on from Gullah (a Creole language begun in the 1600s) to English, such as cooter (tortoise), goober (peanut), gumbo (okra), juke (as in jukebox) and voodoo (witchcraft).

Gullah speakers often simplify English words and constructions, speak rapidly with no Southern drawl and use an intonation unlike that of English.

Representative sentences in Gullah are: *Dey fa go shum* ("They went to see her," literally "They take go see her"); *Shishuh tall pass una* ("Sister is taller than you"); and *Uma-chil' nyamnyam fufu an t'ree roll-roun', but 'e ain't been satify* ("The girl ate mush and three biscuits, but she wasn't satisfied").

— DAN HUNTLEY

A Club Foot in the Door: Diary of a Mad Promoter

BY JOHN JETER

The e-mail signature lines of too many concert-industry people bear the following quote, attributed to Hunter S. Thompson: "The music business is a cruel and shallow money trench, a long plastic hallway where thieves and pimps run free, and good men die like dogs. There's also a negative side." Hardly a role model but hardly (or hardly wholly) inaccurate, Thompson sounds like many a bands' road manager or tour manager, cranky as all get out after a nine-hour ride on a bus stuffed with eight other malodorous gentlemen of dubious habits calling themselves artists, crew members—a band—stumbling into your live-music venue to perform for the evening.

Welcome to the world of show business, in clubland.

Why would anybody subject himself, herself, oneself or any friends or relatives to the Thompsonian vagaries of such a business as running a concert-promotions business, a nightclub?

Since 1994, The Handlebar in Greenville, S.C., has promoted more than two thousand concerts, hosting some three dozen Grammy Award winners, countless Grammy nominees and at least a half-dozen Rock and Roll Hall of Fame inductees. Performers have included legends such as Joan Baez and Leon Russell, legends-in-the-making like John Mayer and South Carolina icon Edwin McCain, plus Woodstock performers Richie Havens and David Sanborn and even *American Idol* finalist Chris Sligh.

A dozen years is a long time to be in the club business. Most promoters have the reputation of being shady types who rip off artists at the end of the night, chain-smoking cigarettes under five-day beards, running cash businesses that make more money on alcohol than they do on music—what else, after all, pays the rent?—coke-addled booze hounds hunched over their own bars past last call until the business goes bust because their reputations (and health) can't outlast the artists who refuse to play for them anymore.

Then you have the agents, the guys—primarily—whom the artists hire on commission to build tours. These are the powerhouses who believe all promoters keep their shaky clubs afloat *only* by ripping off their artists. Agents, in fact, run today's American live-music business. Most work semi-normal hours, nine to six or so, five days a week, and take substantially fewer risks than the promoters with whom they deal because of the *sine qua non* of concert booking called the guarantee.

Agents require promoters (in a lot of cases, also the venue owners) to pay artists guarantees, upon which the agents earn their commission. The promoter only hopes the artists will draw enough customers to satisfy the guarantee; otherwise the promoter must make up the cash difference and absorb losses that can run to thousands of dollars. The artist only hopes the doors to the club are still open when she arrives to play the gig.

What's it like to run a club in South Carolina?

You try to keep your staff of a dozen twenty-five-year-olds coming to work on time; you try to pay your mortgage, multiple and costly insurances, eighteen different kinds of taxes, payroll and utility bills; you try to keep your PA equipment and furniture and fixtures from falling apart. To keep your customers coming, you have to keep your band calendar full. That requires working with agents, lots of them, and they're a tricky lot.

You have the agent who tells you—from what must be one cushy Emerald City office whose monthly rent has to exceed your yearly income—that under no circumstances are you to call or e-mail there. *He* will contact *you* with "avails" for his artists. Maybe. Fact is, you know they'll play the "majors," the big markets: Charlotte, Atlanta, even Asheville.

Never mind that his roster includes some big names, among the best performers on the road. These are bands and solo artists who would sell out your venue in no time and set revenue records at your bar. And never mind that those same artists would get off the tour bus after a too-long drive, look around your award-winning room, where Joan Baez just played a few weeks before, and say, "Whoa, this place is totally cool. I've never heard of this room before. Dude, what's your name again?"

Then you have the road manager, fired up with enough attitude to launch the space shuttle, who wonders why you haven't bought the band their $70 bottle of Grey Goose—the liquor is right there, clear as vodka, on the band contract's two-page "hospitality" rider. And he demands to know: where are the six bath-sized towels? ("You do have a shower here, right?") And where's the runner with her SUV to pick up rest of the band from the hotel, since they had to relax after flying in from a charity golf tournament earlier that day?

Customers are good for business. And they're the people who are never wrong, the ones who carry the very lifeblood of your bank notes and the very livelihood of your musicians. They are, in fact, hard on the soul. Take the stoner who calls the club as you're recovering from a long and grueling show the night before. He calls early in the morning (you do own a *night*-club) and asks the office assistant (which you're fortunate enough now to afford), "Yo, I was there last night, and . . . dude, I was wondering. Has anybody there seen my pants? I left them there, uuuuhhhh . . . " And the questions—all of them real: "Is the band y'all got there any good?" "Is your food good?" "What kind of music does the Dave Matthews Cover Band play?"

Then you have the artists. By and large, they are good and generous (and exhausted) people, who night after night, reach for a mystical brass ring only they can see and who create art only they can make, which we as promoters can buy if we want to and customers can forsake because they can't find babysitters, money, companions, interest or taste.

Then you have venue, the building, the club, the concert spot, where all your life and hard-earned life savings have gone to build and often sustain your dream—an investment that, at least, in terms of hard currency, likely never will come back out.

According to the U.S. Small Business Administration, only 44 percent of small businesses—which account for 95 percent of the American economic engine—survive past their fourth year.

It's been a dozen years since Livingston Taylor, brother of the famous James, told us we had a tough row to hoe after he played our 1994 Grand Opening.

"You do realize," he said, "that you, as the promoter, you're at the bottom of the food chain?"

He told us that after we were already a quarter of a million dollars in debt, pretty much where we've stayed—until we pay off all our lingering loans.

But I've just sold one of my novels, and maybe I'll sell some more, or maybe one will get turned into a movie—one of my own pieces of art. But this whole essay boils down to the only truth in the music business: If you want to make a million dollars in the music business, you better start with two million.

Still, my wife, Kathy, and I haven't forgotten our original mission, our business plan, the one that keeps us in our morning Grape Nuts, debt and stories enough to last us both our lifetimes, and the only reason for opening shop in the first place: For millennia, humans and their tribes have chanted their stories to anyone who will listen. For ever and for always, some will pay, some will lose their shirts, some their pants and some their minds. But at the end of the day, what really matters is music played live, most assuredly beyond CDs and iPods and albums and stores and computers and whatever music-delivery systems that have come and will go. Nothing comes close to the spontaneity and visceral experience of watching and listening to an artist create a song.

And that's why you open your own live-music venue. In Greenville, South Carolina.

"Chevy Van"

BY TOMMY TOMLINSON

Lots of people will tell you they have always had great taste in music. They will say they latched onto Springsteen in first grade, that they played Dylan for kids at the pool, that they spent their first chunk of allowance money on "Kind of Blue."

These people are liars.

Kids listen to junk. It is the same impulse that makes them crave cotton candy. When our taste buds are young all we want is a sweet rush that melts on the tongue and puts one thought in our mind: *Again.*

Which brings me to a song called "Chevy Van" by a Charlotte boy named Sammy Johns.

In the summer of 1975, to my eleven-year-old mind, there were two great American record labels: K-Tel and Ronco. They crammed twenty hits onto a single LP and sold it for $4.98. A slab of vinyl can't hold as much as a CD, so every song had something edited out: the third verse, or the keyboard solo, or the long fade at the end. In almost every case this made the song better.

I'm imagining some guy at the Ronco splicing machine thinking, *The Beatles got in and out in two minutes and 15 seconds, I'll be damned if Paul Anka gets more than that.*

Because of the sweet glorious Internet I am now looking at the track listing for a record I bought the summer when I was eleven. If I am remembering right, it is the second LP I ever bought. It is a fine K-Tel production titled *Music Express.*

"Chevy Van" is track 9, side 1.

The record leads off with "Love Will Keep Us Together," the Captain and Tennille's megahit—the best-selling record of the entire year—and because this is a personal essay, and you should be honest in personal essays, I will now tell you that back then I belonged to the Captain and Tennille Fan Club. Actually, it could have been a lifetime membership, so I might still be in. We members got a special 8x10 photo of the Captain and Tennille with their bulldogs.

If you tell anyone this I will track you down and kill you.

We will get to "Chevy Van," I promise, but first let me list the other tracks on *Music Express* by category.

SONGS I STILL LIKE ENOUGH TO HAVE ON MY IPOD 32 YEARS LATER:

"Get Down Tonight," K.C. and the Sunshine Band

SONGS THAT STILL SORT OF HOLD UP:
"I'm Not In Love," 10cc
"Jackie Blue," Ozark Mountain Daredevils
"The Rockford Files," Mike Post
"Long Train Runnin'," The Doobie Brothers

SONGS I PROBABLY SHOULDN'T LIKE BUT STILL DO:
"Cat's In the Cradle," Harry Chapin
"Swearin' To God," Frankie Valli

SONGS I USED TO LIKE, BUT IT TURNS OUT
I WAS WRONG:
"Love Will Keep Us Together," The Captain
    and Tennille
"Philadelphia Freedom," Elton John
"Mandy," Barry Manilow
"Poetry Man," Phoebe Snow
"Sky High," Jigsaw
"My Eyes Adored You," Frankie Valli (again!)

SONGS I DON'T REMEMBER ANYMORE:
"Brazil," Ritchie Family
"Dynomite," Tony Camillo's Bazuka
"Black Superman," Johnny Wakelin and the
    Kinshasa Band

SONGS THAT, EVEN AT AGE ELEVEN, SUCKED:
"Run Joey Run," David Geddes
"Rocky," Austin Roberts
"Get Dancin'," Disco Tex and the Sex-O-Lettes

If you are around my age, and you are realizing that this is a fair sampling of the music you loved when you were eleven, part of you might be wishing that when you were ten you had fallen down a well.

But as Woody Allen said in a totally different and really creepy context, the heart wants what it wants. Which brings us back to "Chevy Van."

On YouTube there's a sad little video of "Chevy Van." *Video* is not even the right word; the only image is a still photo of a Sammy Johns album cover. He is dressed in the full '70s singer-songwriter uniform—longish hair, matching beard and mustache, wide-collared shirt open two or three buttons down. The opening act for Dan Fogelberg.

But the song doesn't sound right. It's a remake he did somewhere along the way.

Poke around a little more and you find another video, a shirtless guy in a Hamm's Beer cap goofing around on a farm. It's your basic YouTube special, made for 99 cents and some weed, but the background music is the original "Chevy Van."

It starts to play and in my brain a drawer opens and the words and music come tumbling out.

I gave a girl
A ride in my waaaaagon . . .

There's not much to it: a couple of layered guitars, some nice harmonies, a keyboard of some kind tugging at the chorus. But it all flows together, as shallow and pretty as a trout stream, and Sammy reaches for the high notes, as if he knew when he wrote it, *this one's got a chance.*

She was tired, 'cause her mind was a-draggin'
I said get some sleep and dream of rock 'n' roll . . .

I should stop right here and admit the best thing about this song, back when I was eleven: Sammy got some.

Right there in his Chevy Van. My dad drove a Chevy van back then, mostly to haul around his tools, but I could (and did) imagine giving a girl a ride and shortly thereafter—two minutes and 48 seconds later, if the song was any indication—getting some of my own. Although I wasn't sure how to get some, or how much I needed to be getting, or exactly what "some" was.

When I was eleven there was a lot I didn't know. One of the things I didn't know was how hard it is to write something that is simple and pure and sticks with people thirty-five years down the road.

> 'Cause like a picture she was laying there
> Moonlight dancing off her hair
> She woke up and took me by the hand
> We made love in my Chevy van
> And that's all right with me.

"Chevy Van" sold more than a million copies and made it to No. 5 on the pop charts. It was the only time Sammy Johns made the Top 40.

Twenty years later I was a music writer in Charlotte and Sammy Johns was trying to make a comeback. He came by the newspaper for an interview. He had written a few hits for country singers—Waylon Jennings, Conway Twitty—but wanted another shot on his own. He knew he had a better chance living in Nashville. But he decided he liked it better in Shelby. That was the last I heard of him.

As far as I know he's still knocking around, and he may well be writing his giant comeback hit at this very moment. But chances are that his gift to the world at large is one song, a shade under three minutes long, that they played on the radio three decades ago.

I've been listening to "Chevy Van" over and over as I've been writing this, ten or twelve times in a row, and I keep expecting to get sick of it, the way most of us get sick of the music we used to love before we became mature and smart and cool, the way grown men and women lose the taste for cotton candy.

But instead I keep pressing play, keep clicking and listening and writing, and somewhere in all this I turned eleven years old again, and "Chevy Van" is playing on my K-Tel album on my Sears Roebuck stereo, and spun sugar melts so good on my tongue, and that's all right with me.

2
THE ENTERTAINERS

Duelin' Banjos: Arthur Smith and Don Reno

BY FRYE GAILLARD

It was one of those magical, virtuoso moments that occur periodically in country music, when Arthur Smith and Don Reno came together to pick out a tune they called "Feudin' Banjos." The year was 1955, and both musicians had already made a name for themselves in their native Carolinas and beyond. Smith was a mill-worker's son from South Carolina, a slow-talking, quick-witted man with a lopsided grin and dancing blue eyes, who had long ago decided that music was the key to a better way of life.

Born in 1921, he was still in his teens when he and his brothers, Ralph and Sonny, put together a Dixieland band and played a little jazz on radio broadcasts out of Spartanburg. But they quickly made the switch to country music, and after a few years, Arthur moved to Charlotte and became a regular performer on the clear channel station WBT. His breakthrough hit, "Guitar Boogie," was recorded first in 1945 and soon became an international success, selling more than three million copies. As he began touring the South with other country stars, including Hank Williams, his friend Don Reno was rapidly building a career of his own.

Growing up on a farm in Clyde, N.C., Reno took up the banjo at the age of five, and learned the instrument mostly by ear as he listened to the powerful radio stations of the South. He admired Earl Scruggs, the legendary picker from North Carolina, who had transformed the way the banjo was played, and one night late in the 1940s, he tracked down Scruggs and bluegrass legend Bill Monroe at a gig in Taylorsville, N.C.

"When I got to Taylorsville," Reno would write in his autobiography, "I . . . took my banjo out of the case and walked on stage and started playing. Bill said, 'Boy I've been trying to find you,' and I said, 'Well, I finally made it.'"

In the early '50s, Reno went to work with Arthur Smith on his radio and television shows in Charlotte, and in 1955 the two of them recorded what would become a legendary track. "Feudin' Banjos" was a rollicking, nimble-fingered, Appalachian duet that the two of them had written together. As it made its steady climb up the charts, they were happy to have a solid country hit. But they never suspected that nearly twenty years later, with the help of a blockbuster movie called *Deliverance*, the record, in a sense, would define their careers.

Both musicians had had bigger hits. After touring the South with his well-named band, the Tennessee

Cut-Ups, the irreverent and happy-go-lucky Reno—the prototype of the '50s country star, with his slicked back hair and tight-fitting suits—turned reflective on his first major record, "I'm Using My Bible for a Road Map." It was one of those sentimental ballads that quickly struck a chord in the towns and countryside of the South. One country fan, an elderly woman in a nursing home, had tears in her eyes as she told a music writer, "I still live my life just like the song says."

Reno went on to record more than 500 songs, and Arthur Smith was not alone when he declared, "I think Don was just about the best five-string banjo player I'd ever heard."

Smith, meanwhile, was even more visible in the world of country music. In the infancy of live television, he became a regular on WBTV in Charlotte and soon had his own nationally syndicated show, which was called, appropriately, *The Arthur Smith Show.* The program would run for thirty-two years, and the guests would include a Who's Who of national talent—Johnny Cash and George Hamilton IV, the Statler Brothers and George Beverly Shea. He also opened a recording studio, and over the years, played host to a wide variety of artists: Roy Orbison, Flatt & Scruggs, Don Reno and David Allen Coe. But perhaps the most improbable was the king of rhythm and blues, James Brown.

In February of 1965, the great soul singer and his entourage came to the little brick studio on Monroe Road, and recorded "Papa's Got a Brand New Bag." Released in the summer of 1965, the song became Brown's first Top 10 hit, and foreshadowed a sound that would make him, arguably, the most dynamic singer of his day.

"James was completely in control of the session," Smith remembered later. "He knew exactly what he wanted to do."

Throughout those years, as he was building his career, Smith had quietly earned a reputation as one of the shrewdest businessmen in the industry. It was not, he said, that he had the desire to amass a lot of wealth. "But the process of *making* money," he explained, "I love it. I really do."

All of that would serve him well in 1973 when Warner Bros. Studios released *Deliverance*, the movie version of the great James Dickey novel about a white-water trip through the southern Appalachians. One of the most memorable scenes in the film—and certainly the highlight of the movie soundtrack—occurred when actors Billy Redden and Ronny Cox faced off in a version of Smith and Reno's 1955 song, which the film makers renamed "Dueling Banjos."

Believing that the song was in the public domain, just an old instrumental from deep in the mountains, Warner Bros. failed to credit the writers. As Smith recalled, when he telephoned Warner's to talk about the problem, it took him a couple of weeks to get the company's lawyers on the phone—to convince the secretaries out in Hollywood that this slow, drawling voice from the other end of the continent belonged to somebody to be reckoned with.

When he finally got through, Smith said, the lawyer told him, "Mr. Smith, you haven't got the time or money to take Warner Bros. to court."

"So I told him," Smith remembered, 'Sir, I do have the time, and I believe I can get the money.'"

Smith's case was overwhelming. He had original recordings, a valid copyright and the character testimonials of other people in the business. "I told the opposing lawyer," said Nashville record executive Fred Foster, "'If Arthur Smith told me he wrote "The Star-Spangled Banner," I'd believe him. I might not know quite how it was possible, but I'd know it was true.'"

Faced with all that, Warner Bros. agreed to settle as the case went to court. The settlement itself was about $200,000, which paled beside the royalties that began to flow in. And when it was over, Smith was able to affirm with a grin: "Even my wife was pleased."

In the years after that, both Smith and Reno kept on doing the things they loved, which, in Reno's case, mostly consisted of playing the banjo. He began recording for CMH Records, a new bluegrass label that Smith helped launch in 1976. For Smith, it was a tidy business operation. Some of the finest bluegrass musicians—Lester Flatt, the Osborne Brothers—began to cut their records at his studio, with Smith, most often, serving as producer and playing back-up on many of the sessions. And some of the artists, including Reno, began writing songs for Clay Music, the publishing company owned by Smith.

It was, for Smith, the perfect blend of music and money. For Reno, the joy of the moment came almost entirely from the banjo, and he played it with passion until tragedy struck in 1984. On October 16, he died from complications after what was supposed to be a simple surgical procedure in Virginia. He was only fifty-seven. In the years that followed, Smith and other friends remembered Reno's fun-loving style almost as much as they did his music. "He never got real serious about anything," Smith concluded, "except his banjo playing."

Smith, meanwhile, remained active and involved in the music business, performing occasionally with his friend Johnny Cash, and writing new songs until well into his eighties. From the vantage point of his advancing age, he seemed to regard his multiple accomplishments with a quiet and unapologetic satisfaction. "I knew what I wanted to do by the time I was fourteen years old," he explained. "I wanted to marry a wonderful woman, have children, have a nice home and car, write music and entertain people . . . and I've done just that."

He also recorded his share of classic songs, including the one made famous by a Hollywood movie in which the producers, initially, failed to give him credit. But Smith was happy with the way it turned out.

"The royalties," he concluded with a smile, "keep on coming."

Etta Baker: One-Diming It

BY CLAIR DELUNE

Roots and blues music have long been passed down through families as a living legacy.

Blues music in the late nineteenth and early twentieth centuries differed because of many factors. Piedmont blues was singular among the many styles of rural blues in the South owing to the geography of the region. Strong dividing lines, such as the Appalachian Mountains, cut the Carolinas off from much of the Deep South. The high cost and limited means of transportation created further rifts.

Thus, European and African musical influences were mixed together in the Southern Appalachian states, resulting in the creation of Piedmont blues.

Piedmont blues "married" the rhythmic pentatonic scales of African music which had spawned the roots of the blues, with European tones, styles and instruments. The outcome was a merging of styles that produced not only the ragtime-based Piedmont blues but served as the foundation for bluegrass and "hillbilly" music as well.

Emerging from the mixing of those cultures, both musically and through her own family's European, African-American and Native American heritage, was Etta Reid, later known as Etta Baker, master of Piedmont finger-picking style.

Baker was born in Caldwell County, N.C., in 1913 to Sallie and Boone Reid, a banjo player who taught his daughter to play at the age of three. Reid, like many early bluesmen, took standards and folk songs and made them his own. The family played for white, black and mixed-race listeners, although accounts of early recording attempts around 1955 noted very few performances by the once-active street and community party players.

Baker recounted that early on she knew she would have to make music her life and she played for almost ninety years. She learned guitar before she was old enough to hold one, and had to set the instrument on a chair to play it. Baker also learned her father's instrument, the five-string banjo, as well as the fiddle, a popular mountain addition to eastern blues.

Home and hearth were central to the Baker family's performances. One of Baker's early tunes is a rendition of her father's rewriting of "Spoonful," which he called "Carolina Breakdown." She played with her family, including a sister, Cora, her six other siblings, and later with her own nine children.

However, in 1956, Baker's dazzling finger-picking appeared on a compilation album, *Instrumental Music of the Southern Appalachians*, which put her in the spotlight during the 1960s folk revival and garnered her a following among such notables as Bob Dylan and Taj Mahal. "One-Dime Blues" was among her contributions to the album. The musical catch phrase "one-diming it" was coined around that time and indicated that a musician could keep up with Baker's rapid fingering style.

It was not until 1991 when her first full CD, *One-Dime Blues*, garnered critical and public acclaim. However, her influence had been felt long-before her "overnight" success. Baker and her sister, Cora Phillips, were honored jointly with the North Carolina Folklore Society's Brown-Hudson Folklore Award in 1982. Baker also received the National Heritage Fellowship Award from the National Endowment for the Arts in 1991.

* * *

During concerts throughout the Carolinas and other Piedmont states in the 1990s, Baker would perform and tell tales, recounting the good and the sad aspects of life. At an early '90s concert at Gambrell Hall, a small auditorium at the University of South Carolina, she appeared with her friend Walter Liniger, a Swiss-born blues musician and professor of blues and southern studies at the University of South Carolina.

After playing acoustic guitar for a set or two, Baker pulled out an electric Les Paul—one that her daughter gave her in the 1950s—and, before playing it, spoke of her deep love for her family while she stroked the neck of the vintage guitar.

"It was the surprise of my life and one of my many blessings," Baker said, with a sweet smile, evidencing the emotions she felt at her daughter's generosity.

Although the Les Paul was a prized possession, clearly nothing took the place of family for Baker. She and the family suffered when, in 1964, Baker's husband Lee suffered a stroke and she lost a grandson in an accident; then within a month in 1967, her husband died and she lost a son in Vietnam.

To keep her family going, she had worked in a textile mill for two decades, "retiring" at age sixty to play full time. But as a widow on her own, she worked hard at home, too.

Liniger considered Etta Baker his mentor. He recalled one visit to her home in particular. He walked up the road to her house and heard noises, but didn't see Baker. He called out to her and was awestruck when this eighty-year-old woman called down to him from the roof. And then she asked him to climb the ladder and bring her some roofing shingles.

He said, "You shouldn't be up there doing that!"

She matter-of-factly replied, "If I don't the rain will get in. And if I don't, who will?"

* * *

Etta Baker died in 1996 while visiting a daughter in Virginia who had suffered a stroke. "Etta was a special friend to me," Liniger said more than a decade after her passing. "I know that we were special to each other. We had known each other for over twenty years. She taught me that her music was an intricate part of her life, but so was cooking and eating, and constantly working on improving one's balance in this world.

"Etta Baker opened a door to my spiritual world, he said, "a place I had not looked for, a place I had not believed in, a place of my own. Over the years she continued to assure me that she would *always* be my friend. And she was. She still is."

Baker was a master of the Piedmont Blues finger-picking style, a woman who put home, family and friends first; a winner of awards and homages; a teacher and inspiration to guitar pickers everywhere; mentor to many; and one incredible woman with the strength and fortitude of the North Carolina mountains in her soul.

Etta Baker's many contributions will live on in her artistry as well as in the music made by those who have learned so much from her.

～～～

Earl Scruggs: The Banjoman

BY JOE DEPRIEST

The banjoman—Earl Scruggs—is still making music in his eighties.

He got his musical start at the age of four on a farm near Boiling Springs, N.C., playing a mail-order banjo. Without any formal music training, Scruggs was able to rise to the top of the music world, riding all the way on his unique three-finger picking style he perfected on the banjo.

His new style, introduced for the first time at the Grand Ole Opry in Nashville, Tennessee, in 1945, revolutionized the five-string banjo and helped transform the face of American music. Today, Scruggs is considered one of the most important pioneers of bluegrass music.

Even people who don't know bluegrass music recognize his masterpiece, "Foggy Mountain Breakdown," the blistering banjo number that was the score for the movie *Bonnie and Clyde*. It was played on the radio more than one million times and became an American classic. Along his journey to greatness, he has released dozens of albums, been nominated eleven times for Grammys—winning twice—and has played with some of the biggest names in the music world for over the last fifty years.

He's also grateful to still be playing. Scruggs has survived a car crash, plane crash, chronic back pain and a near-fatal heart attack. His wife and longtime manager, Louise, died in February 2006.

"My attitude now is I'm eager to play," said Scruggs in 2001, sitting in his Nashville home, wearing a sporty dark suit, shirt and tie. "The joy and the urge—those are the major ingredients. What keeps me young at heart is playing with good, talented musicians. It's been a joyful thing.

"I'm feeling the best I have in years. It's exciting to go into new directions. And it's fun."

In 2001, Scruggs recorded his first album in seventeen years. *Earl Scruggs and Friends* was a tribute to the bluegrass banjo master with help from superstars Elton John, Sting and Melissa Etheridge. Those who know Scruggs weren't surprised that he was back and sharing the studio with a new crowd.

"Since Earl Scruggs stepped out on the Grand Ole Opry stage December 8, 1945, he's been a progressive," said Eddie Stubbs, Opry announcer, country music historian and National Public Radio commentator. "Every time he plays the banjo he makes a statement. He's one of the most influential instrumentalists not only in country music but music of the world."

FROM THE MILL TO NASHVILLE

Scruggs and his brother Horace, who died in July 2007, taught themselves to pick the banjo on a cotton farm in the Flint Hill community near Boiling Springs in Cleveland County. Their dad, George Elam Scruggs, had learned to play on a mail-order banjo before he died in 1928. It was then that four-year-old Earl picked up his father's banjo to play. It meant so much to his life, Scruggs still has the banjo today.

As a kid, Scruggs walked down to the Broad River on Saturday nights to play for dances at Ollie Moore's fish camp. Even at work in Shelby's Lily Mill textile plant, banjo tunes raced through his head. "Most of the time, whether I was doffing or spinning, I was thinking about music," Scruggs said. "I couldn't get it off my mind."

In 1945, the twenty-one-year-old Scruggs quit the mill and left on a musical journey that within a surprising few months took him to the home of country music, the Grand Ole Opry. He was a sensation from the beginning with Bill Monroe's Blue Grass Boys band. Later, Scruggs and another band member, Lester Flatt, left to form their own group.

In the 1950s, Flatt and Scruggs popularized bluegrass with folk music audiences outside the South and reached an even wider audience during the 1960s playing the theme song on TV's *The Beverly Hillbillies*. They also influenced new generations of bluegrass musicians such as John Hartford and Bela Fleck.

Later, Scruggs immersed himself in country rock with his sons in the Earl Scruggs Review, jammed with jazz great Dave Brubeck and recorded with everybody from Loggins and Messina to the Nitty Gritty Dirt Band.

GETTING THROUGH THE PAIN

The musical journey took Scruggs on many a hard mile. First there was recurring back pain for decades from a 1955 car wreck in Knoxville, Tennessee.

Scruggs and his wife were headed back to Shelby, N.C., where his mother, Lula, had suffered a stroke. Broadsided by another car, Louise Scruggs' face hit the windshield, and Earl's hips were dislocated. Both were hospitalized for months and missed his mother's funeral.

After the wreck, Scruggs got a pilot's license. Early one morning in 1975, flying home from a concert, his plane flipped while landing in heavy fog at an unattended airfield in Nashville. He was trapped in the wreckage because of an injured left ankle and wrist. "I saw cars pull up, and [I] hollered. But nobody could hear me," he recalled. Police later found him after family members reported him missing. Doctors worried a severe injury to his left hand might end his picking career, but he recovered.

In the 1980s and 1990s, his chronic back pain made it hard for him to perform. He cut back on performances and recording. After hip surgery in 1996, Scruggs suffered a near-fatal heart attack in the hospital recovery room. He immediately went back for more surgery to repair six blocked arteries.

Recuperating at home, he wondered what could possibly happen next. Then, unexpectedly, the pain began to ebb—and Scruggs' passion for the banjo was rekindled.

RECLAIMING HIS PASSION

Scruggs lives in a gated home in an exclusive Nashville neighborhood. A winding drive threads past contemporary sculptures sprinkled around ten neatly trimmed acres. When he rides his golf cart down for the paper in the morning, he waves at tour buses full of fans checking out the homes of country music stars.

Inside his roomy contemporary-style house, a banjo theme rules—banjo books, banjo photos, crocheted banjos and even a banjo refrigerator magnet. Scruggs is a relaxed, thoughtful, grandfatherly man, who speaks with a soft North Carolina twang.

When Scruggs made his 2001 album, his son Randy, a veteran Nashville record producer, lined up the artists, which included Grand Ole Opry star Vince Gill. "Earl's the man," Gill said backstage at the Opry. "People from all musical walks of life know who Earl Scruggs is. He's the real thing."

At eighty-four, Scruggs continues to perform—everywhere from North Carolina's MerleFest to the B.B. King Blues Club in New York. And he's always looking for new projects.

"I won't exclude anything when it comes to music," Scruggs said. "If it's good, use it. Yeah, boy!"

~~~

DeWitt "Snuffy" Jenkins

BY SAM BOYKIN

Much like today's purveyors of modern rock have early bluesmen and jazz musicians to thank for helping create the art form's distinct sound, fans of country and bluegrass owe a big debt of gratitude to folks like DeWitt "Snuffy" Jenkins. Jenkins, born in Harris, N.C. in 1908, helped pioneer the distinct three-finger picking style that influenced some of the greatest bluegrass banjo players, including his protégé Earl Scruggs.

Music, it seems, was literally in Jenkins' blood. He was the youngest of ten children, all of whom excelled at music. As a child he tried to play fiddle, but the bow proved too big and cumbersome, so he picked the instrument as if it were a mandolin. As a teenager he moved on to the guitar, and played with banjo players Smith Hammett and Rex Brooks, during which time he developed his three-finger picking style. In the late 1920s, he and his brother, Virl, along with two other musicians, formed the Jenkins String Band. They played at local dances, on Charlotte's WBT Radio, and always dominated at the regional fiddler convention contests.

In 1936 Jenkins joined J.E. Mainer's Mountaineers and recorded on Bluebird Records, including the standout tune "Kiss Me Cindy." Although he played fiddle and guitar as well as the harmonica, by the late 1930s Jenkins started to focus on the banjo. In 1939 Jenkins' musical career began to truly blossom when Byron Parker, the manager of WIS Radio in Columbia, S.C., took the helm of Mainer's band, and expanded its sound to include an additional fiddle player named Homer Lee "Pappy" Sherrill, as well as harmony quartet singing. The musicians performed as WIS Hillbillies on radio and Byron Parker's Mountaineers on record. By 1940 they had recorded sixteen sides with Bluebird Records.

Jenkins and Sherrill emerged as the stars and main attractions of the band and eventually developed the "Snuffy and Pappy" comedy routines. After Byron Parker died in 1948, the duo took over the band, changing their name to the Hired Hands. Jenkins and Sherrill continued to fine-tune both their musical and comedy acts, and when WIS added television to their line-up in 1953, it proved to be a perfect format, and in no time the Hired Hands and Snuffy and Pappy were famous.

The Hired Hands continued to perform on radio and television, and record for various labels, including a 1962 album on the Folk Lyric label, and a 1971 LP

Jenkins and Sherrill recorded for Rounder. With the growth of bluegrass festivals, Jenkins and Sherrill, by then legendary figures, were able to share their music with audiences outside their native Carolinas. By the time the group recorded their last album in 1989, Jenkins was in poor health, and was only able to play banjo on a few songs. He passed away on April 30, 1990. He is still remembered as one of the fathers of bluegrass, and a key figure in the music's evolution to the fluid and graceful sounds heard today.

~~~

Doc Watson: Idol Conversation

BY TIMOTHY C. DAVIS

"Hi. Is Doc there?"

"Just a minute. Are you an interviewer?" It's Rosa Lee Watson, Doc's wife.

"Yes, I am," I say.

"Just a minute. You're an interview? Now you hold on, hear?"

"It's an interview, honey . . ." Rosa Lee calls out to her husband of many years. She's probably done this a thousand times over the years, but there's no trace of artifice or routine in her voice. "Here's the phone," she says, guiding her husband to the receiver. Her husband, of course, is one of the most revered folk and roots musicians to ever set foot in the United States, much less Deep Gap, N.C., where I'm calling him at his home. Blind since infancy, Doc is lucky to have a woman like Rosa Lee around. Not that he needs to be babysat, mind you. I recall a story Watson's sometimes-sideman Jack Lawrence once told me about Doc building a 16 by 20-foot utility building behind his house all by himself, and try to picture it in my mind. A second later, I'm shot back to the present.

"Hello?"

"Mr. Watson?"

"Who's this?" Fair enough. He's Doc Watson, and it's morning, the same week as MerleFest, and I'm bothering him.

"It's Tim Davis," I say. "Sorry I'm a bit late. Still a little early for me . . ."

"Man, this ain't early. I've been up for hours!"

My heart stops. Then Doc begins to laugh. Air once again courses through my respiratory system. I check my notes, search for questions. The few seconds of silence pound my head like a drum.

"So, this concert in Charlotte is a celebration of your eightieth birthday, right?"

Doc laughs. "Well, that's what they say! I don't know. My eightieth birthday was the third of March, and they're trying to tack on birthday celebrations all the way down the line! I don't even know what eighty years old signifies. I'm just thankful for my health."

"I guess it's a big round number for people to latch on to," I say.

"I guess that's it. But if a man is eighty and still able to pick and sing a little bit, I think it is a blessing, don't you?"

"Did you think back years ago that you'd still be touring at eighty?"

"I never thought about it one way or another," Doc

says. I begin to feel like that character Chris Farley used to play on *Saturday Night Live*, where he says all the wrong things to his idols. Switch gears, Davis!

"With MerleFest growing every year, did you imagine in the beginning that it would turn into such a big event?"

"I don't think anyone that had anything to do with MerleFest ever dreamed it would happen the way it did," says Doc. "Originally some friends—'B' Townes, Bill Young, Ralph Williams—wanted me to do a concert to put a little memorial garden there at Wilkes Community College in memory of Merle" (Doc's son and playing partner who died in a tragic farming accident in 1985). "I told them sure, I'd do that, and we talked about it for a while. My wife and daughter, Rosa Lee and Nancy, said, 'Why don't you hold it over till spring, and do a little one- or two-day festival so Merle's friends can come?' About 5,000 people showed up for it—they did some good promotion on it. It did so well we decided to do it one more year, and then it just mushroomed and took off like a big storm cloud or somethin' a buildin' right fast. Only it wasn't a storm. It's been a wonderful thing—been well handled, the people, the volunteers, everybody. It's safe for children to come to—they have a petting farm and all that stuff, good little things for youngsters to do, and people aren't afraid to bring their children. To me, it's a real festival—a fellowship and a get-together as much as a festival."

"A lot of the festivals nowadays, the big bluegrass festivals, you can't necessarily bring children to," I say. "They're big *drinking* festivals, sometimes."

"You don't have to drink and carouse, as Dad used to put it, to have a good festival. You need fellowship, which is much more important than the music.

You need a good variety of music, and not something wild to drive people into some kind of orgies, ya know? That's what a good kind of festival is about, and it has proven itself in MerleFest."

Doc's really rolling now, and I'm staying quiet as possible. Did Doc just say "orgies?" Focus.

"Since Ralph Stanley is opening the show here in Charlotte, how long ago did you first meet him?"

"I've listened to Ralph on the radio, you know. I listened to him and Carter, the Stanley Brothers, before I ever got into music as a profession. My wife and I, shortly after we were married and moved out on our own, we listened to 'Farm and Fun Time' on WCYB Bristol. It was a regular station, and the Stanley Brothers were favorites. I met Ralph a time or two as they would come to Boone and do shows. I got to know Ralph personally and worked with him to get him to come to MerleFest. Ralph, he holds a pretty big spot in bluegrass and old time music, you know, and that's why he is there. And that Jim Lauderdale, he's a character, man, that guy is something else." Doc begins laughing hard. I do as they do in Deep Gap, and laugh too.

"I had the occasion of meeting him once," I say.

"I like the man. You know, I haven't met him, but I have through his music," Doc says.

I feel like a name-dropper.

Doc continues. "You get an idea of a fellow's personality if you listen to him a little bit in song, especially songs the person has written themselves. I intend to shake a howdy with old Jim, this time, though. I won't let him get away."

He seems happy to talk about others. I ask him about touring with Richard Watson, Merle's son. His voice lowers a half-step, it seems.

"I believe Richard began touring solid with me nearly two years ago," Doc says. "He did some shows with me before that, and we did a CD, *Third Generation Blues,* together. It sure has been a pleasure having Richard out there. It's an extension of his dad in a way. He hasn't developed his music as far as Merle has, because Merle was with me for years on the road. [Merle] never got half the credit. He kind of stayed out of the limelight. Somebody once asked why he didn't speak on stage, and he said, "Dad talks enough for both of us!" He tried introducing the boys one time and did a good job, but he didn't care to do that. He wanted to let his guitars talk, and his slide, and his flat pickin', and his fingerstyle. Richard is a good blues man, and other things. If you heard the album, you'd have a real good idea what Richard could really do."

Doc can talk real easy about Merle and Richard, so we chatted a few more minutes about that, and about subjects that probably don't concern anyone reading this. Truth be told, they probably didn't concern Doc all that much, either. I think he could sense my genuine interest, though, and gave genuine answers to everything I asked. I thanked him for his time, and wished him luck.

In the beginning, I felt bad about bothering Doc during an especially busy week. By the end, the hard part was just hanging up.

~~~

John Coltrane: Key Notes

BY RICHARD GARRISON

As the tones of tenor sax poured through the speakers of my '67 VW, they had no connection to a name or any other exterior frame of reference. It was one of those pure moments when you are exposed to something completely new to your senses, and you can only respond on a wordless, emotional level. I had gone to visit my parents in Raleigh, N.C., from my home near Chapel Hill. My car radio was tuned to WDBS in Durham, which at the time had a nightly jazz program. I was not really a jazz fan, not until that night. Not until I heard that tenor softly, intelligently, and so soulfully playing. The music spoke to me with passion, sadly and joyfully. It spoke to me in a new language as I sat alone in the car. What was this song? I had to know. I couldn't do anything else until I knew. I waited to hear.

"Dear Lord" by John Coltrane.

Dear Lord, yes; it was like a prayer, honest and reverent. No music had ever affected me so deeply. I had no idea music could. I wondered how such wonderful music had eluded me for so long, and I was thirsty for more.

The next day, first chance I got, I thumbed through a bin of Coltrane records, feeling privileged to have been let in on this "secret." At the time, I didn't know anyone who listened to jazz, so as I looked at each record I felt it was a step into uncharted territory amid rumors of gold. Which direction to take when faced with a recording legacy as large and varied as Coltrane's? An amazing legacy especially when you consider that he recorded with his own bands for only seven years in the 1960s.

Not long into my Coltrane education I was delighted to learn he had North Carolina roots. He was born on September 23, 1926, in Hamlet, and later moved to 118 Underhill Street in High Point, where he lived during his high school years. His father's love of music and proficiency on several instruments was an inspiration in Coltrane's youth and his dad encouraged him to take up the E-flat horn and clarinet. After hearing Lester Young and Johnny Hodges, Coltrane switched to alto sax and later, to tenor.

Beginning in the late '40s, after some time in music schools in Philadelphia and a stint in the Navy during World War II, Coltrane played with several other bands including Eddie Vinson, Jimmy Heath, Dizzy Gillespie, and the Miles Davis Quintet. He really began to stretch out playing with Miles in the late '50s, and then recorded with his own bands beginning in 1960, perhaps most famously with Elvin Jones on drums, McCoy Tyner on piano, and Jimmy Garrison on bass.

For five years or so this quartet recorded and performed together until they were like those flocks of birds you see that make sudden hairpin turns in complete unison. They were a group of individuals with one mind, telepathically connected. During some live performances Coltrane would begin playing a number the band had not done before, knowing the others would follow.

The recordings he made with that quartet and with other groups eventually brought Coltrane fortune and fame as an important and innovative musician. But his path to fame was not easy as he struggled with heroin and alcohol addiction throughout most of the 1950s. When drugs began to adversely affect his work, though, he was somehow able to quit and turned to a deeply spiritual relationship with God. From that profound point of epiphany forward, this spirituality became the inspiration and the driving force for his life and music. Coltrane was indeed driven. His day-long practice sessions were legendary as he pushed the limits of his instrument to make the music he heard in his mind, and to honor the love of God.

His openness to a wide variety of spiritual ideas, including those found in Christianity, Islam, Buddhism, and Hinduism, mirrored his openness to a wide variety of musical influences: Lester Young, Johnny Hodges, and Charlie Parker early on; then Miles Davis, Thelonious Monk, and later Pharoah Sanders, Ornette Coleman, John Gilmore; and Indian classical music, especially that of Ravi Shankar. Through his relentless dedication, experimentation, and a deep sense of spirituality, Coltrane eventually took his well-earned place among the greatest figures in jazz who elevated and expanded the music into new places.

Signs of his unique power were displayed early in his work with Miles Davis, and in his push to new places through the rest of his life, he gave standards like Ellington's "In a Sentimental Mood" a new edge and infused love ballads like "My One and Only Love," accompanying singer Johnny Hartman, with a poignant tenderness. He vented extreme sadness and anger in his own composition "Alabama," which memorialized the four young girls killed in a church bombing in Birmingham and is probably one of the saddest songs I've ever heard. He composed songs that became standards like "Giant Steps" and "Naima," and he took simple, commonly recognized tunes like "My Favorite Things," and "Bye Bye Blackbird," to reinvent them as avenues for his own self-expression and as frameworks on which to build endlessly inventive solos. He spontaneously breathed absolute fire with abstract virtuoso performances like "Chasin' the Trane" and "Traneing In."

His 1964 album-length masterpiece of reverence and praise, "A Love Supreme," in the four parts "Acknowledgement," "Resolution," "Pursuance," and "Psalm," was extremely well-received when it was released and continues to grow in stature. Since its release, the recording has, perhaps more than any other, given Coltrane an almost saint-like reputation. How many musicians have a church named after them, with their music and quotations as the central focus, like the "Saint John Coltrane African Orthodox Church" in San Francisco? Still, it is good to keep his life in perspective and remember he was a man who was extremely dedicated to his craft.

Before Coltrane's death in 1967 at the too-young

age of forty-one, he ventured into "free jazz," with the album *Ascension*. Perhaps inspired by the work of Ornette Coleman and Pharoah Sanders, *Ascension* was comprised of one forty-minute session of improvisations built around four different scales, with very little chord structure. Like many of Coltrane's recordings and performances in his later years, *Ascension*'s sustained intensity demands an open mind and perhaps repeated listens to appreciate fully. The overall texture of the music becomes more important than any one phrase or solo.

The house where he lived in High Point was purchased by the city, which plans to renovate it. There is already a Coltrane statue at City Hall, as well as a permanent Coltrane exhibit at the High Point Museum that contains, among other artifacts from his life, the piano owned by his family and which he continued to use in his professional life. In 2006 I saw an article in my local paper about the museum's wish to purchase the piano, and I jumped at the chance to be one of the eighty-eight contributors—one for each key—as it was an opportunity to express in a small way my great admiration for the man, as well as the love and gratitude I have had for his music since the first time I heard "Dear Lord."

Thanks, John.

〜〜〜

Thelonious Monk

BY SAM STEPHENSON

Silence one of Monk's languages, everything he says laced with it. Silence a thick brogue anybody hears when Monk speaks the other tongues he's mastered. It marks Monk as being from somewhere other than wherever he happens to be, his offbeat accent, the odd way he puts something different in what we expect him to say. An extra something not supposed to be there, or an empty space where something usually is.

—JOHN EDGAR WIDEMAN, "THE SILENCE OF THELONIOUS MONK," FROM GOD'S GYM

On Friday May 15, 1970, fifty-two-year-old Thelonious Monk and his wife of twenty-three years, Nellie Smith Monk, flew into Raleigh-Durham Airport and took a cab to a local hotel. In that day's edition of *The News and Observer* a photo of Monk ran with a caption heralding "Star Returns" and text stating: "Pianist and Composer Thelonious Monk returns to his native North Carolina for a 10-day run at Raleigh's Frog and Nightgown beginning Friday Night. The Rocky Mount native, long in the avant garde of jazz, has written several standards, including the well-known ''Round About Midnight [sic].'"

The existence of a successful jazz club in Monk's home state in May of 1970 was an anomaly. Woodstock (August 1969) marked the era and Led Zeppelin, the Beatles, Simon and Garfunkel, Stevie Wonder, and the Jackson 5 topped the charts. Jazz clubs were closing in bigger cities across the country while Raleigh, with a population of 120,000, wrestled with integration. But Peter Ingram—a scientist from England recruited to work in the newly formed Research Triangle Park—opened the Frog and Nightgown, a jazz club, in 1968 and his wife Robin managed it. Don Dixon, house bassist at the club who later gained fame as the co-producer of R.E.M.'s first album, *Murmur*, says, "It took a naive Brit like Peter to not know that a jazz club wouldn't work in 1968."

The Frog, as it was known, thrived in a small, red-brick shopping center nestled in a residential neighborhood lined with nineteenth-century oak trees. Surrounded by a barber shop, a laundry mat, a convenience store, and a service station, the Frog often attracted large crowds; lines frequently wrapped around the corner. Patrons brown-bagged their alcohol (the Frog sold food, ice, and mixers), bought cigarettes from machines, and some smoked joints in the parking lot.

Ingram booked such jazz icons as Dizzy Gillespie, Clark Terry, Zoot Sims, Art Blakey, the Modern Jazz Quartet, and Stan Getz, as well as lesser-known but adventurous musicians like Booker Ervin and Woody Shaw. Due to its mixed clientele, the club came under threat from the Ku Klux Klan, but Ingram never blinked, and the Frog held on, exceeding all odds.

Six weeks earlier, Monk postponed his originally scheduled engagement at the Frog because of pneumonia, which hospitalized him from March 16 to March 31. He spent the month of April and the first half of May convalescing in his apartment in New York City. He probably had no business traveling anywhere for ten days, much less playing three sets a night, but the Frog offered his standard rate of $2,000 per week and Monk needed the money.

Despite two decades of recordings that made him a cornerstone of jazz, Monk's life and career were spiraling downward in 1970. Columbia Records dropped him from the label and he was nearly evicted from his longtime New York apartment. Moreover, as he battled various illnesses and chronic exhaustion, his schedule became unpredictable, making it difficult to hire and keep musicians in his band.

On the morning of May 15, 1970, with the flight to Raleigh later that day, Monk still didn't have a saxophonist for the trip. Monk's old friend and bassist at the time, Wilbur Ware, first called alto saxophonist Clarence Sharpe but he couldn't make it. He then called tenor saxophonist Paul Jeffrey, who jumped at the offer. Jeffrey tossed a portable Uher tape recorder and a new box of reels into his bags and met the band at LaGuardia Airport. "Part of the reason I got that job at that time," says Jeffrey, a native New Yorker who had been considered for the Monk quartet before, "is because a lot of cats were afraid to go down South then. I'd toured the South in B.B. King's band in 1959 so I knew the ropes. Plus, I wouldn't turn down the opportunity to play with Monk if the gig had been on the moon."

Over those ten days, Jeffrey recorded much of the music the quartet made at the Frog and Nightgown, and his tapes are remnants of Monk's only major engagement in his home state. Jeffrey remembers the opening night: "I was nervous. I mean, this is Monk we're talking about and his music isn't easy. I remember the first night like it was yesterday. It is emotional for me to think about now. We played 'Blue Monk,' 'Hackensack,' 'Bright Mississippi,' 'Epistrophy,' 'I Mean You,' ''Round Midnight,' and 'Nutty,' in that order."

Jeffrey's recordings reveal a band in good form, driven by bassist Wilbur Ware's familiarity with Monk's shifting rhythms. Following a blistering, four-minute solo on "Nutty," Jeffrey expresses a warm, deft sound on the ballad, "'Round Midnight," bearing the influence of Dexter Gordon. Drummer Leroy Williams provides a rhythmic platform for the band. No matter his physical condition, Monk sounds remarkable.

* * *

Monk's arrangements blended gospel, blues, country, and jazz influences with a profound, surprising sense of rhythm, often using spaces or pauses to build momentum. The idiosyncrasies of his music made it difficult for some fans and critics who considered his playing raw and error-prone. But those criticisms came from classic European perspectives in which piano players sat still and upright in "perfect" form. Monk played with flat fingers and his feet flopped around like fish on a pier while his entire body rolled and swayed. In the middle of performances, he stood up from the piano, danced, and walked around the stage, then rushed back to the piano to play, sticking a cigarette in his mouth as he sat down.

In a remarkable 1963 appearance with Juilliard professor and friend Hall Overton, at the New School in New York, Monk demonstrated his technique of "bending" or "curving" notes on the piano, the most rigidly tempered of instruments. He drawled notes like a human voice and blended them (playing notes C and C-sharp at the same time, for example) to create his own dialect. Overton told the audience, "That can't be done on piano, but you just heard it." He then explained that Monk achieved it by adjusting his finger pressure on the keys, the way baseball pitchers do to make a ball's path bend, curve, or dip in flight.

Influenced by his devoutly church-going mother, Monk's music was born out of black gospel. When he was sixteen years old, he dropped out of New York's prestigious Stuyvesant High School, where he had gained admission on merit, and soon embarked on a two-year tour playing piano for a female evangelist. This experience solidified his extraordinary musical architecture. The pianist Mary Lou Williams first met Monk in Kansas City while he was traveling with the evangelist and she reported that he was already playing the music he later brought to the jazz scene in New York.

The syncopated Harlem Stride style is said to be the foundation of Monk's music and that's not false. It's just not the deepest root. Here is how the father of Harlem Stride, Willie "the Lion" Smith, described his own music: "All the different forms can be traced to Negro church music, and the Negroes have worshipped God for centuries, whether they lived in Africa, the Southern United States, or in the New York City area. You can still hear some of the older styles of jazz playing, the old rocks, stomps, and ring shouts in the churches of Harlem today."

Lou Donaldson, a member of Monk's band that recorded "Carolina Moon" in 1953: "My father was an AME Zion minister in Badin, N.C., and the Albemarle area and one of the reasons I was so drawn to Monk's music was because I recognized right away that all of his rhythms were church rhythms. It was very familiar to me. Monk's brand of swing came straight out of the church. You didn't just tap your foot, you move your whole body. We recorded 'Carolina Moon' [in 1952] as a tribute to our home state, with Max Roach on drums. Max was from Scotland Neck."

The seventy-nine-year-old saxophonist Johnny Griffin, who played with Monk often in the 1950s and '60s, said in late 2007, "I never knew a musician whose music was more him—I mean *him*—than Monk. His music was like leaves on a tree. His music grew from nowhere else but inside him."

＊＊＊

The jazz books agree that Monk was born in Rocky Mount, N.C., in 1917, but beyond that his family background is mostly unknown. His Frog and Nightgown engagement is treated as merely another entry in scholarly chronologies of his career, no more significant than gigs in Michigan or California. From the research of Gaston Monk (a retired school principal and NAACP leader in Pitt County, N.C., whose grandfather was the half-brother of Thelonious' grandfather), Erich Jarvis (a neurobiologist at Duke whose mother, Valeria Monk, was a cousin), and Pam Monk Kelley (an educator in Connecticut, whose father Conley Monk was a first cousin), some of Thelonious Monk's roots emerge.

His father, Thelonious Monk Sr., moved with several relatives to the tobacco and railroad hub of Rocky Mount, in the 1910s, where he met his wife Barbara Batts Monk, who gave birth to one of the most original musicians in American history, Thelonious Jr., on October 10, 1917. The family lived in a neighborhood called "Around the Y," named for the Y-shape intersection of the Atlantic Coastline Railroad roughly a hundred yards from their home on Green Street (later renamed Red Row). Henry Ramsey, who grew up in "Around the Y" before becoming a judge in Oakland, California, is writing a memoir in which he describes black railroad workers lighting campfires outside boxcars, playing harmonicas and guitars, and singing blues tunes—all marks of a tradition carried on by such North Carolina country-blues musicians as Sonny Terry, Blind Boy Fuller, and the Reverend Gary Davis. Thelonious Sr. played harmonica and piano in almost certainly this Piedmont rag style. Three and four decades later, Thelonious Jr. would write compositions mimicking train sounds such as "Little Rootie Tootie" and "Locomotive."

The Monk family struggled. Jim Crow was in full force and, by all accounts, Thelonious Sr. and Barbara had problems with their marriage. Barbara moved to West 63rd Street in New York City in 1922 and took Thelonious Jr. and his older sister Marion and younger brother Thomas with her. Barbara Monk was an only child and both of her parents died before she moved away from Rocky Mount at age thirty. The pain of those losses is one explanation for her moving to New York—to get away. But Barbara was a North Carolinian through and through. Her accent, the food she cooked, and, most profoundly for young Thelonious, the churches she attended with the family in New York, were steeped in Southern culture.

The Monks weren't the only family in their neighborhood with ties to the South. The 1930 census shows that of the 2,083 people who lived in the immediate vicinity of the Monks' apartment on West 63rd Street, 480 were born in North Carolina, South Carolina, or Virginia. Another 489 were born in other Southern states, the rest in the West Indies and New York. The census also shows that the Monks had a boarder named Claude Smith who was also born in North Carolina. When Nellie joined the family in 1947, she moved into the three-room apartment with Monk, Marion, and Barbara.

Monk rarely emerged from his apartment in New York without wearing a suit and tie and an exotic hat. (And according to *Time* magazine, Monk often wore a "cabbage leaf" lapel pin. Though he would have called it a collard green.) "Even when Monk and Nellie were living like paupers," says his longtime manager, Harry Colomby, "he always looked like a king. He was only about six feet tall but the way he dressed and carried himself made him look six-foot-nine."

Monk's royal-like aura made him an effective bandleader. Musicians weren't sure how to act around him, so they followed him seemingly spellbound, often learning to play music they didn't know they could play. But Monk's demeanor sometimes worked against him in the conventional world. In 1951, police discovered heroin in a car occupied by Monk, his friend Bud

Powell, and two other passengers. Monk silently took the rap for the heroin, which by all accounts, except the cops', wasn't his. He spent sixty days in jail. "Every day I would plead with him," said Nellie in an interview in 1963, "'Thelonious, get yourself out of this trouble. You didn't do anything.' But he'd just say, 'Nellie, I have to walk the streets when I get out. I can't talk.'" When Monk got out of jail, his all-important New York City cabaret license was revoked and he wasn't allowed to play in clubs for six years—all during the 1950s jazz heyday. He recorded several masterpieces during this period, but, without the license to play in clubs, he had limited opportunities to promote them. Nobody ever heard him complain.

When judged by the workaday world—or even by the working jazz musicians of his day—Monk's personality and social habits were eccentric. Some observers believe Monk suffered from manic depression, with tendencies for severe introversion, and perhaps some over-the-counter dependencies (alcohol, sleeping pills, amphetamines). One of Monk's bassists, Al McKibbon, told a story about how Monk showed up at his house unannounced and sat down at his kitchen table and didn't move or talk the whole day. He just sat and smoked cigarettes. That night McKibbon told him, "Monk, we're going to bed now," and he and his wife and daughter retired. The next morning when they awoke, Monk still sat at the kitchen table in the same position. He sat there for another day and night without moving or talking or seeming to care about eating, just smoking. "It was fine with me," said McKibbon, "it was just Monk being Monk."

On a national front, Monk's return to North Carolina in May of 1970 coincided with a period of his-

toric chaos during which American casualties in Vietnam officially totalled over 50,067 dead and 278,006 wounded, and college campuses, from Georgia to New Mexico, erupted in protest and violence.

On the local front, meanwhile, two white men shot and killed Henry Marrow, a twenty-three-year-old black Vietnam veteran, in broad daylight in Oxford, N.C., on May 11. On Saturday May 23rd, the last night of Monk's engagement at the Frog and Nightgown, seventy African Americans were marching forty-one miles from Oxford to the State Capitol in Raleigh to protest the passive judicial treatment of Marrow's murderers. On May 24th, the day Monk flew back to New York, the caravan of protesters, led by a mule-drawn wagon carrying a symbolic coffin, grew to four hundred people and passed two blocks from the Downtowner Motor Inn, a four-story hotel near the State Capitol in Raleigh where Peter Ingram put up the Frog's visiting musicians.

Neither Leroy Williams nor Paul Jeffrey recall the political events of 1970 as being on their minds during their Frog engagement. The attendance in the 125-seat club was, by most accounts, solid but not overwhelming. Bruce Lightner, the son of a funeral home owner and Raleigh's first black mayor, Clarence Lightner, came home from mortuary science school in New York that week and was stunned to find Monk playing in Raleigh. "The night I attended the band was on, really on. I took a date and we got to shake Monk's hand and it was a thrill," says Lightner. Paul Jervey, the son of the owner of the black newspaper in Raleigh, *The Carolinian*, remembers the audience as being mixed but predominantly white. Henry M. "Mickey" Michaux, a black state legislator from Durham, remembers Monk wearing a medieval robe and boots that had pointed toes that curled upward. He recalls the Frog being about half full for the set he attended.

Leroy Williams recounts the night the Frog's staff presented Monk with a white homecoming cake ornamented with a fez in honor of Monk's famous passion for odd hats. "It had icing that said, 'Welcome home to North Carolina,' and Monk was very enthusiastic about it," Williams says. "He was smiling and he said, 'Thank you. I'm from Rocky Mount. Thank you.' Monk loved it."

∗ ∗ ∗

Monk's trip to Raleigh seems to be the last visit he made to North Carolina and it was one of only a handful of times, at most, that he returned to his home state. That spring, just thirty-two miles from the Downtowner, Monk's ninety-year-old uncle, John Jack Monk, was living near Newton Grove. Seventy miles away in Pitt County lived Monk's cousin, Gaston. In Raleigh, maybe seven miles from the Frog and Nightgown, were cousin Almetta Monk Revis, her husband, and their seventeen-year-old son. These are just a few of the many relatives who lived near Raleigh at that time. When Gaston Monk inaugurated the annual Monk family reunions in 1979, four hundred people showed up. But there is little or no evidence that any of Monk's relatives attended the Frog and Nightgown shows, or that Thelonious and Nellie sought out the family.

Biographer Robin D. G. Kelley, in his forthcoming book, says that at this point in Monk's life he normally spent the entire day in bed resting for his gigs. But one wonders if it occurred to Monk or Nellie to try to track down family members in eastern North Carolina while in Raleigh. The relatives may have seen the "Star Returns" write-up in *The News and Observer* or they may have seen Peter Ingram's newspaper advertisements for the Thelonious Monk Quartet or his fifteen-second spots on Johnny Carson's *Tonight Show*. On Sunday, May 17, Monk and Nellie may have had time to attend church and get back for that night's gig at the Frog and Nightgown.

∗ ∗ ∗

Monk died in 1982 after a long, infirm seclusion. He was sixty-four years old.

Soon after his death, Nellie and Monk's sister Marion began attending Gaston Monk's annual family reunions in Pitt County, N.C. Gaston's son, William, picked them up at the train station in Rocky Mount, the same station where the five-year-old Thelonious had left for New York with his mother, sister, and brother in 1922.

During the mid-1980s, one of the Monk gatherings was dedicated to the late Thelonious Monk and his family. While working on his Monk genealogy, Erich Jarvis interviewed many Monk elders, including Nellie, in 1993, when she was seventy-two. (She died in 2002.) "Nellie started coming to the reunions," says Jarvis, "in order to feel a closer connection to her dead husband. She also knew it was important to him or else she wouldn't have done it. She was closing a circle for Thelonious."

〜〜〜

Dizzy Gillespie

BY DAVID PERLMUTT

Stand at Cheraw's immaculately kept Town Green with eyes closed and mind rewinding to the early 1930s, and you can almost hear the music at full throttle.

On the second floor of Town Hall, or a ballroom in the former Hotel Covington over 2nd Street, whites danced and sweated in the sultry summer air to the blaring jazz rhythms.

Bill McNeil was usually on trombone. Cleveland Powe on bass; Bernis Tillman on piano. And on trumpet, hips swaying and feet swarming, John Birks Gillespie.

It was the Great Depression. So they did anything for a buck, especially Gillespie. He'd pick cotton. Perform "monkey acts" off the high dive at a private pool for whites. Dance on street corners, or at all-white dances. Yet even at an early age, he longed for the stage. The world would know him as Dizzy. At home in South Carolina, he was John Birks.

Still is. John Birks. Both names.

Even when he died in January 1993, his relatives and longtime friends never referred to him by his famous nickname. Always John Birks.

"He had a great personal inner peace," lifelong friend Norman Powe of Cheraw said in 1993 just after Gillespie's death. "He knew who he was, where he was and was at peace with himself."

Both grew up in the turbulent times of a segregated South. But a week after Gillespie died, blacks and whites respectfully filed into a downtown theater—where as a boy Dizzy would watch movies from the "colored only" balcony—to pay tribute and watch a video from 1990, when he was honored at the Kennedy Center in Washington.

"When you're from a small town like Cheraw, and a legend from your town like Dizzy dies, you really feel a sense of loss," said Sarah Spruill of Cheraw. "He brought a lot of excitement into our lives, blacks and whites.

"Even though he belonged to the world, Cheraw will always be remembered as Dizzy Gillespie's hometown."

NEVER IN TUNE

Gillespie was the youngest of nine children—two died early—and grew up in a small wooden house on Huger

Street, four blocks from downtown. It's gone now. The Cheraw of his youth was a farming community—just south of the North Carolina border. Blacks, who comprised a third of the town's 3,700 residents, generally found menial work picking cotton.

His father, James, a builder and bricklayer, ruled his large family with a leather strap. But James Gillespie loved music, too, and at any chance, was off playing East Coast gigs. He spent his money on instruments: a stand-up bass with one string, a piano, guitar, mandolin and set of drums that filled the Gillespies' living room.

John Birks would sit on the floor and marvel at his father banging at the keys as his band rehearsed. James died when John Birks was ten. He'd never know the boy's incomparable talent and contributions to jazz.

That summer, John Birks, his family poor and needing money, went to pick cotton. He hated the work and the little money it generated. He went home one day and told his mother he'd never pick cotton again—he wanted to be a musician, just like his father.

When not in school, John Birks and other kids were forever banging on those instruments. "We were never in tune," said Powe, six months older than John Birks, a trombone player who played for Cab Calloway and Louis Armstrong, and who grew up across Huger Street from the Gillespies. "We'd listen to Duke Ellington and Cab Calloway on the radio and try to imitate them.

"When I met John Birks, he was about eight and playing anything by ear."

Then they met Alice Wilson. She was their teacher at Robert Smalls Public School, the only public school in Cheraw for blacks, grades one through nine.

When John Birks was a fifth grader, Wilson and the principal got money for new instruments. They asked for volunteers to form a band. John Birks was the youngest so the older boys got first pick on instruments. Only a slide trombone remained for John Birks. His arms were still too short to reach the higher notes. He never missed a practice.

A neighbor taught him rudimentary techniques on trumpet. Soon he was playing trombone and trumpet in Wilson's band. "He told most of his friends that I started him off in jazz," Wilson later said in Gillespie's memoirs. "And so I told him: 'Boy, you got me now, 'cause what you play now, I don't understand.'"

SEEKING HIS OWN STYLE

That was the music John Birks, Norman Powe and other kids were playing in the Gillespie home and local watering holes. By then, he and his trumpet were inseparable. Wilson said she'd always see that horn under his arm, never books. His music became mischievous, as he tried different styles to find his own. The boy was also mischievous, "devilish, a little rascal," remembers first cousin Margaret Malloy of Cheraw. Back then, they called him "Lion."

"When he wanted something that someone else had, he'd always get it, even if it meant he fought you for it," Malloy said in 1993. "He wasn't mean-spirited, just single-minded. I think that served him well."

His mischief took him to the former Lyric Theater, where the manager hired him to keep out nonpaying customers. His pay: movies. It was the first time he saw Duke Ellington on the screen, dressed in white tails. There, he'd dream.

Even at age eight, his talents—he was a dancer, too, a cut-up—were known by whites. In a segregated town, he was the only black person invited to entertain at white dances. His first gig: the all-white high school.

He'd also go to the old Ice House bar at the end of Church Street and perform on the piano and trumpet for white patrons.

PLAYING CAROLINAS TOWNS

But he learned rhythm listening to the congregation rock at the black Sanctified Church, a half-block from his house. After ninth grade, Gillespie and Powe won music scholarships to Laurinburg Institute, twenty miles east in Laurinburg, N.C.

The two roomed together and continued to play, their jazz meshing with the greats they heard on radio. Gillespie began to develop his legendary style—always suspenseful, with breakneck runs interrupted by pauses, and notes that shot through the roof.

They kept a band in Cheraw and a Laurinburg insurance agent booked them in towns like Pinehurst, Southern Pines and Clio. His last year at Laurinburg, Gillespie's family moved north to Philadelphia. Gillespie came back to Cheraw for six months, then in 1935 left for Philadelphia.

And there he'd sneak into clubs and listen to jazz. Soon, he was playing with them, and soon he was Dizzy.

He never let the world forget that his urban sounds came from small-town Carolinas beginnings. Wherever he went—Russia, Holland, Nairobi, New York—it was the same: "I come from Cheraw, South Carolina."

"I know I'm always physically and mentally some-place else, but I always feel a link to my hometown," Gillespie said in a 1983 interview.

Malloy never remembers him boasting of fame. "He was always John Birks," she said. "He never acted the part of being a legend. Never. When he saw you, he was never above taking time to say hello, or addressing you by name.

"He learned that here."

Gillespie came home often. He got a key to his hometown in 1983, addressed the S.C. Legislature in 1976 and after he became a devout member of the Baha'i faith, often visited the growing Baha'i community in Hemingway, S.C.

By then the Cheraw he'd known as a boy had vastly changed.

"There is a big change in attitude here," he said after he was honored by Cheraw. "Before I came here, [ex-mayor] Charles Jackson offered me his home to stay in. That's how things have changed. Used to be when we came down here to perform we'd have to stay with friends, or hotels run by blacks.

"There's no jive here anymore."

The last time he was in Cheraw, Malloy and others took him to Charlotte to fly home. He stopped at a ticket counter to cash a check.

"I need some identification, please," said the cashier.

As he'd done thousands of time before, Gillespie put a finger to his mouth, and blew. His trademark bull-frog cheeks inflated to the size of two ripe grapefruits.

"Thank you, that's all the identification I need," the cashier said. "You're Dizzy Gillespie, aren't you?"

~~~

Billy Taylor: Music For The Millennium

BY T. BROOKS SHEPARD

I
f "all diplomacy is a continuation of war by other means," then jazz pianist Billy Taylor, from Greenville, N.C., is a diplomat nonpareil. He is the supreme commander in the struggle for a more enlightened understanding of the art of jazz. In fact, this seventy-seven-year-old gentle giant of jazz is the voice of jazz. When he speaks and when he plays, people listen.

They listen when Taylor speaks because he communicates in so many ways. As a teacher, composer, musician and recording artist, author, lecturer, producer, and television and radio personality, Taylor is all about jazz. In an inimitably affable but determined way, he gets the message out.

You see his smiling face on CBS *Sunday Morning* and hear his friendly voice on National Public Radio's *Billy Taylor's Jazz* at the Kennedy Center. And live from C.D. Hylton High School, in Prince William County, Virginia, which has its own satellite, Taylor broadcasts master classes to students around the country. Taylor also trumpets jazz in his books on music, including *Jazz Piano: A Jazz History* and his latest, *The Billy Taylor Collection*.

His list of academic titles is just as impressive: He is a Duke Ellington Fellow at Yale University, and he occupies the Wilber D. Barrett Chair of Music at the University of Massachusetts at Amherst, where he earned his doctorate in music education. He has been awarded nineteen honorary degrees.

The list goes on: He is a member of the International Association of Jazz Educators Hall of Fame. He has two Peabody journalism awards, an Emmy and an award for Best Direct Satellite Broadcast/Special Events, from the National Academy of Television Arts and Sciences.

Of his many accomplishments, he says, simply, "Everything I do is related, and I'm indebted to music for putting me there."

When it comes to jazz education, a major contribution of his has been Jazzmobile, New York City's premier music clinic and free concert series, which he co-

Editor's Note: T. Brooks Shepard's story on Billy Taylor was written in 1999. Now in his eighties, Dr. Taylor, though recovered from a 2002 stroke, is retired from active touring and recording but still does speaking engagements, radio and television appearances and educational activities. In 2003, he lent his name to East Carolina University's annual April jazz festival. And, according to his website, he now holds more than twenty-three honorary doctoral degrees.

founded with former jazz musician David Bailey. Taylor describes the genesis of the idea for Jazzmobile: "In those days, because we couldn't get jazz taught in the schools to the extent that I wanted to see it, I started a workshop in New York City. And we've turned out a lot of folks that are doing well in the field—people who studied with Frank Foster, Frank Wess, Jimmy Owens, and some of the teachers that we have there. They put folks out there that can play."

People listen when Taylor plays because his protean pianistic skills encompass so many great piano jazz styles and meld them into a splendid oneness. His latest album, *Ten Fingers, One Voice*, is an exquisitely sensitive, virtuoso solo statement on piano. On the tune "Joy Spring," Taylor plays one melody with his right hand and another with his left with confidence, ease and dexterity. "That's something I enjoy doing," he says. "When I was studying classical music, I always wanted to find something to do with the way that Bach handled melodies with both hands. There's something going on here, and there's something going on there. It took me a long time, but I finally found some things that I was comfortable with that allowed me to use my left hand melodically as well as harmonically."

After Taylor graduated with a Bachelor of Science degree in music from Virginia State University, Petersburg, he split straight for New York City. In town less than a day, he was jamming with tenor saxophone master Ben Webster at Minton's, the renowned Harlem jazz club. A year later, he was playing the famed Birdland jazz club on Broadway. Monte Kay, Diahann Carroll's first husband (who later managed Flip Wilson and the Modern Jazz Quartet), hired Taylor because, he said, "I have to have one musician who shows up."

"He liked the fact that I was dependable and could play with anybody—any style, whatever," Taylor explains. "I looked at it as a challenge and was happy to be there. You see, my first job at Birdland was with Charlie Parker and Strings. To start off with Bird in Birdland was just terrific. All of the memories I have from there are pleasant. It was a two-year period in my life, man, that was New Year's Eve every night."

By the 1950s, Taylor's jazz club star was on the ascendant. He was leading his own trio, with Charles Mingus on bass and Charles Smith on drums. "In those days, I could play in Greenwich Village, take a week off and play out on Long Island for a week or so, go to Jersey and play for a couple of weeks, and then go to Connecticut," he recalls. "I could be right at home, playing in this neighborhood, and it was like going to different towns."

By the 1960s, however, the jazz club scene was winding down for him. "What drove me out of the clubs," Taylor says, "was that I was recording for Capitol Records when they discovered The Beatles, and I was so frustrated because nobody could get their records pressed, and you needed to record, especially in my position at that time. You needed to be played on the radio so people would hire you."

Jazz clubs fell on hard times, and jobs disappeared. "In the days that I was traveling with my trio," he continues, "at least for the entire decade of the '50s, you could get a gig and play for a month, then go to another place for two weeks, go to another place for three weeks. It wasn't a one-nighter. You got a salary that you could live on, on the road. So you could make it by doing the club scene. When that fell apart, it was very difficult for a lot of guys to make the adjustment of going into colleges, doing concerts and stuff like that, because now you're talking about one or several concerts together so that you could make up for what you used to make in two weeks."

With the jazz club era dying, Taylor knew that he was going to have to make the transition to another part of the business. "I began to look into radio a little more, and finally a guy hired me at WLIB in New York City. I was supposed to do a jazz show, just on Saturdays, which I could tape and still continue to play. I did, and it was so successful that when one of the guys got busted for payola, they brought me in on a daily basis, and I came in off the road."

Having survived that era, Taylor is confident that there will be no diminution in the status or stature of the art of jazz. He describes the power of jazz this way, "The music touches people in ways that transcend language. That's the thing that I think makes jazz so popular in places where they don't speak the same language we speak.

"When I've gone to India or to South America, China and places like that, I can't talk to those people. They listen to me and respond to what I play. I can't exchange any ideas with them unless they speak English because of my limitations. The exciting thing for me is that you play something for them and they just get it. As an artist, who can ask for anything more?

"This is the millennium coming up, and I think that since jazz has been the most influential music of this century, it's going to continue like that. I don't see anything else, at the moment, that can take the place of the contribution it's making now.

"People who play jazz are influencing people around the world rhythmically, harmonically and melodically," says the honorable doctor. "Those are three of the key aspects of music. So if you're doing those things collectively and separately, then you're covering a lot of territory."

The Carolina Bebop Kings

BY STEVE CRUMP

Several of America's best-known and most-beloved jazz standards came from gifted artists with humble Carolina beginnings.

" 'Round Midnight," "A Night in Tunisia," and "Giant Steps" are treasured works of three individuals whose roots are deeply planted in Tar Heel and Palmetto soil.

Consider this: trumpeter John Birks Gillespie, better known as Dizzy, and saxophonist John Coltrane were born sixteen miles apart, and pianist Thelonious Monk came into the world on October 10, 1917 nine days before Dizzy's arrival.

* * *

The church, as it has for so many musicians, offered an early forum that became a meaningful outlet to develop fundamental skills.

Born in the railroad town of Hamlet, N.C., in the Sandhills in September 1926, John Coltrane's early introduction to music came in what would later be his new hometown of High Point.

He was the grandson of the Rev. William Blair who preached at Saint Stephen AME Zion. That church was an early showcase where Trane's talent as a lad would shine through.

"We had a very happy childhood, and John was well taken care of," remembered Betty Jackson, who grew up near the Coltrane family. She also recalled his early musical feats. "I was in the choir and we used to do 'Jesu, Joy of Man's Desire,' and I remember him singing that bass part and playing that bass part on the saxophone."

Dizzy Gillespie discovered music at the old red-brick Wesley United Methodist Church in Cheraw, S.C., but his first horn came from Robert Smalls Elementary School. Surprisingly, it wasn't the instrument he would excel with. "They gave him a trombone," said Gillespie's cousin Norman Powe, who was there to see the early challenges. "His arms weren't long enough to get to the fifth and sixth positions."

Although Dizzy Gillespie, John Coltrane, Thelonious Monk and Billy Taylor are recognized as jazz icons, most people don't know how closely their lives intersected—as Carolinians. This piece by award-winning filmmaker Steve Crump, adapted from his documentary *The Carolina Bebop Kings*, explores the connections among these men and their music.

Clearly challenged with the trombone, Dizzy was given a trumpet. His musical skills were so solid he won a scholarship at North Carolina's Laurinburg Institute.

That was years after Thelonious Monk by the age of five would leave his birthplace of Rocky Mount, N.C., with his mother. They settled in New York, on the path taken by many African Americans during "The Great Migration."

Getting out of the Jim Crow South and settling in Northern cities eventually offered them opportunities for their creative talents to soar.

Philadelphia later became home to Dizzy and Trane. Like Monk, these Carolinians would also find success in New York City.

* * *

Saxophonist Jimmy Heath of the well-known Heath Brothers, a family with connections to Wilmington, N.C., took an early chance on John Coltrane. "I was daring enough at a young age to have a big band, and I asked Trane if he would play in my big band, and he said yes."

Heath's bass-playing older brother Percy would also land a gig in one of Thelonious Monk's bands in New York.

Eventually Jimmy and Trane would share the stage with Dizzy. Jimmy recalls being singled out by the hard-blowing trumpet player. "We were big bebop fans; we assumed the costume of the beboppers. We got us some berets and our artist ties and we would follow the band."

Jimmy says it was an entree into Dizzy's big band. "Eventually, I got in the big band, and Coltrane, who was in my band, got into Dizzy's band. We got into Dizzy's band in 1949 together."

Jazz musicians from the Carolinas had a way of looking out for each other.

Saxophonist Lou Donaldson of Badin, N.C., became one of Monk's sidemen. "He thought about stuff that other people didn't think about musically," Donaldson said.

That meant being prepared for anything onstage, he added. "And [Monk] would never write the stuff out for you to play. You would have to memorize it."

With Donaldson and drummer Max Roach from Newland, N.C., Monk would record a tribute to the Tar Heel state, "Carolina Moon."

* * *

At the peak of his popularity in the 1960s, Monk appeared on the cover of *Time* and won several reader polls in the highly regarded *Downbeat* magazine.

Dizzy would be known as America's jazz ambassador and lead several touring bands around the world for the U.S. State Department. One of them had a young trumpet player by the name of Quincy Jones. He would later lead the United Nations orchestra.

Trane not only stood on his own as a performer, but also shared the stage and recorded with the legendary Miles Davis.

* * *

In many aspects they were perhaps larger in death than they ever were in life.

Coltrane died of liver cancer in 1967, but forty years later his contributions would be honored with a special Pulitzer Prize for his improvisation and contributions to the history of jazz.

Monk, whose death made the front page of the *New York Times* in 1982, would also be honored with a Pulitzer in 2006. His son, drummer T.S. Monk, carries on his work and legacy through the Thelonious Monk Institute of Jazz, which keeps jazz alive in inner-city communities and awards scholarships.

Before he died in 1993, Dizzy lent his name to a hospital in Englewood, New Jersey, to help struggling musicians. That's where the Jazz Foundation and its network have given jazz musicians more than $200,000 a year in donated funds for heart surgery, cancer treatment, tests and other medical care.

The work and good deeds of all three live on.

Understanding their many gifts inspired another Carolina jazz giant, Billy Taylor (known as America's jazz professor), to make this observation about their talents, "They were linked by race. They were linked by experience, and they were linked by art."

These links help music fans remember Dizzy, Monk, and Coltrane together as the "Carolina Bebop Kings," whose musical visions transcended the confines of the segregated South to the deserved recognition on the stage of Carnegie Hall and beyond.

~~~

Charlie Daniels

BY WOODY MITCHELL

Charlie Daniels made his mark on 1970s Southern rock as a bandleader/fiddler/guitarist, helping define the budding genre with songs like "The South's Gonna Do It" and "Long Haired Country Boy," successfully straddling the fence between rock and country. But in recent years, he's equally renowned as a voice for conservative values, uber-patriotism and good-over-evil.

Born in Wilmington, N.C., in 1936, Daniels was steeped in Pentecostal gospel, bluegrass and early R&B before he left home after high school with a traveling band. In 1959, he joined the Jaguars and traveled with them until 1967. Along the way, he met Nashville producer Bob Johnston, who eventually talked him into settling in Music City as a session player.

It was a good move—Daniels played on Bob Dylan's albums *Nashville Skyline*, *New Morning* and *Self Portrait,* all produced by Johnston. He also cut *The Prophet* with guitar legend Roy Buchanan (never released) and produced the Youngbloods' highly regarded *Elephant Mountain.*

By 1970, Daniels was building his own band and hit pay dirt with the minor hit "Uneasy Rider" in 1973. His career picked up steam as his material caught on with the "headneck" crowd, and he began the Volunteer Jam series, daylong festivals that included such leading Southern-rock lights as the Allman Brothers and Lynyrd Skynyrd. This stage was capped in 1979 by "The Devil Went Down to Georgia," which went to No. 1 on the country charts and crossed over to hit No. 3 on the pop charts.

The Iran hostage crisis in 1980 spawned Daniels' first venture into hard-core jingoism with the song "In America." Themes of vigilantism and American dominance permeated subsequent albums through the '90s, generating notoriety that attracted media attention. Meanwhile, he made a string of gospel albums on the side.

After 9/11, a number of country-flavored performers recorded fervently patriotic songs, and Daniels chimed in with his contributions. But his zealous nationalism and biblical sense of vengeance was too much for Country Music Television—he pulled out of the network's Country Freedom Concert benefit when they took issue with the lyrics in some of his material.

Daniels still tours, but not at the frantic pace of the past. He continues to hold forth with frequent political statements on his website's "Soapbox" page. His 2007 album, *Deuces*, features Daniels' duets with artists as diverse as Brenda Lee and Hootie and the Blowfish lead singer Darius Rucker on some classic country tunes. In January of 2008, Daniels was formally inducted into The Grand Ole Opry.

~~~

Ben E. King

BY PHILLIP BROWN

Possessing one of the most elegant baritone voices ever, Rock and Roll Hall of Fame alumnus Ben E. King's imprint on the musical landscape is so indelible that an optimum barometer has been set for countless aspiring performers. From a youngster in Harlem to an embraceable solo artist, Ben E. King's contributions to the pop music spectrum are incalculable.

From the first cut of his 2006 release *I've Been Around* to the very last track on this superlative disc, Ben E. King magnifies his presence as a monumental force in the ever-changing entertainment arena. *I've Been Around* is a twelve-track rainbow collection of fresh, eclectic tunes, including the title track, "I've Been Around," which is a rapturous mix of R&B and indefatigable jazz-funk; "Comparing Her To You," is a lingering ballad laced with a smidgeon of new country; and "I Bet You That" is a vocally infectious jam with a uniquely frenetic pulse. In addition to these and a plethora of other novel selections, keep an ear open for the surprise bonus track.

Born Benjamin Earl Nelson, in Henderson, N.C., young Ben's family relocated to New York City when he was the tender age of nine. While attending junior high school, he discovered a unique talent: singing harmony in a group with other gifted youngsters. Little did precocious Ben realize that these after-school, impromptu doo-wop sessions were mere tune-ups for a dynamic musical career that would exceed his wildest dreams, span decades, and enchant millions of music aficionados the world over. Benny's precocious young group became known as The Four B's and earned the reputation of being one of the finest young acts in the area. One evening, while competing against other aspiring acts at the world-renowned Apollo Theater, their sacrifice and success was handsomely rewarded as they walked away with a prized second-place finish.

In 1958 Ben reached the big-time as a member of the Five Crowns, a local group that opened shows for well-known groups. In that same year they were privileged to open an Apollo Theater concert for the most popular R&B group in the world, The Drifters. Because of the departure of their popular lead singer, then manager George Treadwell sensed a colossal vacuum and staleness in the group. His solution? Replace the whole Drifters group with members of the graceful Five Crowns! That daring move would open the door for Ben to sing lead for the greatest R&B group at that time and create full exposure for his musical compositions. Their first recording in 1959 was Atlantic Records' trend-setting smash-hit titled "There Goes My Baby"; that ballad (which Ben co-wrote with Jerry Leiber and Mike Stoller) distinguished The Drifters as the first popular group to feature strings (violins) on major musical recordings.

As a member of The Drifters, Ben sang lead on such chart toppers as "Dance With Me," This Magic Moment," "Save The Last Dance," and "I Count The Tears." In 1960, and in the midst of unimaginable success as a Drifter, Ben made the decision to aim even higher by pursuing a lifelong dream—to choose and perform many of his own tunes as a solo artist. This also called for Ben to create a stage name to distinguish the solo artist from the Drifter. By shortening his original name, by using his middle initial, and by displacing his last name, he now became known universally as Ben E. King.

In 1961, as Ben E. King, the icon that the world has come to cherish, his first hit was one that even the Queen of Soul was moved to cover, the magnificent "Spanish Harlem." But his second heart-melting single, "Stand By Me," reached gargantuan proportions. That No. 1 R&B hit and Top 5 pop jam (written by King, Leiber and Stoller) has been sung or covered by almost everyone who ever walked into a recording studio. Why, even Hollywood film-director Rob Reiner was inspired to select "Stand By Me" as the title for his 1986 feature film and sound score by the same title. During that same period "Stand By Me" was re-released as a single, rose to the Top 10 in the U.S., and rocketed to the No. 1 spot in the U.K.

In 1962 King's hits kept coming: "Don't Play That Song" became another commercial success and was complimented by "I Who Have Nothing" and the Latin-flavored "Amor."

With quite a musical track record already established by the early '60s, King seemed to be unstoppable. However, the English, who had been studying and rehearsing R&B and early rock sounds of America for nearly a decade, were finally ready to export the very music that inspired them back to its creators. As King once remarked, "The British launched the greatest entertainment promotional campaign ever. They took our music and sold it back to us!" But despite invading America with countless bands imitating the great blues, R&B, and rock groups of the day with watered-down versions of the same music, artists like the incomparable King continued to weather the trans-Atlantic storm. And if that wasn't enough to contend with, disco, as if rising from the dead and sporting simplistic, up-tempo, and mostly rhythmic reiterations, saturated the airwaves across the nation and around the globe. Yet, despite all of this, compromise was never a consideration with King, as the balladeer remained true to his music and loyal to his devoted following.

While in Miami in 1975, the head of Atlantic records, Ahmet Ertegun, caught one of King's dazzling shows. He was so impressed that he encouraged King to re-sign with Atlantic Records. King acquiesced, and the result of this reunion was a No. 1 on R&B charts and a Top 5 on pop with the funk-laced groove titled "Supernatural Thing, Part 1." Ertegun said of King: "Ben E. King is one of the greatest singers in the history of rock 'n' roll and rhythm and blues. His style and the tempo of his voice have a magic all their own. I'm sure his fans all over the world will relish his new album." This set the stage for one of the most interesting collaborations of the '70s, the soulful King and the progressive Average White Band. The result was the 1977 release, intimately titled *Benny and Us.*

In 1999 King's versatility was accentuated through collaborations with Milt Jackson and the late Ray Charles' protégé David "Fathead" Newman; this resulted in the unique project titled *Shades Of Blue.* Of course, this was not King's first collaboration; he recorded a duet with legendary diva LaVern Baker when he was just twenty-two.

King's first release of this century (2000) was the studio project, *Person To Person*, which is a tribute to his love of jazz and blues standards along with his passion for fine arrangements. This album is a live recording at New York's famed Blue Note Club. King plans a new CD soon and he continues to perform live at top venues around the world. He recently performed a mini-tour with a legend-filled ensemble titled Four Kings, which featured superlative vocals and timeless arrangements from a stellar cast.

As a philanthropist, King's love for the youth and disadvantaged of America has inspired him to establish a charitable foundation to address some of their needs. The Stand By Me Foundation sponsors a yearly celebrity-golf tournament and other fund-raising endeavors. This also provides an avenue for the great King to reinvest in the community that is so precious to him.

In 2005, with hip-hop enjoying major groundbreaking success, King is still recording and pleasing fans from Tokyo to the streets of L.A. Truly one of the premier group and individual artists to ever clutch a microphone, King's rich, velvety voice is a priceless

national treasure. *I've Been Around*, a True Life Entertainment production, was released in 2006 and was followed up by his 2007 national television appearance on *The Late Show* starring David Letterman. The CD is full of melodious delicacies interspersed with versatile vocal gymnastics. King's career was poetically summed up this way: "As the auburn moon glows and the grand sun keeps shining, Ben E. King's contribution to the world of music is one that will not only stand the test of time but one that will flourish incessantly."

Loonis, Alec and the American Songbook

BY JERRY SHINN

They were the unlikeliest of collaborators. When they met in the early 1960s, Alec Wilder was well into his fifties, a bachelor supported by an upstate New York banking family trust fund, living at the Algonquin Hotel in New York City or on trains. Loonis McGlohon was barely into his forties, a native of rural Eastern North Carolina, happily married and raising a young family in a leafy Charlotte suburb.

Alec had been composing music since 1930, and had written or co-written popular songs performed and recorded by Frank Sinatra, Bing Crosby, Peggy Lee, Tony Bennett, and other celebrated singers and musicians of the '30s, '40s and '50s. He also had written "serious" compositions for small ensembles. He was a sort of cult figure among aficionados of classic jazz and cabaret music.

Loonis was something of a piano prodigy growing up in Ayden, N.C. (home of the annual Collard Festival). He had played in dance bands as a student at East Carolina Teachers College (now East Carolina University) and with the Army Air Corps during World War II. In Charlotte he had regular gigs with his jazz trio in nightclubs and at social events, but he made his living as music director and occasional special-projects pro-

ducer at WBT radio and WBTV. He had composed and recorded a few songs, and he was something of a musical celebrity in and around Charlotte. But he was not widely known outside his home state.

Alec, product of a privileged but emotionally miserable childhood, had cut most of his remaining family ties and was eccentric, sometimes moody, and often rude.

Loonis, from a loving, solidly middle-class extended family and now with a lively, loving family of his own, exuded good cheer, Southern charm and graciousness and was generally polite and respectful.

Alec was an agnostic who despised the sentimentality and secular excesses of Christmas.

Loonis directed the choir at Carmel Presbyterian Church and wrote hymns. Christmas was his favorite time of year.

Alec was a heavy smoker and had a problem with alcohol, occasionally going on drinking binges.

Loonis was a model of moderation in all things, except maybe Eastern North Carolina barbecue and country ham.

They also had a few important similarities, including their unpretentious but inviolate personal integrity and their large capacity for loyal friendship and for humor, whimsy and joy. But what made their differences ultimately insignificant was what they shared, which was their taste in music and the aesthetic values on which it was based.

Loonis was aware of those shared values long before he got to know Alec. As a student at East Carolina, he was already enamored of Alec's music. Recordings were on brittle discs that spun on turntables at 78 revolutions per minute, and the name of the composer was printed on the label in the center of the disc. When Loonis went shopping for records, he looked for the name of his musical hero Alec Wilder on labels.

It was the time of Cold War crises and nuclear standoffs, of Elvis and the Beatles, of miniskirts, Playboy Clubs and the pill. It was also a time when radio and television stations still took pride in producing some of their own programs, using their own talent. At WBTV, Loonis was producing a series of musical programs featuring talented local teenagers. For the series finale, he chose songs by Alec Wilder. He had no mailing address for Alec but had read that he lived at the Algonquin Hotel. He wrote him a letter in care of the Algonquin, telling him about the program. Alec surprised him with a prompt reply, saying he would like to come to Charlotte and see the show. He came by train, and a nervous, excited Loonis met him and took him to meet the young people in the cast, gathered by the lake at Freedom Park. Alec told them all how flattered and grateful he was that they were doing an entire program of his songs.

That evening Alec was treated to Nan McGlohon's cooking at the McGlohon home, and he and Loonis talked. They talked about music, of course, about what they liked and what they didn't like. What they didn't like was rock 'n' roll, which was increasingly dominating radio playlists. Their musical tastes had been formed in the era of the great swing bands and the classic Broadway and Hollywood musicals, when most of what became known as the Great American Songbook was written. As boys and young men they loved those songs and the way jazz musicians interpreted them to create America's great indigenous art form. In comparison, rock 'n' roll was crude and simplistic. They considered it a shameful corruption of the glorious musical heritage of African Americans epitomized in the music of Louis Armstrong, Duke Ellington, Dizzy and Bird, Billie and Ella—music of great energy, emotional depth and sophistication.

Loonis and Alec were committed to the preservation and expansion of the Songbook. They had plenty to talk about.

Alec was old-fashioned in that he kept in touch with friends by mail. After he returned to New York, he and Loonis began exchanging letters. Loonis sent Alec some of the songs he had written. The response was a phone call from Alec, who said, "Where the hell have you been? I've been looking for you. Send me a lyric."

That was the beginning of a collaboration that would last until Alec's death in 1980, producing dozens of songs, including a few that rank among the best anyone ever wrote. Over the next decade, songs by McGlohon-Wilder and Wilder-McGlohon were recorded by Sinatra, Eileen Farrell, Teddi King, Cleo Laine, Mabel Mercer, Marlene VerPlanck, Meredith d'Ambrosio, Dick Haymes, Julius LaRosa, the great jazz pianist Keith Jarrett and many others.

They wrote songs over the telephone, one dictating

the key and the notes in each bar while the other wrote it all down, or sometimes one dictating the words and asking the other to set them to music. They wrote songs at Loonis' piano in the McGlohons' home, where Alec came for extended visits. While Loonis was at work during the day, Alec would start something for Loonis to help him finish that night. Sometimes Loonis wrote the words and Alec wrote the music. Sometimes it was the other way around, or both of them working on both the words and the music. The genesis of a song could be just a few notes, a musical phrase that one would establish and the other would build on. Or it could be just a few words, or an idea for a title. A song recorded by Sinatra began that way. Alec thought of an intriguing phrase—"South to a Warmer Place"—and challenged Loonis to write a song with that title.

One day Loonis and Nan returned from Greensboro, where they had just left the youngest of their three children, Laurie, to begin her freshman year of college. Suddenly they were "empty nesters," and they were feeling a bit sad. Alec was there and, oblivious to those parental sentiments, showed Loonis a tune he had written. He said it was a sort of crazy love song, and he asked Loonis to write some lyrics, maybe something about balloons and polka dots and young love. Loonis didn't feel like writing anything, but he sat down and made the effort. He wasn't in the right frame of mind to write a love song. Instead, he wrote about what he was feeling, about how empty the house felt. Alec pronounced "Where's the Child I Used to Hold?" perfect. On another occasion Loonis came home from work to find Alec noodling a few bars at the piano, fascinated with the strings of eighth and sixteenth notes he had crafted. Alec asked Loonis to complete the melody,

write a bridge and come up with some words. The first five descending notes reminded Loonis of a term he had heard since childhood: blackberry winter, referring to a brief return of cool weather in the Southern spring, after the blackberry bushes bloom. Loonis wrote lyrics on that theme, and a bridge that added a bit of drama to Alec's gently cascading melody. "Blackberry Winter" was possibly the best song they wrote together, and about as good as a song can be.

In addition to their prolific songwriting, the unlikely McGlohon-Wilder collaboration bore other kinds of artistic fruit. In the late 1960s, they wrote music for a new theme park, based on the book and movie *The Wizard of Oz*, built as a summer attraction at the new ski resort on Beech Mountain, in the North Carolina High Country. Perhaps the most important McGlohon-Wilder collaboration was a public radio series.

For several years Alec had been working on a book called *American Popular Song: The Great Innovators, 1900–1950*. Published in 1972, it was monumental in concept and in execution, a volume of more than 500 pages. Alec had chosen some 800 songs out of the more than 300,000 submitted for copyright during the first half of the twentieth century, and analyzed each one, offering his opinions on its strengths and weaknesses. He devoted a chapter to each of the major songwriters of that period, and other chapters to outstanding songs by lesser composers. The only important composer whose name and songs were never mentioned was Alec Wilder, who refused, despite his publisher's pleas, to include anything about himself.

Among the people impressed by the book was Dick Phipps of the South Carolina Educational Radio and

Television Network. He wanted to produce a series of radio programs using the book's title, hosted by Alec Wilder, and featuring outstanding singers performing the songs being discussed. He mentioned the idea to Loonis, who thought it was a great concept but said that Alec would never agree to do it. He told Phipps that Alec was very shy, avoided the spotlight and hated microphones. They would never be able to get him into a recording studio, he said.

Phipps didn't give up so easily. They wouldn't have to get Alec into a studio, he said. They could record the programs at his home on Lake Murray, outside Columbia. He would hide the microphones in some potted plants. Alec was finally persuaded. Loonis would serve as co-host, and his trio (Terry Lassiter on bass, Jim Lackey on drums) would accompany the singers.

Loonis recruited Thelma Carpenter as the guest for the first show, recorded in spring 1976 in Phipps' living room, with its large picture window overlooking the lake. As promised, Phipps had hidden the microphones, but he may have overdone the greenery, with ficus trees and exotic potted plants. When Alec walked in, he asked, "Where is Jane?"

"Who?"

"You know, Jane. Tarzan's mate."

Phipps got a grant from the National Endowment for the Arts to support the program. After hearing a pilot, National Public Radio agreed to distribute *American Popular Song with Alec Wilder and Friends* to 190 affiliates across the nation. The first show aired in fall 1976, and it was an immediate hit with listeners hungry to hear those kinds of songs and singers again. It also exposed a new generation of listeners to the Great American Songbook.

From the beginning, Loonis and Alec had no problem getting the singers they wanted, including Teddi King, Dick Haymes, Margaret Whiting, Tony Bennett and Mabel Mercer. Once the program was on the air, singers began calling them, asking to be on the show. The program revived the careers of some singers who had once been well known on radio or in movies or nightclubs but had faded from view in the rock era. It also revived an interest in cabaret music in New York City bars and lounges. It was the catalyst for a new record label, Audiophile, created to take advantage of the renewed interest in the great songs and singers being heard on public radio.

After taping twenty-seven programs, Alec and Loonis were persuaded to do thirteen more. The series won a Peabody Award, radio's equivalent to the Oscar. It also expanded the horizons of Loonis' reputation and career. He continued to live in Charlotte and work at WBTV, but his gigs were now not only in Charlotte and the Carolinas, but also in New York, Los Angeles, San Francisco, and even the Far East. The singers who performed on *American Popular Song* and the audience learned that Loonis was a world-class accompanist. He spent a season as musical director, accompanist and arranger for Eileen Farrell, the erstwhile opera and concert diva who had started singing popular music, traveling to concert venues across the nation.

He and Eileen later co-hosted another public radio series on great singers.

Not long after the last taping of *American Popular Song*, Alec was diagnosed with lung cancer. He died in Florida in 1980, on the day before Christmas.

Despite his growing international reputation and exposure, Loonis kept his roots firmly planted in Charlotte. He was usually available to play at a local wedding reception or social event, and he brought some of the fine singers who were now his good friends to perform with him in Charlotte. In the mid-1980s, he and Charles Kuralt created a much-acclaimed musical tribute to their home state, *North Carolina Is My Home*.

In early 1994, Loonis was diagnosed with lymphoma, and the prognosis was not good. But he lived eight more years, sometimes depressed by his condition and debilitated by chemotherapy, but they were productive and often joyful years. He continued to perform, to record, to write music, to enjoy good times with friends and cool summer days at his mountain house. When he died in January 2002, there were unfinished songs and unfinished projects cluttering his studio.

Like his friend Alec, he left a rich legacy, not only of his own music, but of all the music that he and Alec together had revived, refreshed and reestablished as the Great American Songbook.

~~~

Nina Simone Put A Spell On Us

BY CHARLES BLACKBURN JR.

Nina Simone grew up in a pretty little tourist town in the North Carolina mountains, but by the time of her death in 2003 at her home in the south of France, she belonged to the world. Her deep, raspy, forceful voice, along with a gift for composition and a piano style that reflected her classical training, made her a unique figure in jazz and popular music for nearly fifty years.

Her music embraced jazz, folk, classical, pop, gospel, blues, Broadway, rock, and opera, in more than fifty albums. As one reviewer said of her style, "It's Bach, boogie, and bebop all mixed together."

What's more, she often sang with a larger purpose, providing a lift to the American Civil Rights movement and helping to raise the consciousness of a nation.

MUSICAL UPBRINGING

She was born Eunice Kathleen Waymon in 1933 in Tryon, about forty miles south of Asheville. "The house on East Livingston Street where she was born is being restored by its current owners," according to Crys Armbrust of Tryon, who was among the singer's fans long before he became executive director of the Waymon-Simone Memorial Project.

Launched in 2006, the effort to honor the world-famous diva is ahead of schedule in providing scholarships to deserving students in all disciplines. Plans also call for an annual Nina Simone Music Festival, as well as a bronze statue of her by renowned local sculptor William Behrends.

A former university English professor, Armbrust is an accomplished musician in his own right and working on an original piece called "Five for Nina Simone," based on writings of significance to her. The memorial project is his brain-child, in pursuit of which he has become an authority on the singer/songwriter. "She's the most famous person ever to come from Tryon," he notes, "and I felt we should recognize her. Local people were very supportive of her during her formative years here."

He says Waymon came from a musical family and was playing the piano by the age of three. Her father, a businessman and jack-of-all-trades, was a performer earlier in his career. Her mother was a religious woman who later became a Methodist minister. By the time she was six, Waymon was the main accompanist at St. Luke's CME Church.

Armbrust says, "Mrs. George Miller agreed to pay for formal lessons here for a year with Mrs. Muriel Mazzanovich, a transplanted Englishwoman known to the community as Mrs. Mazzy."

In her autobiography, *I Put A Spell On You*, Nina Simone said of those lessons: "Mrs. Mazzanovich only allowed me to practice Bach, and soon I loved him as much as she did." At the end of the year, when the money ran out, Mrs. Mazzy started the Eunice Waymon Fund so the gifted student could continue her studies.

Everything in the prodigy's adolescence revolved around music. When the time came, it was decided that she would attend Allen High School in Asheville, a four-year boarding school for African-American girls.

EARLY INFLUENCES

In Asheville, she studied with the school's music teacher and had private lessons from Clemens Sandresky, now dean emeritus of the Salem College School of Music. In the late 1940s, he was a young man just starting his own career, following military service and studies at Dartmouth and Harvard.

"She was my first private student when I opened a piano studio in my Asheville apartment," Sandresky recalls from his home in Winston-Salem. He was impressed with the fifteen-year-old from the start. "I remember saying to friends, 'There isn't anything I say to this girl about music that she doesn't understand immediately.' I found she had an extraordinary affinity for Bach and decided that she should be heard."

He arranged a recital for her at his studio. Everyone was enthusiastic about the performance, "It was apparent that Eunice had to go on," Sandresky says. "Money was raised in Tryon to send her to the Juilliard School of Music in New York."

ROAD TO SUCCESS

After a year at Juilliard, she had hoped to attend the prestigious Curtis Institute of Music in Philadelphia, but was refused admission on the grounds that she wasn't good enough. This rejection would haunt her for the rest of her life.

She moved to Philadelphia anyway. "She still wanted to pursue a classical career," Armbrust says. "She gave piano lessons to make money and studied as a private student with the same instructor she would have had at the Curtis Institute. When he remarked one day that she should have been a scholarship student there, it confirmed to her that she had been rejected because of her race, not because of a lack of talent."

On a trip to New York around this time, Sandresky stopped in Philadelphia to visit his former student. "She had just started playing in a nightclub in Atlantic City," he says, "and didn't want her religious mother to find out. That's why she changed her name to Nina Simone."

She had discovered a nightclub performer could make more money than a piano teacher. "The club owner suggested she sing as well as play," Armbrust explains. "She had a regal presence onstage and demanded that her audiences respect her by being quiet during her sets."

She gained a following among local college students and attracted the attention of a record producer. Her 1959 recording of "I Loves You Porgy," from the opera *Porgy and Bess*, became a Top 40 hit and made her a star.

Later, she began composing songs of her own. The searing lyrics to "Mississippi Goddamn," written after the 1963 murder of Civil Rights leader Medgar Evers, were both an indictment and a plea for justice. Her other songs included "To Be Young, Gifted, and Black" and, in memory of Martin Luther King, "Why? The King of Love Is Dead."

GREAT COLLABORATION

One of her best collaborations was with Grammy-winning jazz pianist and educator Billy Taylor, who grew up in Greenville, N.C. Now retired, Taylor has been the Kennedy Center's artistic adviser on jazz for a dozen years. Each spring, East Carolina University holds a jazz festival named for him.

"Nina Simone was a student at Juilliard when my bass player brought her to see me perform in a club," Taylor recalls from his home in New York. "She heard me play a song titled 'I Wish I Knew How It Would Feel To Be Free.'"

He had written the song for his daughter and considers it his most important work. "Later, when Nina got a record deal with RCA Victor, she called me to say she'd like to include it and invited me to the recording session," Taylor says. "I was enthralled listening to her play it. She asked, 'Does it have any words?' And I told her it did."

Did it ever. The lyrics resonated with the times. It was 1967. Her version of "I Wish I Knew How It Would Feel To Be Free" became an anthem of the Civil Rights movement.

FAME AND EXILE

Simone left the United States in 1973 and lived in the Caribbean and Africa before settling in Europe. She said she felt freer there than she did in her native country. She returned in 1985 for a concert tour and remained a top draw in her later years, making records into the 1990s.

"Nina last visited Tryon in 1992 and played music at St. Luke's CME Church here, where her career began," Armbrust says. One of her greatest performances came at Carnegie Hall in 2001. She was somewhat frail, having battled for a number of years the cancer that would ultimately claim her. Fans wildly applauded every song and demanded an encore—to which she responded by shouting affectionately, "Go home!" Support for the Waymon-Simone Memorial Project in Tryon has come from far and wide. "While local people are interested in the life of Eunice Waymon," Armbrust notes, "the world is still in love with Nina Simone."

Link Wray

BY BRENDAN McKENNEDY

I came to Link Wray late, and ignorantly, but honestly. About five years ago, I bought a used LP set, a Columbia compilation called *Rockabilly Stars*: Carl Perkins, Sleepy LaBeef, Rick Nelson, those guys. On first listen, one track snagged my ear like barbed wire: "Mary Ann," a Ray Charles song, cut by Link and his band the Raymen. Their "Hand Clapper" also appears on the compilation, as well as "Rawhide." But it was "Mary Ann" that collared me, with its gravel-crunch guitar, its jungle tom-toms suddenly thrown beneath the tires of a crazed swing backbeat. And more—Link's desperate howling:

I say HEYYY-uh MARy Annnn. I say baaaabuh— cuh'mon hooommmme.

Of course I'd heard "Rumble," in the film *Pulp Fiction* if not before then, but the song hadn't punctured my consciousness. I didn't know that what I was supposed to hear was the *guitar*. It was Link's voice here that rattled me awake. He sounded both leering and heartsick, burning love and burning rubber. Ray Charles's original is a seduction song, a dance-floor pick-up line: "Oh Mary Ann, can I take you home tonight?"

Where the Raymen find the story, Mary Ann has come home, stayed, moved in, and run off. Listening to Link Wray's feral, bloodshot phrasing, it's not difficult to imagine what drove her to flight. When he drawls, "Baby come on home," it's a typical codependent love-song entreat, but it's also a threat.

Hey Mary Ann, come on home: I dare you.

✳ ✳ ✳

Link Wray was born a middle child, in a dirt-floor shack in Dunn, N.C., a truck-stop town forty miles south of Raleigh. His mother was a fiery Shawnee street preacher, and his father had been gassed in the trenches of Europe and survived. When Link was eight, he met a circus performer called Hambone, who introduced Link to the blues, fixing Wray to an archetype that also claims Hank Williams, Sam Phillips, and the Carter Family: the recording star tutored by a black bluesman who is himself swallowed by history.

At the time he recorded "Mary Ann," Link had one lung. The army had sent him to war in Korea, where he contracted TB, later causing a pneumonia bout that cost him his left lung. The doctors told him to take it easy on the singing, the consequence of which we can suss is that he developed his famous guitar style: the speaker cones punctured by switchblade knives, the feedback, the power chords, whence floweth the rocky river of punk, garage, grunge and metal.

I'd submit that Link's rare vocal tracks, carried on his one lung, were as innovative as his vaunted guitar picking. I can't draw any lines to and from—I've never read anyone cite his dragging dead-dog voice as a singing inspiration. But listen. Listen to his rotten, choking, obsessed take on the Jimmy Reed stalker blues, "Ain't That Lovin' You Baby," in which Link Wray gasps and rasps as though his lover really had, as he suggests she might as well try, dropped him into the ocean, or imprisoned him, dead, deep in the earth. As if he really had come crawling out of the roiling darkness, out of death itself, breathing nothing in his one lung but love, or hatred, or both at once. Tell me that voice doesn't inspire you.

~~~

Peg Leg Jackson: The Last Medicine Show

BY JERRY BLEDSOE

The afternoon heat was heavy in the room, oppressive like the heat of July or August. Almost no air stirred. The window was closed, still covered outside with the clear plastic that had kept out the winter winds. A fat wasp took flight from a corner of a windowpane and buzzed lazily over the bed where the old man lay.

The old man had a dark, lean face with a vicious scar across the right side. "Twelve-gauge shotgun done that," he said later, offering no further explanation. The scar had claimed half his ear. His gray goatee seemed to stand on his chin. Even in the heat his body was under the covers. The wooden leg was propped against the foot of the bed.

Peg Leg Jackson hadn't been up all day. The miseries were upon him, had been for several days. There had been considerable debate about just what had brought on this attack. John Glenn's wife maintained it was those green beans, so heavy with grease, that he had eaten the other night. But in Peg Leg's mind the matter was settled.

"Eat too much po'k," he said. "High blood, you know . . . I love hog meat, you see. Appetite's goin' to be the death of me, I reckon."

Another white boy had come. He sat by the bed fiddling with a tape recorder that wouldn't work. In recent years, there had been a lot of eager white faces, mostly young, drawn to Peg Leg's side. He always made time for them, even when he had the miseries. They often had tape recorders, and they wanted him to tell his lies into them, sing his songs and play his mouth harp. Some had been almost reverent, convinced, it seemed that locked somewhere inside Peg Leg's harmonica were the very secrets of life.

It was true Peg Leg need only play his mouth harp and all of life's miseries and joys would come tumbling out. He could make that thing talk and laugh and cry. And if those who had come were lucky and got him liquored up enough, got him *right,* Peg Leg might even dance. Yes, dance, with that peg leg flying, that leg he carved himself kicking high.

"Shoot, he can dance better'n he can play them

Peg Leg Jackson got to feeling better after I visited him, and in the summer of 1977 went to Canada to make another appearance at a folk music festival. It was his last. He fell ill again after returning home and died in September. He is buried in a small church cemetery not far from the shanty he called home. —JERRY BLEDSOE harps," Peg Leg's friend, John Glenn, said. "Oh Lord, you should see him dance. He can put on a show, I tell you that."

Once, a few years back, some white folks had come from New York to see Peg Leg. They had brought sophisticated recording equipment and plenty of liquor and that night Peg Leg had got right, he and Baby Tate. The result was playing loud now on John Glenn's record player. And for the first time all day, Peg Leg began to stir, responding to the music.

"*. . . Ain't but one thing, buddy boy, give a man the blues . . .* " his voice was singing from the other room.

"Yes, Lord," he said, nodding to the music.

A guitar boogie came on with Peg Leg playing harmonica accompaniment, and he tried to snap his fingers. "That ol' Baby Tate. Yeah, Baby Tate Boogie. He stayed in Greenville. Ol' Baby Tate pump 'at thing, don't he boy? He's dead now. Yeah, Lord, that the first record I made. Full of whiskey. Good corn likker . . . I had my likker settin' in 'tween my legs when I was makin' 'at record in Spa't'nburg. Right out there behind the Co-Cola plant, John. Spa't'nburg."

Peg Leg had been at John Glenn's house for about two weeks this time. Through the years, he had known he always had a place at John Glenn's. They had been raised together, dirt-poor, in the country near Jonesville. Glenn settled down close to home, but he knew his friend (he calls him Ol' Peg and seems to chuckle every time he says the name) was born to roam.

***

Arthur Jackson was ten when he first ran away from home. "First time I run away, I stayed three weeks. Next time, I stayed away, I think about four months. I kept stayn' longer, goin' a little farther all the time . . . I didn't know what I was goin' do. I was doin' some of anything. I wanted to be anything."

He learned to ride the freight trains, and he was riding one in Raleigh when he lost his leg. "I was just down from Cincinnati when I got my leg off. I believe I was asleep. All I know, when I woke up, part of my body was gone." He recuperated at home. An old man made him a peg leg, and when he stared to learn to walk on it, his mama began to worry he would take off again. John Glenn drew the task of seeing that he didn't. An impossible job, he discovered. One day in the woods Peg Leg slipped away from him and was gone. Glenn recalls going back to report, "Peg done run ag'in."

After that, nobody ever knew when to expect him around Jonesville. It might be two years, or it might be eight. He always came back, but he always was just passing through. "Drifter," he said, "just a drifter."

He learned to play the harmonica when he was eight or nine, and he hooked up with a medicine show man. "I drawed a crowd for 'im, you see. We had a little stage like. I'd put on an exhibition for 'im. I played a harmonica, then tell lies. I'm the biggest liar you ever seen. When the crowds got heavy enough, then he'd talk and I'd pass it out. He have three or four different items, you know, snake oil, tonic . . . "

Arthur Jackson started calling himself Peg Leg Sam. He considered himself a showman. In the late summer and fall he worked the tobacco warehouses. In the colder months he hoboed about the country playing in joints and on the streets. "I wear out a harp a day when I was buskin'. You don't know what buskin' is, do you? Buskin' passin' the hat aroun' for nickels, dimes and quarters."

His health stayed good . . . "All but when I'd get in a knife fight. Great God a'mighty." And somehow he always got by, always kept moving. "Yeah, I been over the United States a hundred times." Always, too, he went back to the medicine shows. In the early '30s, he met a medicine show man in Smithfield, N.C., who called himself Chief Thundercloud, an Indian from Oklahoma. Off and on, they worked with each other for nearly forty years.

"Sometimes I wouldn't see Chief for a year, two years, but he'd come back and git me." Right up until a few years ago, Peg Leg and the chief would hit the road in the springtime, just as they always had, and work the country towns in the Midwest and Deep South. Peg Leg believes they were the only medicine show still going. "Last. We was the last one. Me and Chief. Ol' Chief died about three years ago."

The Last Medicine Show was the name of Peg Leg Sam's first record album, the one that he and his friend, Baby Tate, made while they were drunk in Spartanburg that night. It was still playing on John Glenn's record player. Songs such as "Skinny Woman Blues," "Peg Leg's Fox Run," "Greasy Greens." Peg Leg lay on the bed listening.

"I just had a second grade reader," he said, as if talking to himself. "Wonder how I could make up all them songs?"

The wonder is that it took the young people and folklorists so long to discover Peg Leg Sam. That happened only six or seven years ago. Peg Leg can't remember exactly. They started coming to him wanting him to play at "folk festivals." He always was happy to go. First thing he knew, he had a record album and a booking agent in New York. "I played Chicago," he said, "Philadelphia, a big one. El Paso, Texas. All them. Washington, D.C., New York City. See, they pay my way up there and back. Pay for all my eatin', all my sleepin'. Don't cost me nothin'."

Four more record albums followed that first one (Did Peg Leg make any money on them? "So much it leak right out my pocket."), and he cut another one back in the winter when he was passing through New York on his way home from Canada. Since then, he hasn't been anywhere, sticking close to the shanty he shares with his brother a few miles out of Jonesville, or putting up at John Glenn's. He's been turning down appearances, he says, and for the first time in his life, he hasn't felt like moving on.

"Done run out," he said. "I give up, might near. Too old. Good God. Half sickly too. Devil gittin' to me now for the deeds I done, I reckon. But I ain't never hurt nobody. Naw suh. *My* lies ain't like them other lies I tell, you know."

The white boy had one last question. "If you could live your life over, would you do it differently?"

Peg Leg looked at him for a long time saying nothing, as if the question were not worthy of an answer. "Yeah," he said finally, "I'd start earlier."

June, 1977
Whitestone, S.C.

Hope Nicholls

BY COURTNEY DEVORES

When people talk about women in punk rock, indie rock, new wave, no wave, or experimental music in North Carolina, all roads lead back to Hope Nicholls. Now in her late forties, she's still fronting an experimental rock band, Snagglepuss. Over the past twenty-plus years Nicholls has become an iconic figure in the music scene. She's our Siouxsie Sioux, our Exene Cervenka—a completely original musical and stylistic force that's become the mother figure of at least a considerable pocket of the region's indie-rock scene. She never received the international recognition that many of her contemporaries did, but has fronted three renowned bands, served as a mentor to other musicians, and contributed her distinct vocals to works by Marilyn Manson, Pigface, and Kat Bjelland's soundtrack to the Witchblade comics while managing and eventually owning her own alternative clothing boutique in Charlotte.

In the 1980s, Nicholls, a Davidson, N.C., native, began her career fronting Fetchin Bones, which included her future husband and musical partner Aaron Pitkin. A fixture on college radio, the group toured and opened for the Replacements, the B-52s, and R.E.M. They recorded four albums between 1985 and 1989, three for Capitol/EMI. Fetchin Bones' swansong, *Monster*, entered *Billboard's* coveted Top 200 and its 1989 single "Love Crushing" cracked *Billboard's* Modern Rock Top 20.

Too progressive for the hair-metal atmosphere of the late '80s, Fetchin Bones had already broken up by the time the alternative-rock boom of the early '90s hit. Nicholls and Pitkin moved on to their next band, Sugarsmack. A colorful convergence of rock and jazz and all points in between, Sugarsmack was my first encounter with Nicholls' brilliant stage presence. She was a wild child whose pink hair and Day-Glo fashions weren't just stage costumes—she dressed that way to sell CDs at the used record store. Sugarsmack released three full-length albums in six years before disbanding due to distance—band members lived everywhere from Connecticut to Atlanta.

Around that time Nicholls was also busy hosting monthly "Bucket Parties," karaoke-meets-live music, at Charlotte's Tremont Music Hall. These fun events served to attract crowds eager to put their own spin on '80s fare like Blondie or the Knack while checking out indie bands. She also organized seasonal Ooh La La parties at the Visulite Theater and co-founded the fictional band the Bar-B-Que Grillz, which performed a handful of theatrical shows (enacting its fictional history on stage) during the late '90s.

In 1999, with a desire to focus on family and her non-music business, she and Pitkin handed instruments to friends and founded a new avant-garde project, the seven-member Snagglepuss. Pitkin, a bassist, took up drums. So the musical approach—not being completely familiar with your instrument—was a new one for the couple. "When you've made music for so long and done it as your livelihood, you have to come at it from a different way for it to be fun again," Nicholls said. Over the course of three albums, she says, the band learned to play. Theirs is an adventurous, spontaneous, horn-laden sound complete with songs about cartoon characters He-Man and She-Ra, Princess of Power, that continues to pack small Charlotte clubs even though the days of national touring in a van are long past.

"One of the really memorable things for people about Snagglepuss is seeing me play a show at Tremont one month to the day before [my daughter] Bell was born," she said. "I was tremendously huge and rocking out. I wasn't sure how I was going to feel, but the more I started jumping up and down, the better it felt."

What's more punk rock than that?

~~~

Gary Erwin: Charleston's "Shrimp City Slim"

BY CLAIR DELUNE

As you drive toward the Lowcountry of South Carolina, pine trees and scrub oaks give way to huge Live Oak trees that spread their branches to meet each other across roadways. They dangle spidery webs of soft gray Spanish moss by way of greeting. And if you are fortunate enough to make your way to Charleston, South Carolina, as your car stubbles over cobblestone streets, you will pass rows and rows of two-story homes behind stucco-walled garden gates. Beautiful, graceful abodes adorn this Grande Dame of a city that was too beautiful to burn, according to General Sherman, as he scorched "lesser cities" to the ground on his battle to the sea during the Civil War. At the farthest point of the city, soft pastel colors decorate the houses of the Battery as they look upon Fort Sumter out in the Atlantic Ocean. The Atlantic returns its regards by slapping a rhythm on the high sea wall of "The Holy City," so called for its many churches and their high steeples, visible from land and sea.

But there is another name for Charleston, one much less elegant: "The Shrimp City." This downhome name was earned from the thriving maritime industry in the Lowcountry. As a matter of fact, you can often smell shrimp on the boil when you drive into the city.

That is where blues musician, DJ and promoter Gary Erwin got his band name, Shrimp City Slim. Born in Chicago, his blues roots were assured, but in 1986, Erwin adopted Charleston as his new home town and began what has grown into a veritable Carolina blues legacy.

Erwin's keen ears are attuned to finding obscure Carolina blues players. He has rediscovered and showcased, in stateside and European tours, such talents as Walter "Lightnin' Bug" Rhodes, Big Boy Henry, Chicago Bob Nelson, Drink Small, Beverly "Guitar" Watkins, Wanda Johnson, Neal "Big Daddy" Pattman, John Lee Ziegler and the recently deceased Kip Anderson.

Erwin also plays keyboards and writes music. His band members are red-hot players and, while some appear almost as urbane as jazz musicians, some have the blues stamp of authenticity and appear to have lived life on the underside of down. The current lineup includes long-standing member Silent Eddie Phillips on guitar, LaMont Garner beating the drums, Jerome Griffin holding down the bass, and Mike "Mr. Big" Kincaid ripping it up on saxophones. And Shrimp City Slim, smiling and wearing his signature beret, brings it all home on keyboards.

During one memorable period a decade or so ago, Shrimp's concerts featured gritty singer and harmonica player Juke Joint Johnny, who stormed the stage looking like the Che Guevara of the harmonica set, his chest criss-crossed with belts loaded with harps of every key, singing about his most recent divorce in "She Got Papers," included on Shrimp City Slim's 1994 CD, the popular *Blues on the Beach*. Recorded in Lowcountry blues tradition, guests included Skeeter Brandon, Steve James, Roger Bellow. *Gone with the Wind*, in 1992, featured Silent Eddie Phillips on guitar and Juke Joint Johnny on harmonica.

In addition to promoting blues concerts in Charleston, the always dapper Erwin is the promoter or artistic director for many if not most of South Carolina's notable blues concerts, including annual blues festivals such as the Lowcountry Blues Bash, which is held in Charleston every February; the Carolina Downhome Blues Festival, in Camden the first Thursday through Saturday in October; Blues by the Sea, on Kiawah Island in May; and the Greenwood Blues Cruise in July.

You can also catch Erwin in action on S.C. Educational Television's "Juke Joints & Honky Tonks." On this edition of the *Carolina Stories* series, Shrimp City Slim performs with sensual vocalist Wanda Johnson at Doc's Gumbo Grill in Columbia, one of the few venues in the Capitol City that features live blues. "Juke Joints & Honky Tonks" features many South Carolina blues legends, including Johnson, Drink Small and Freddie Vanderford, who each play and talk about venues that feature blues music.

Erwin has been a radio host for various blues radio shows in the Lowcountry for twenty years and recently ended a year fronting the house band on the local ABC features show, *Lowcountry Live!* He produces CDs, books performances for artists, and works closely with basso profundo-voiced blues guitarist and South Carolina legend, Drink Small; and he is building legendary status for the Upstate's Wanda Johnson, for whom he writes material as well. Erwin's latest solo CD, *Dark Piano*, is his best since *Blues on the Beach*.

But Erwin is not all business—he has a big heart. When the need arises, it is Shrimp City Slim who can be depended upon to brainstorm, book and promote a fundraiser such as the annual Ric Strome Memorial Blues Rumble, a benefit festival for the Lowcountry Blues Relief Fund, which aids downhome blues musicians in need.

In a business built on the downbeat, Shrimp City Slim is seemingly inexhaustible and upbeat. He is truly a Carolina treasure who is keeping downhome blues alive.

Tommy Faile: Crackerjack Country

BY JACK DILLARD

Anyone who lived in North or South Carolina in the '50s and '60s will remember the deep baritone voice of Tommy Faile, a talented musician, singer and songwriter who hailed from Lancaster, S.C. Faile was probably best known as a member of The Crackerjacks, a group of crackerjack country musicians who backed up Arthur Smith on his syndicated country music television show at WBTV in Charlotte. As a regular on *The Arthur Smith Show* for eighteen years, Faile was a versatile performer who could touch the heart with a stirring verse of "The Old Rugged Cross" in his trademark brushed-velvet voice or keep an audience in stitches with his good-natured, cornpone humor as "Cousin Phud," a hayseed character developed for the show. He developed enough of a following that when Smith jumped to a rival station, WSOC-TV, Faile was hired by WBTV to host his own half-hour, prime-time TV show, *The Tommy Faile Show*, which ran from 1968 to 1974. The program was the local lead-in to *Gunsmoke*, the popular CBS western on Saturday night.

His love of old-time traditional music led Faile to quit his job at Springs' Lancaster cotton mill in the late 1940s to become a singer and play with a country band from Columbia, known as the Hired Hands. He was

fifteen at the time. As he developed as a musician, he was asked to sit in on recording sessions for a variety of bluegrass and country artists, including the Tennessee Cut-Ups. In 1951, Faile was hired by Arthur Smith to join The Crackerjacks.

Throughout a musical career that spanned fifty years, he returned to his humble roots and made appearances at county fairs, bluegrass festivals, and school auditoriums throughout the South. Yet he also performed at the Grand Ole Opry and even Caesar's Palace. For a time, he was a featured performer on weekends at Tweetsie Railroad, and he returned to Lancaster to host the Carolina Legends musical festival the last ten years of his life.

Faile was also an accomplished songwriter with nearly sixty published songs to his credit. "Big Joe and Phantom 309," a song he wrote about a ghostly truck driver named Joe who delivered a hard-luck hitchhiker to a safe place, sold 1.5 million copies in 1967 for country singer Red Sovine. The song was later covered by Tom Waits on his album *Nighthawks at the Diner*. Faile also wrote and sang "The Legend of the Brown Mountain Lights," which became a popular bluegrass hit for him in the early '60s. It's a folksy song about the mysterious lights on Brown Mountain near Linville Gorge that have never been scientifically explained. When Faile died in 1998 of a heart attack, his ashes were scattered on Brown Mountain.

Tommy Faile appeared on many record labels, including Dot, Admiral, Sapphire, Caddy, Choice, Lawn, Sho-Boy, CMC, and Lamon.

~~~

Little Eva

BY MICK PATRICK AND MALCOLM BAUMGART

When Little Eva quit the music business in 1971, she returned home to North Carolina a single parent of three young children. She found employment as a housekeeper, caretaker and cook. When work wasn't available, she and the kids survived on welfare.

At the time of her hit records in the '60s her weekly salary had been $50 plus expenses. That and her previous job as a $35-a-week live-in nanny for songwriters Carole King and Gerry Goffin must have seemed positively well-paid by comparison.

Eva Narcissus Boyd was born on June 29, 1943 in Belhaven, N.C., the tenth of David and Laura Boyd's thirteen children. The family home was situated on (prophetically) Railroad Street. She always wanted to be a singer and was inspired by the gospel, country, R&B and rock 'n' roll records she listened to on the radio. For a while Eva and four of her siblings had their own gospel group, the Boyd Five.

In the summer of 1959, Eva went to spend the school holidays with her eldest brother Jimmy and his wife in Coney Island, N.Y. She returned to Belhaven for a few months but, having acquired a taste for life in the big city, quit school and, in 1960, got the bus back to New York and found a job as a maid in Hempstead on Long Island.

Eva's sister-in-law was friendly with Earl-Jean McCrea of the Cookies, an established vocal group then making demos for publisher Don Kirshner. Among the many writers signed to Kirshner and business partner Al Nevins' Aldon company were the husband-and-wife team of Carole King and Gerry Goffin. When the Shirelles' version of Goffin and King's "Will You Love Me Tomorrow" reached No. 1, the young scribes devoted themselves full-time to song writing.

With a home, a husband, a baby daughter and another on the way, King decided to hire a nanny. Meanwhile, the Cookies, their line-up in flux, were on the lookout for a new member. McCrea encouraged Eva to apply for both jobs, which she did by performing "Will You Love Me Tomorrow" at her interview/audition. Eva landed both positions and, in 1961, moved into the Goffin apartment in Brooklyn.

With Goffin supplying the lyrics and King the melodies, the team were on a roll. Over the next year or so they wrote for the Drifters ("When My Little Girl Is

Smiling," "Some Kind Of Wonderful"), Tony Orlando ("Halfway To Paradise") and Bobby Vee ("Take Good Care Of My Baby") plus many others.

The Cookies, who had released a handful of singles of their own in previous years, were now working primarily as a session group. In March 1962, Eva joined the three other Cookies on a four-song Ben E. King session and can be heard clearly on "Gloria, Gloria" and "Don't Play That Song (You Lied)."

When Dee Dee Sharp shot to No. 2 with "Mashed Potato Time" in May 1962, Kirshner suggested to Goffin and King that they write a similar number for him to pitch at her label, Cameo Records, as a possible follow-up. The result was "The Loco-motion." The hot writers had their babysitter Eva record a demo version. Goffin himself produced the session at Dick Charles' studio, where most Aldon demos were cut. Kirshner flipped when he heard the disc. He decided it was good enough to release, and he would form his own label to do so.

Goffin and King rushed Eva to Mirasound, their preferred studio, to re-record "The Loco-motion." They were unable to reproduce the fabulous sound of the original demo, which, with the simple addition of some overdubbed backing vocals by King and Eva, was the version used as the initial release on the new Dimension label in June 1962. Eva, who was less than five feet tall, was renamed Little Eva and two years were lopped off her age by Kirshner's publicity machine.

Within weeks, Little Eva was appearing on *American Bandstand*, lip-synching "The Loco-motion" and demonstrating the required dance steps, which were her own creation. The record entered the Hot 100 in the last week of June. By the end of August it had replaced Neil Sedaka's "Breaking Up Is Hard To Do" at No. 1.

An album, *LLLLLoco-motion,* was recorded and rush-released to capitalize on Eva's newfound fame.

Eva's follow-up single, "Keep Your Hands Off My Baby," was probably a better record than "The Loco-motion" but was destined to be forever overlooked in favor of its famous predecessor. It peaked at a very respectable No. 12 on the final *Billboard* Hot 100 of 1962 (No. 6 R&B). Little Eva celebrated her success by marrying her long-time boyfriend James Harris on December 18, but didn't let the special occasion prevent her from appearing at the Apollo in Harlem that evening.

For Little Eva's next single, "Let's Turkey Trot," King borrowed heavily from "Little Girl Of Mine," a huge R&B hit for the Cleftones in 1956. So heavily, in fact, that the melodies of the two songs were virtually identical. "Let's Turkey Trot" was one of Eva's best records and provided her with another Top 20 hit.

Like her role model Dee Dee Sharp, who was eulogized in song by Vinnie Monte with "Mashed Potato Girl," Little Eva was also the subject of a tribute record: "Little Eva" (the title) by The Locomotions (the group), released on the Gone label in 1963.

Meanwhile, in the spring of that year, Little Eva made her first trip overseas, sharing top billing with Brian Hyland on a tour of Great Britain. She also traveled to Paris to perform but her father passed away while she was in France and the trip was cut short.

If Little Eva's singles were lacking in anything, it was original ideas. And that criticism was certainly deserved by her next attempt, "Old Smokey Loco-motion," a too-obvious amalgam of "On Top Of Old Smokey" and "The Loco-motion." However, it sold well and reached a chart peak of No. 48.

Throughout her career as a Dimension artist, Eva

continued cutting demos for Goffin and King. They obviously felt that she had a voice that could help sell their compositions. One such song was "One Fine Day." Legend has it that the Chiffons' producers, the Tokens, simply took Eva's demo, wiped her voice from the track and over-dubbed the Chiffons' vocals.

Little Eva's next release, hot on the heels of "Old Smokey Locomotion," was a terrific return-to-form which paired "What I Gotta Do (To Make You Jealous)" and "The Trouble With Boys." Production wise, they sounded perfect for their time. Unfortunately, neither side really caught on and "What I Gotta Do" stalled just one place outside the Hot 100. "Let's Start The Party Again"—a joyful racket with Eva doing her best Gary U.S. Bonds impression—fared even worse, bubbling under the charts at No. 123 for just one week before disappearing. Hidden on the B-side was "Please Hurt Me," a previously unused gem from the *LLLLLocomotion* sessions. Never again would Little Eva grace the American charts.

There was only one Little Eva record released in 1964, possibly her most contrived. Unfortunately for Eva, the powers that be at Dimension were still intent on marketing her as a singer of novelty dance tunes. "Making With The Magilla" was an ode to Hanna-Barbera's cartoon gorilla. The following year, Little Eva got some tasty adult material in the shape of "Wake Up John" and "Takin' Back What I Said"—both rather fine Chip Taylor compositions, sharply arranged by Charles Calello and produced by Jack Lewis. ("Get Him," also recorded at this session, remained unissued until the Murray Hill label unearthed the master tape and included it on their *Best Of Little Eva* album in 1988.) But it was too late—Dimension was on its last legs and

the record received little promotion. The label ceased operations shortly afterwards.

Following the demise of Dimension, Little Eva recorded several other singles for the production team of Feldman/Goldstein/Gottehrer and for Verve but none did very well.

For the next two years or so, she worked the club circuit to earn a living and to support her children. In 1970 Eva signed to the Spring label, future home of soul stars Millie Jackson and Joe Simon. She was billed as Little Eva Harris, her married surname, on the funky Motown medley "Get Ready/Uptight." A frantic update of the Shirelles' "Mama Said" was followed by a much-needed original, "Night After Night," supplied by her producer John Lombardo. Eva thought highly of Spring's owners, the Rifkin brothers, who were very good to her financially.

Laura Boyd, Eva's mother, died in 1971. The event prompted the former star to re-evaluate her life. Down on her luck, with an estranged husband, Eva quit the music business and went back to Belhaven to live. She immersed herself in her new life and tried to forget how unhappy she'd become in New York.

When "The Loco-motion" re-entered the United Kingdom charts in 1972, Eva remained blissfully unaware. Grand Funk Railroad's version of the song was No. 1 in the U.S. two years later. For the next fifteen years, Eva lived in total obscurity. She became a regular churchgoer, patched up her marriage and had two more children. James Harris died in 1983.

In 1988 yet another version of "The Loco-motion" became a huge worldwide hit, this time courtesy of another tiny pop princess, Australian Kylie Minogue. At the time, Eva was working as a cook in a soul food diner. The media tracked her down, and numerous press, radio and television features and interviews resulted, as well as the aforementioned *Best Of* album. Realizing that she was not a forgotten figure, Eva decided to ease herself back into showbiz and to fulfill a new ambition to record a gospel album. Later that year she went to California to record the selections that would comprise her *Back On Track* album, issued by the tiny Malibu gospel label late in 1989. One track, "In Memory Of C.J.," was a poignant epitaph to her late husband.

Eva also returned to the stage, touring the U.K. on an all-star bill with Little Richard. Among her last shows was a mammoth charity event to raise funds to help pay the medical bills of ailing legend LaVern Baker.

Eva died in April of 2003 following a long battle with cancer.

~~~

Dad, Sam Moss and Me

BY PETER HOLSAPPLE

When I dragged my father to Reznick's Records Downtown in Winston-Salem after he got off work at Wachovia Bank, it was raining, mixed with snow, in the waning weeks of December. The slush was high in the sewers, and Christmas lights reflected in the little lakes that lined Liberty Street. Not the nicest night to be guitar shopping, but teenage rock 'n' roll fervor was not going to be denied by inclement weather.

Since I was a little kid, my father and I spent many Saturday mornings downtown together, first going to Sears and looking at hardware, and then crossing the street to George's Hobby Shop to look at car kits and metalflake spray paints. Or we'd go to Separk Music, down a little further on 4th Street and poke around in the sheet music. My dad is not a musician although he took some piano lessons after he retired, but he humored me with a lot of time spent in record and guitar stores of Winston-Salem throughout my youth.

This particular evening, Dad closed his dripping umbrella as we stood in the tiled foyer of Reznick's. We were surrounded by lit glass display windows filled with shiny new band instruments and violins, sheet music books and batons, metronomes and student acoustic guitars. Jimmy Woods was seated on a stool behind a counter to our left. Mr. Woods was the resident guitar expert at Reznick's, having special-ordered Gibsons made for himself from the factory. He was a gentle, reserved soul with whom I had very little conversation, being in a state of general awe around him. But this evening, I asked him to show me the guitars I'd seen upstairs in the attic just a few days prior.

Mr. Woods took us past the jeweler's kiosk in the back and up the wooden stairs to the attic. There among ancient record albums and dusty abandoned cellos, he pulled down two alligator chipboard cases and laid them on the floor. In one, there was a cherry red Gibson Les Paul Junior. I opened the other case,

---

Peter Holsapple now lives in Durham, but grew up in Winston-Salem where Sam Moss was, as one writer put it, "the quintessential guitarist in Winston-Salem for 40 years." Moss also owned and operated a music store there, Sam Moss Guitars, for many years and is credited with introducing vintage guitar collecting to the area. Moss died in May 2007. Holsapple is a member of The dBs and has toured as a sideman with R.E.M. and Hootie and the Blowfish.

and there was the next model up, the Les Paul Special with two pickups. The price tags read $65 and $75 respectively. Even at thirteen, I knew these were incredible bargains, but it was my task to explain that to my hopelessly naive-about-guitars father, since it would be his money paid out to get one.

Either guitar would have been a great step up from the Japanese Kent electric guitar that I'd gotten the prior Christmas from my grandparents. The Kent was fine and dandy, but it was not very cool. These were actual Les Pauls, as played by my hero Michael Bloomfield and locally by Sam Moss of Rhythm Method, who could play better than anyone in town.

Sam, only three years older than me, seemed grown-up in terms of what one could do with a guitar. He was already a professional in my mind, the local guitar blues master, presiding over a tight band with a horn section. His cool factor was way high. He had plenty of friends and acolytes who listened to his licks and tone, then learned from listening, myself among them.

I pulled out the Special and hit a few nascent blues licks for my father without benefit of an amp. The little red Gibson felt sweet, so natural under my fingertips, and in my heart, this was the one for me.

I sensed, and tried to express to my father, that the Les Paul would inspire me to play better, to learn more, to reflect my commitment to the instrument. It may have come out like "Daddy, buy me this pretty red guitar," but I pursued it doggedly. He has always been somewhat inscrutable, and this evening, my father's reaction was pretty much as I had expected. "You know, son, you can lead a horse to water . . ."

It was getting late, and my father was hungry for dinner. I closed the cases, and reluctantly bid a possibly permanent farewell to my dream guitar. We descended the stairs, bade Jimmy Woods goodbye and opened the door to the rain and Liberty Street. As if by heavenly dispensation, there, in the foyer of Reznick's, stood Sam Moss.

Nervously (I was, I felt, an invisible neophyte in his eyes), I sputtered a hello, introduced him to my father and then tried to explain to Sam how I needed the Special up in the attic. Sam listened, then he turned to my father and respectfully and clearly laid out how good an investment the guitar would be, what a talented player I was becoming, and why it was such a great match. I listened, stunned.

I could not believe Sam would take this kind of time and interest in helping me get the guitar when he really didn't know me very well. I realized later this was just Sam's nature, encouraging young players who "got it." Sam could talk to parents as easily their progenies, even as a teenager himself. This neat ability matched his guitar prowess, and probably served Sam well eventually as owner of his own guitar store.

Some days after our providential encounter with Sam, my father took me back to Reznick's, and we bought the Les Paul Special. I wish I had that guitar today, but it got hot-rodded and traded away many years ago. Sam was right about it being a good investment, too; had I not messed it up with humbucking pickups and fancy-dan tuning pegs, it might be worth a pile of money to whoever owns it today. I can't say that it was his endorsement alone that got me the guitar, but I know it helped. It was the first of a thousand times I was grateful for the attention Sam Moss paid me throughout the rest of his life.

Richard "Big Boy" Henry

BY JANET HARTMAN

The music style of Richard "Big Boy" Henry, called the "Patriarch of Carolina blues," developed from his life experiences as a musician, a fisherman and a preacher.

The Piedmont blues have a lighter feel, unlike the harder-edged Delta blues that migrated north and became electrified. While other blues singers often sound like they are in or headed for clinical depression, Henry's singing style conveyed the hurt, but showed he was going to get through it.

Henry was born in Beaufort, N.C., in 1921, and his family moved to New Bern when he was twelve. As a small teenager, he spent so much time listening to the music emanating from The Honey Hole, a New Bern juke joint, the patrons nicknamed him "Little Boy" Henry.

A chance meeting with guitarist Fred Miller grew into a musical partnership that launched Henry's career playing and singing at local events. By then, the tall, handsome young man had outgrown the "Little Boy" label. In the late 1940s, he performed on the New Bern WHIT radio program *Jive Time*. When Miller moved to New York, Henry also spent time there and met other Piedmont blues musicians including Sonny Terry and Brownie McGhee. Henry, Terry, and McGhee recorded four songs together in 1951, but they were not released.

Disheartened, Henry returned to North Carolina and gave up singing professionally for over twenty years. He preached in local churches and supported his family by running a grocery store, crewing on menhaden fishing boats, and fishing on his own. He did not stop singing entirely, though. The menhaden fishing crews sang chanteys to coordinate the pulling of the nets.

In the early 1980s, some younger musicians recognized him and encouraged him to return to music. According to Henry, "The minute I picked it up, it all come back to me."

But Henry did more than recall the past. Current events also inspired his music. His 1983 song, "Mr. President," an angry response to Ronald Reagan's social welfare cuts, earned him a W.C. Handy Award from the Blues Foundation.

During the late 1980s and into the '90s, he performed regularly at national folk festivals and toured Europe. He recorded in the enclosed back porch of his house, and produced and marketed his music under his independent Down Home label. In 1989, he won the Brown-Hudson Folklore Award for folk arts from the North Carolina Folklore Society, presented to people who have contributed in special ways to the appreciation, continuation, or study of North Carolina folk traditions. Contrary to his imposing stature, he was known for his gentle nature and the encouragement he gave younger musicians.

Songs from his menhaden fishing days were included in his new repertoire, and he helped organize retired menhaden fishermen into the Menhaden Chanteymen to perform and record work songs. The Chanteymen performed at Carnegie Hall and for the North Carolina General Assembly. Plus, their music is part of the menhaden fishing display in the North Carolina Maritime Museum in Beaufort.

Memories of his days as a preacher found their way into his lyrics, and perhaps influenced the name of the backup group on his 1995 recording, *Poor Man's Blues*: the Ministers of Sinister. *Living Blues* magazine called that compilation "the best down-home blues CD of 1995." In 1995, Henry received the North Carolina Folk Heritage Award for lifetime contributions to the folk culture of the state. The North Carolina Arts Council called Henry "a master musician in the blues tradition from eastern North Carolina, which is one of the important parts of the roots of blues in our state."

Some refer to his style as the "old hollar blues," based on the call-and-response songs field hands sang as they worked. While that influence can be seen in the songs sung by the Menhaden Chanteymen, that label is an oversimplification of his music. Henry's songs told stories—stories that he sometimes made up as he sang. He even made up a new song while performing

with Mike "Lightnin' " Wells at New York City's Lincoln Center.

For Big Boy, singing the blues was a blessing. As he put it, the blues are "in my heart, not because I'm troubled that much now, but I just love to look back." He died in 2004, but in 2007, Beaufort paid homage to him by dedicating a portion of its annual music festival to his music and memory. His daughter Carolyn summed it up at the festival by saying, "It's all about the heart. The blues have to come from the heart."

〜〜〜

Gina Stewart: Go Your Own Way

BY SHEILA SAINTS

Gina Stewart didn't know any Fleetwood Mac songs and certainly didn't want to go to the *Rumours* (1977–78) concert with her sister, but there they were. Gina was fifteen and her sister was five years older—a gap that seemed worlds apart. When they approached the Charlotte Coliseum, her sister said, "Don't act like you know me. Just meet me back here. Go!" Wounded, Gina cut through the pot smoke, patchouli and people. Young and small, she needed only a smile and gentle "excuse me" to get to the front row. A burly man lifted her on his broad shoulders and told her to pull his hair when she wanted down. Gina floated above the crowd, adrenaline pumping, body vibrating, and mere inches away from the lead singer. As Gina watched the chiffon twirling, the glitter shining, the crowd screaming . . . a gossamer fantasy formed. She wanted to be Stevie Nicks. "I never really questioned it until I turned forty and wondered if I should do something else," she said.

Gina Stewart has the chiseled features of Jodie Foster and the comfortable drawl of Holly Hunter. Wearing a brown T-shirt from her latest band, Volatile Baby, and a black baseball cap, she is unassuming yet intense.

Her career as a musician, actor, and songwriter has spanned nearly three decades. She reflected upon her journey while eating California rolls at a trendy eatery in uptown Charlotte.

"At the time, my sister was dating a guy who was a terrific keyboard player in a band," she said. "He let me sing and he very wisely told me I needed to play an instrument because if I could play an instrument, I was twice as likely to get in a band. Girl singers were a dime a dozen, but girls who could play were rare." So, at fifteen, she studied music theory, picked a voice teacher out of the phone book and taught herself guitar. "I knew," she said, "this is what I wanted to do."

Like a blacksmith forging iron, Gina shaped her dream. "I was determined. I get tunnel-vision when I want something, especially artistically," she said. She majored in music at UNC-Charlotte, specializing in musical theater, and dropped out three times to join bands. Her parents told her, as all good parents do, to have a safety net—but they underestimated her resolve. In 1984, she joined an edgy punk band called Fetchin Bones. Up until then, Gina had been drowning in music theory and key change. Now, she was in a band that was breaking all the musical rules. "I was like, O.K., that's hectic, but it works and that was huge for me," she said.

Pound, pound, pound. Gina kept hammering away at her craft. "What motivates me is simply wanting to be good, and to put my voice in it somehow," she said. "I want it to be true. I want to grow." From 1986 to 1989, she played guitar for The Blind Dates, a local all-girl band. Then, in the 1990s, she emerged with Doubting Thomas, a folk-rock band popular on the Southeast circuit. She and the musicians played smoky clubs and outdoor festivals. Fans sang along to "Lost Generation." Band members came and went. The years became a whirlwind. The CDs. The fame. The traveling. The entourage. The effort. The exhaustion. The burn-out. The end.

Gina regrouped. She had been taking acting roles while playing in bands—television, stage, and film— and she naturally found a home there again. "Because I was an actress and because I could play guitar, I wound up in a position to write music for theater and movies. If I read a story I like, I hear the soundtrack," she said. "It's like I hear some sort of emotional line to stories."

Ventures in 2005 and 2007 merged her talents. With a wig, a wide skirt, and an acoustic guitar, she played Maybelle Carter in stage productions of *Wildwood Flowers: The June Carter Cash Story* and *Keep on the Sunny Side*. Cross-training has kept her busy— and employed. "It's the biggest thing that has brought me jobs," she said. "That's not the 'be all, end all,' but it does come down to trying to make a living and being happy doing what you do."

Maturity is reflected in her Americana trio, Volatile Baby, and with this band she recorded with June Carter Cash's daughter, Carlene Carter, a personal career highlight. This time, the focus is on collaboration. There's no goal of wider exposure, just to find joy again in making music. "I'm different because I think the last remnants of wanting to be famous are gone," she said. "I've seen enough of it, experienced enough of that tension to know it's the last thing I want. It's very freeing to not want that. I think fame is something you learn how to manage and handle. It should never be a goal. I'm not sure, certainly at fifteen, that I understood that."

Using the precision of a skilled artisan, she has followed her bliss and advises others to do the same: "Don't fool around with learning how to wait tables, go for it. Life has taught me if you're on the path you're supposed to be on, you're not going to starve to death. You're not going to be lacking in anything you need if you follow your heart."

Regrets? None about failing, only failing to try.

"Looking back on it, I knew so early what I wanted to do. I was fifteen. There's a part of me that will always wonder what would have happened if I had had a little bit more abandon . . . been more daring," she said. "I once had my bags packed for New York but didn't go. I didn't hit a bigger market. I think it was something I could have learned from. Not that I wouldn't have ended up in the same place."

Success came not at once, but in determined increments along the way.

Pound, pound.

Pound.

Maurice Williams

BY ANN WICKER

Maurice Williams & the Zodiacs' "Stay" hit the Carolinas in 1960, touching off a musical explosion unprecedented in the region. After a sleepy summer of Percy Faith, Frankie Avalon and Connie Francis, teens besieged radio stations with an insatiable demand for the song. The ripple effect eventually carried it onto the *Billboard* charts, where it rode the top spot for fourteen weeks.

The original record, featuring Williams on lead vocal and Shane Gaston on the compelling falsetto part, loped along to a Latin-tinged groove spiced by soulful vocal harmonies.

Williams, a Lancaster, S.C., native is like many R&B singers—he first sang in church choirs. But by 1953 he'd formed a group called the Royal Charms. Around this time—he was thirteen—he wrote the first of his hits, "Little Darlin'."

The Royal Charms were renamed the Gladiolas at the behest of Ernie Young, head of Exello Records, before the band recorded "Little Darlin'." Released in 1957, this version went to No. 11 on the R&B charts, but a Canadian group, the Diamonds, recorded a later version that went to No. 2 on the pop charts.

When the Gladiolas moved to the Herald label, the band's name changed again to Maurice Williams & the Zodiacs. They recorded another song he'd written, "Stay," released when Williams was twenty. Another of Williams' songs, "May I?" charted for Bill Deal and the Rhondels in 1969.

Williams, unlike some other singers and songwriters, really paid attention to the business part of the music business. Those lessons have served him well, as he explains in a 2008 interview. "I started learning about publishing when I was sixteen," Williams says. "Through the years I followed it, and I learned there was an awful lot of money in publishing—that's where the money really is. I starting holding on to my stuff then—I was told always hold on to my own songs if I could. It paid off."

***

Williams has lots of good memories from his long career. "Every time I received a gold record, of course, that was a big highlight," he says, "first for 'Little Darlin',' and then of course the platinum for 'Stay.'" He is also particularly proud of having received the Order of the Palmetto in 2001, the highest honor a civilian can be awarded from his home state of South Carolina.

And he's met and played with many great musicians, too. "When I met Johnny Mathis, that was a highlight. We performed together at the Brooklyn Paramount back in the '60s," he says. "Then Sam Cooke—we were friends. Me and Otis Redding, we were friends."

With his trademark throaty laugh he adds, "We hung out—some great guys through the years."

Charlotte guitarist Woody Mitchell was in the Zodiacs in the 1980s. "Maurice was a gentleman who treated me great," says Mitchell, "and taught me a whole lot about show business."

He laughs and adds, "I ran into a couple of current Zodiacs in a bar recently and told them I'd worked with the band in the '80s. Their first question: 'Did you eat a lot of chicken?' I knew they were bona fide then, 'cause Maurice is legendary for stopping *only* at chicken joints on the road. But if you wanted a burger, you could hop out of the van and run across the road to McDonald's or whatever."

✳✳✳

These days Williams, who has lived in the Charlotte area for years, continues to tour and record. "We do a lot of doo-wop shows around the country," he says. "Those are real hot."

He adds he is also, of course, performing with his regular band. "We're playing in the Southeast, mostly." He still mourns the passing of his longtime band director, Calvin McKinnie, in 2006. "From 1958 on, he was the bandleader," Williams says.

Other projects keeping him busy include his upcoming 50th anniversary album (scheduled for a spring 2008 release) and a Christmas DVD released in 2007. He's also working on a book.

Oh, and about that little song of his, "Stay"—it's had several incarnations since the 1960s, too. The Four Seasons and the Hollies covered it. Jackson Browne did a cover version in 1978 that was part of a song titled "The Load Out/Stay." The original recording of the tune was part of the hugely popular soundtrack for the film *Dirty Dancing* in 1987. All this from the tune that some sources say was the shortest song (1:37) to ever hit No. 1.

〜〜〜

Hip-Hop in the Carolinas

BY CLYDE SMITH

The history of hip-hop in the Carolinas is largely unwritten. Individuals may share deep, textured accounts of their local scenes, yet that rarely gives a sense of the larger history of hip-hop in the region. However, we do know that hip-hop came to the Carolinas via multiple pathways and that, in return, a small but growing number of hip-hop artists have emerged from the Carolinas to address a national audience.

Many residents of North and South Carolina discovered hip-hop first through the mass media as early records and media coverage led to a series of movies in the 1980s, such as *Beat Street* and *Breakin'*. The films were often a bit silly yet gave those at a distance from New York a better sense of the hip-hop subculture as a whole.

Another important source of information for Carolina residents, one that predates mass media coverage of rap music, came from the connections between African Americans in the Carolinas and in the New York City area, whether through family visits or relocation. Such connections introduced the Carolinas to early New York hip-hop radio shows by such legendary figures as DJ Red Alert via cassette tapes.

Today, both North and South Carolina are over-flowing with up-and-coming artists representing many different styles of hip-hop, though N.C. artists have been the first to break through to national attention. Three such artists, Ski Beatz, Petey Pablo and 9th Wonder, and a closely related group, Little Brother, reveal the diversity of hip-hop in the Carolinas.

SKI BEATZ

Ski Beatz (David Willis) is a native of Greensboro, N.C., who made the move to New York in 1990 to further his career as a hip-hop artist. After initially working as a member of Original Flavor, Ski Beatz and his manager, Damon Dash, got involved with the then largely unknown Jay-Z and helped create the album *Reasonable Doubt*.

Released in 1996, Jay-Z's *Reasonable Doubt*, now considered a classic of hip-hop, featured four tracks in which Ski Beatz handled the musical elements and overall production. The success of this effort catapulted Ski into the limelight in New York, where he worked with a variety of artists before returning to North Carolina and settling in Winston-Salem to focus on local projects. Recently, Ski Beatz has returned to the spotlight as artists he helped develop, such as HOT-Wright and M.O.S., have matured and sought serious recognition.

PETEY PABLO

Petey Pablo (Moses Barrett III) left his hometown of Greenville, N.C., in the late '90s and moved to New York, where he eventually won a contract with Jive Records. In 2001 the single "Raise Up" caught on with its verses filled with the names of small North Carolina towns. Followed by an All Cities Remix, featuring the names of larger cities across the country, Petey became known as the first artist in the Dirty South genre to emerge from North Carolina, though he actually did so from New York.

However, Petey seemed to quickly hit a glass ceiling as promising opportunities never became great hits and, in 2004, he signed to Death Row Records. Though he soon went into the studio and recorded a great deal of material, there have been no subsequent releases nor explanation to the public. The early press regarding this signing is the last strong wave of publicity we have seen for Petey Pablo, and this extended absence has likely damaged his career.

9TH WONDER/LITTLE BROTHER

The Durham-based members of Little Brother came together as a group featuring DJ 9th Wonder (Pat Douthit) and MC's Phonte (Phonte Coleman) and Big Pooh (Thomas Jones) in 2001. Their 2003 debut album, *The Listening*, brought 9th Wonder to the attention of Jay-Z for whom 9th Wonder produced a track for Z's

The Black Album later that year. Though this opportunity brought 9th Wonder and Little Brother widespread attention, it also hastened the group's eventual separation, as 9th Wonder became a star in his own right.

In the wake of a disappointing response to their major label debut, *The Minstrel Show* (2005), and the recognition that 9th Wonder's sound was no longer unique to Little Brother, 9th Wonder officially went solo while Phonte and Big Pooh continued to work together as Little Brother. 9th Wonder has also been reinvesting time and energy in Durham, N.C., including teaching a course at North Carolina Central University while Little Brother has begun work on its next studio album.

✳✳✳

From Ski Beatz' association with classic New York acts to Petey Pablo's Dirty South party music to Little Brother's underground hip-hop with commercial overtones, Carolinas artists have already produced a great range of hip-hop music. Though the most visible performers have come from North Carolina, many talented South Carolina artists are advancing towards the national stage, and hip-hop in the Carolinas appears poised for even greater achievements.

Pink Anderson

BY PETER COOPER

Alvin "Little Pink" Anderson, son of the most important blues musician in Spartanburg history, meets me on a Sunday afternoon in the parking lot of the Beacon drive in restaurant on Reidville Road in Spartanburg. Two weeks after his release from a Greenville prison, Anderson is glad to be a free man and pleased to answer questions about his life as the son and sidekick of Pink Anderson. We drive to Alvin's girlfriend's apartment for the interview, and I present Alvin with a compact disc called *The Blues of Pink Anderson: Ballad and Folksinger, Volume 3*.

The disc, recorded in Spartanburg in 1961, thirteen years before Pink's death, contains liner notes in which Pink is called "one of the greatest of the Piedmont-style guitar-picking songsters, an inspiration to the British art rock band Pink Floyd and to such folk-blues troubadours as Roy Book Binder and Paul Geremia." The photograph on the cover depicts Pink, then sixty, sitting on the steps of his Forest Street home with his smiling suspender-clad, six-year-old son, Alvin. Alvin has never seen the photograph before, though he remembers precisely the situation and time of day that it was taken. We put the disc on the stereo and the memories return in a flood.

"As we're listening to this, I can see that little boy that's in that photograph," he says. "Samuel Charters came to our house to record those songs. I can see that little boy sitting on the floor in front of the coal heater listening to my father in complete awe. I was sitting there, trying to be as quiet as I could. Hey, they were making a *record*, like you bought in stores."

Pink was not the only Spartanburg bluesman to make a record—the others were Simmie Dooley, Baby Tate, and Peg Leg Pete—but Anderson was a sort of common denominator for a century of musical activity. A protégé of Dooley, a mentor to Tate and Peg Leg, and a performing partner of each of the three men, Pink favored a musical approach that was highly informed by his forty years of traveling with medicine shows and playing Spartanburg street corners. Mississippi bluesmen such as Robert Johnson and Skip James knew how to draw a tear from a listener, but Anderson and his

This is an excerpt from a chapter of Peter Cooper's book, *Hub City Music Makers: One Southern Town's Popular Music Legacy*.

Born in 1900 in Laurens, Pink was playing guitar on the streets in Spartanburg and traveling with medicine shows by 1918. Pink was in top form in 1950 for live recordings made at the Virginia State Fair, now part of a CD called *Gospel, Blues and Street Songs*. In 1962, Charters also filmed Pink for a documentary. After a stroke, Pink rallied to play a few performances up north arranged by Book Binder. Pink died on October 12, 1974.

—ANN WICKER

kind knew how to draw a chuckle. A tear was good for nothing in Pink's world; a laugh was often good for a thrown quarter.

A month after my conversation with Alvin Anderson, Roy Book Binder and I are sitting in Roy's RV after his concert at the Handlebar in Greenville, S.C. The vehicle is a home on wheels, with photographs of some of Roy's musical heroes prominently displayed. Pink's photo is in the kitchen area, while a picture of Rev. Gary Davis, a bluesman who hailed from Greenville and who learned to read at Spartanburg's School for the Deaf and Blind, is located just behind the front passenger seat. Book Binder first traveled with a friend from New York to Spartanburg (in 1970) in order to meet the man who had made those living room records, and he recalls his surprise at some of the other activities that took place in Pink's small home:

"Pink was selling whiskey at the time. You could always wake up Mr. Pink if you needed a drink. He'd sell it to anybody. I remember one time I was there and Pink had one of his albums on the mantelpiece. I said 'You only have one album?' He said, 'I only made one album for Mr. Charters.' I said, 'They put *three* out.' The next time we came down, I brought him the other albums. I brought the records in and there was this drunk lady in the living room. She was a mess: sprawled out on the couch, trying to get a drink from Pink, but she didn't have any money . . . she looked down from the couch, and I had two Pink Anderson albums. She picked one up and looked at it, looked at me, looked at Pink, and said, 'Pink Anderson done made records!' She went up and down the street yelling, 'Pink Anderson done made records!' I guess she had no idea."

Such was the life for Pink Anderson and for his young son. "Yeah, he was a hustler," says Alvin. "I grew up around all this. As a matter of fact, I grew up a part of all this, because he didn't hide anything from me. He used his music to hustle, he played cards, and he sold liquor. In the art of surviving, he was a genius."

***

Alvin is also beginning the process of rediscovering and relearning his father's style of music, and he speaks of carrying on the legend of Pink Anderson. "I'm at peace with myself now, and his style of music is now my style of music. See, that's my roots. I'm not going to try to walk in his footsteps because I need to make my own tracks. I can still walk in his shadow, though. I've always been there, and that's where I'll stay.

"He's influenced a lot of people and he never even knew it. He didn't know about Pink Floyd or Johnny Cash. I just want people, especially in his home, in Spartanburg, to know who he was and what his name really meant. It wasn't that he was the world's greatest singer—to me, he was—but he has passed on something that needs to be kept alive. I think the racial situation from the 1920s to the 1970s caused a lot of the world to miss something that he shared with me, and that he would have shared with anybody. I won't be satisfied until I'm standing in front of audiences again, telling the story of growing up with that ol' fool, as I used to call him sometimes when he'd get crazy."

Carlisle Floyd

BY K. MICHAEL PRINCE

Southern themes and Southern language have been the stuff of art—of both the lowest and highest sort—for generations. They have become a staple of a vast genre in literature, music, the arts and entertainment. Southern writers are widely recognized for their special appreciation of the unique character of the regional tongue and for the universal meanings they plumb from our sometimes odd and homey life stories.

The musical element of the Southern dialect is a delight to all (well, *nearly* all)—those spur-of-the-moment creators who enrich our daily conversations with their quirky verbal inventions as well as to those whose artistic careers are built on their skills in the melodies and harmonies of Southern speech and manners. The vividness of rhythm and intonation, the expressiveness of imagery and pronunciation, the playfulness of our everyday verbal exchanges—all go together to make the rich burgoo of talk and tales that transform mere communication into real community. Our poets, novelists, singers and playwrights have revelled in it, giving voice and attracting a world-wide audience to our regional ways of life.

Given that, how odd it is that the musical world's grandest art—opera—has done so little to tap those same sources of narrative inspiration—especially given the often operatic qualities they possess. Maybe opera seems too rarefied an art form, too high-class and big-C cultured, too European, to adapt itself to the homespun world of Southern folkways.

Carlisle Floyd, however, has been writing operas based on Southern stories for more than half a century—and has done so quite successfully, too. What's more, he's Carolina born and raised. Floyd of Latta, a small town in the sandy-bottomed Pee Dee region of South Carolina, was born in 1926 to a Methodist-minister father and piano-playing mother. He spent the formative first twenty years of his life in South Carolina, beginning his musical studies at the age of sixteen at Converse College in Spartanburg, where he took piano instruction under Ernst Bacon. When Bacon moved to Syracuse University, Floyd followed, completing his bachelor's degree in 1946 and moving to Florida State University, where he remained for the next twenty years. In 1976, he accepted a teaching post at the University of Houston (where he is now professor emeritus) and became co-director of the Houston Opera Studio.

All the while Floyd was composing—mainly opera, many of which are set in the South, peopled by thoroughgoing southern characters. One of his operas, *The Passion of Jonathan Wade* (1962), takes place in Columbia, S.C., and tells the story of a Union officer sent to supervise the federal government's Reconstruction-era program following the Civil War. Another, *Willie Stark* (1980), is based on the Robert Penn Warren novel, *All the King's Men,* a fictionalized telling of the rise and fall of Governor Huey Long of Depression-era Louisiana. And his last completed opera, *Cold Sassy Tree* (2000), draws on the popular novel of the same name by Olive Ann Burns, a story that combines comedy and tragedy set against the backdrop of a small-town scandal in turn-of-the-century Georgia. Floyd has also set to music stories by American writer John Steinbeck (*Of Mice and Men*, 1969), as well as those of Robert Louis Stevenson (*Markham*, 1966) and Emily Bronte (*Wuthering Heights*, 1958).

But his third completed opera, *Susannah* (1955), became Carlisle Floyd's first and most lasting popular success. Based on the apocryphal biblical tale of Susannah and the Elders, the opera is a portrait of conservative religious fervor and small-minded suspicion whipped up against the innocence of youth. Populated by a quintessentially Southern cast of characters, the opera offers the trash-talking Mrs. McLean and her bevy of tight-laced biddies; the fire-and-brimstone hurling, tent-meeting preacher, Olin Blitch; the tenderhearted white trash, Sam Polk, whose alcohol-bated anger trips the story's final slide into tragedy; and Sam's vivacious younger sister, Susannah, whose downfall brought on by social intolerance and self-serving manipulation forms the heart of the drama.

What strikes the listener first about *Susannah* is how thoroughly listenable it is. While muscularly modern, it does not revel in the sort of obtuse angularity and arid atonality typical of so much "serious" twentieth-century music. This opera is at once complex and folksy, without being either off-putting or trite. Two of Susannah's arias—"Ain't it a pretty night" (Act I, Scene 2) and "The trees and the mountains are cold and bare" (Act II, Scene 3)—as well as her brother Sam's soliloquy on the failings of human nature—"It's about the way people is made, I reckon" (Act II, Scene 5)—are by turns warm and heart-rending, little gems of sentiment and substance. And though they may sound like arrangements of folk-tunes, they are Floyd originals, formed from American folk traditions we all recognize almost instinctively.

The second thing that the listener notices is the language. It's the spoken word of the South, albeit the South of Floyd's youth. It's Welty and O'Connor and Caldwell, with a bit of Steinbeck and *Elmer Gantry* thrown in. Until Floyd, who could have imagined a line like "I wouldn't tech them peas a-her'n!" in modern opera? But Floyd recognized that authenticity flows from the bonds formed in the native language of a people. While the picture of Southern life he presents is in some ways harsh, where lust and intolerance form a violent mix that ruins a young woman so full of life, allowing his characters speak in a fashion true to themselves lends them a humanity they would otherwise lack. He lets us see them from the inside out, rather than from the outside in. By joining together folkways with myth, Carlisle Floyd of Carolina crafts the highest art.

~~~

Randy Travis

BY WOODY MITCHELL

The redemption myth pops up often in country music, but rarely as dramatically as in the career of Randy Travis. Music fans know about his gusher of hits, innumerable awards and platinum album sales over the past quarter-century.

Along with performers like George Strait, the Judds, Dwight Yoakam and Ricky Skaggs, he helped forge the New Traditional school of country that roared through the late '80s into early '90s.

But if not for his rich baritone voice, the luck of the persistent and a fiercely loyal woman, he might have ended up a petty criminal in the prison system.

Born in 1959 in Marshville, N.C., and raised in rural Union County, he and his three brothers showed musical talent as kids. When Randy was eight, their ambitious dad pushed them into performance, sporting cowboy suits and shiny guitars.

By the time Randy was ten years old, he and brother Ricky were performing as the Traywick Brothers, touring the Southeast playing fiddlers conventions, Legion huts and such. While Randy's voice hadn't yet deepened, audiences were impressed by its resonance.

But he grew up too fast and rebelled as a teen, drinking, doping, fighting and stealing cars. Numerous run-ins with the law didn't slow him down, and he was on probation when the Traywick Brothers entered a talent contest at Charlotte's biggest country nightspot, Country City USA. Ricky was in jail, so Randy, then sixteen, decided to go it alone. He won.

The club manager, Lib Hatcher, saw something special in the troubled youth and hired him as a singer. When he was busted again for a probation violation, she went to court with him and pleaded his case. The judge let Randy off, but told him if he ever showed up in court again, he'd better bring his toothbrush.

In 1981, Randy took off for Nashville, and Lib soon followed. She took a job managing the Nashville Palace, where Randy worked as a short-order cook/dishwasher and sang at night as Randy Ray.

Lib managed his career and bankrolled his early efforts, but Music Row execs panned his material as "too country." Nashville audiences embraced him, but he couldn't get his foot in the music-biz door until 1985, when Lib snagged him a contract with Warner Bros. Now billed as Randy Travis, he released his first single, "On the Other Hand." It fizzled out at No. 67 on the country charts.

But patience paid off—his second single, "1982,"

hit the Top 10, and a 1986 re-release of "On the Other Hand" soared to No. 1.

After that, Randy's career exploded like a string of firecrackers—radio hits, platinum albums, music awards and top-tier concert appearances, peaking with male vocalist Grammys in 1988 and 1989. His 1988 album *Always and Forever* held the No. 1 spot for a stunning forty-three weeks.

In 1991, Lib and Randy were married. His career lulled in the mid-'90s as he concentrated on acting, appearing in numerous films and TV shows. But he again hit the top of the charts in 1998 with *A Man Ain't Made of Stone.* The 2000s brought a string of gospel albums, including the Country Music Association's 2003 Song of the Year, "Three Wooden Crosses" and gospel-album Grammy winners in 2005 (*Worship and Faith)* and 2007 *(Glory Train).* In 2007, he was also back in the studio working on a country album with producer Kyle Lehning.

In recent years, Randy has cut back on touring, preferring a quiet life with Lib at their home in Santa Fe, New Mexico.

~~~

Shirley Caesar: The Singing Evangelist

BY MATT EHLERS

After nearly five decades in the gospel business, it's a difficult question. So Shirley Caesar takes a few moments before coming up with a three-part answer:

> The first time she heard her name called at the Grammy Awards.

> The day Nelson Mandela said her songs got him through tough times in prison.

> The tear-filled prayer session with Supreme Court Justice Clarence Thomas.

These are the memories that stand out for Caesar from the years since she sold her biology textbook to buy a $9 bus ticket and start her singing career in earnest. It has been a remarkable career, one that transformed itself to include a vibrant ministry, eleven Grammy Awards and a place in Oprah Winfrey's "Legends" ball.

In mid-2007 just prior to a concert where she celebrated the fortieth anniversary of her first solo album, Caesar, sixty-eight, sat down for an interview in her North Raleigh home. The talk began with the beginning—her birth at home in Durham—and ended with

a trip to the entertainment center, where her Grammys are displayed above the living-room television. In between, she talked about traveling, family, church and her theory about why God has chosen her to reach so many people.

"He looks at faithfulness. It's possible that he saw my faithfulness," she says. "Even during my times of discouragement, I've tried to be faithful."

A FATEFUL START

The tenth of thirteen children, Caesar was born into a musical family. Her father, who died when she was young, led a gospel group, the Just Come Four Quartet. Later, she performed with her siblings.

She got her break in August 1958, after the Caravans, a gospel group, came to Raleigh for an afternoon performance. One of their members was sick, and Caesar tried to get a message to the group that she could sing the missing parts. It didn't make it. So she followed the group to Kinston, where they were performing that evening.

This time the message got through, and she was invited on stage. Before the end of the week, the group had asked her mother if Shirley and her powerful alto could join them on the road. Caesar, whose lack of money had forced her to quit classes at what is now North Carolina Central University, sold her biology textbook so she could buy the bus ticket.

Her time in the Caravans helped establish her in the gospel community. The Rev. Marvin Winans, who grew up in the famous Detroit gospel family, remembers those early songs well. "As a little kid growing up in a house where all you could play was gospel music, the Caravans were quite the stars," says Winans.

She left the Caravans in 1966 to start a solo career. Caesar titled her first album *I'll Go*, and, she says, "I've been going ever since."

A SOURCE OF INSPIRATION

Caesar accumulated a number of gospel hits in the ensuing years, including "No Charge," "Hold My Mule" and "Don't Drive Your Momma Away." Famous for her song intros that resemble mini-sermons, Caesar likes to call herself a "singing evangelist."

Busy with her career, she put off marriage until her wedding in 1984 to Harold Ivory Williams, the senior bishop of Mount Calvary Holy Churches of America. About the same time, she received a bachelor's degree from Shaw University and served on the Durham City Council. And she kept making records.

Other than a couple of weeks during high school when she helped out at a local store, Caesar's only real jobs have been singing and preaching. Today, she and her husband are the co-pastors at Mount Calvary Word of Faith church in Raleigh, which counts about 400 faithful members.

A member of the International Gospel Music Hall of Fame, Caesar bridges the gap between gospel pioneers and contemporaries, says David Gough, the hall's president. "She's a big part of both," he says. "We all look up to her for being that source of inspiration and stick-to-it-iveness."

Winans admires the fact that Caesar has managed to stay relevant to gospel audiences for so many decades. On her most recent album, *I Know the Truth*, Caesar rapped on the title track.

"It's almost unreal, the power of her voice and the popularity she continues to attain," he says. "There's no telling where you'll see Shirley."

~~~

Fred Wesley Jr.: Sideman Extraordinaire

BY ANN WICKER

Fred Wesley Jr. is one of those players who is a musician's musician. He was, as he writes in his autobiography, *Hit Me, Fred*, "born into a musical family." His father, Fred Sr., was director of music at Mobile County Training School in Mobile, Alabama, and directed a big band on the side. His grandmother was an accomplished pianist and piano teacher. Although Wesley first played trumpet in his school band, he also learned trombone, which became his main instrument. After high school, even though he was an aspiring jazz player, he toured with the Ike and Tina Turner Revue before enlisting in the army, where he played in the 55th Army Band. In 1967, he was about to take a job as a milkman to support his growing family when he got a call about playing trombone in James Brown's band. He soon learned that Brown was quite a taskmaster and band members were expected to be at every gig, recording session and rehearsal for their small weekly salary. They were also expected to pay for their own food and hotel rooms while the band was on the road. Brown was already infamous among musicians for fining band members for mistakes made during performances.

Mainly because of these pressures, Wesley left Brown's band in early 1970 and moved to Los Angeles. He played with several different bands but decided, when Brown himself called in December 1970, to rejoin that band as music director. He writes, "I returned to the James Brown Band with a new attitude. My experiences in L.A. had taught me that being a good musician was only incidental to becoming a success and making the big bucks in the music business. There had to be something to set you apart from the ordinary good musician. Mr. Brown convinced me that if I took the job as his music director, I could go a long way. Although I still had my dream of one day becoming known as a great jazz player, it didn't seem to be anywhere in my future. What I had in my favor was James Brown. He needed me, and I surely did need him. The only hard part would be enduring the humiliation that he was sure to inflict on me as I had seem him do to all the people who worked closely with him."

Brown told Wesley in that December phone call that the musicians (including Bootsy Collins) he'd hired after Wesley and others left in early 1970 weren't working out. Brown further explained he wanted to put his old band back together. Wesley immediately went to New York and took over as music director for the tour, which included Europe, while Collins and the others were still in the band. After they got back to New York, however, Collins and some of the other musicians left abruptly, and Wesley had two weeks to put together a new band.

Here's how he describes it in *Hit Me, Fred*:

Ordinarily, New York City would be the ideal place to put together a great band, but James Brown's musicians had to possess certain unique qualifications. Just being a good musician wasn't good enough. A musician also had to be willing to leave home for very long periods of time. And he had to have the disposition to deal with the unusual personality of a superstar like James Brown, which means he had to be able to take a lot of musical and personal shit without quitting and/or jumping on and/or trying to kill the bandleader and/or the star of the show. So I had to find musicians who played well enough to learn the show in two weeks and who would be impressed enough with the gig in the first place to stick through the grueling rehearsals I was about to put them through *and* through the final two or three days of rehearsals with J.B. himself—all for the meager salary James Brown was willing to pay. It would have been easy to hire someone to write out the existing show on paper, hire some top studio musicians and rehearse three or four hours a day at union scale, and come up with a decent but not very exciting show. What I was about to do was

start with what I, Jabo, Cheese, St. Clair, Johnny Griggs and Bobby Byrd knew of the existing show, then teach all the notes, chords, and rhythms for every tune, as well as all the dance routines, cues and cut-offs, to totally green people, and make it seem to an Apollo Theater audience like all the great James Brown shows of the past.

Needless to say, the musicians that I ended up with were not the cream of the New York crop. There were plenty of musicians willing and anxious to play with the great James Brown, but they were either astounded by the low salaries and the long periods on the road or had heard stories about fines and strict rules and humiliations.

Wesley and the musicians worked hard and he describes what happened next:

By the time the Boss came to rehearsal, I had everything all together. Little tricks to keep Coleman on the beat. Little tricks and cues to help everyone remember the when and where and what and how of their parts. I had constantly urged everybody, especially Morgan and Fred Thomas, to play hard and keep the groove strong and threatened everyone with fines and verbal abuse by the Boss if they didn't do everything exactly right.

I felt that we were ready. I didn't expect everything to be perfect, but at least we had a good place to start from. We did the opening and brought on the Man, and what happened next was the most amazing thing I had ever seen. This ragtag group of mostly unrelated, half-ass musicians that I had strung together with spit, chicken wire and chewing gum latched onto James Brown's vibe and became a group of BAAD MOTHERFUCKERS. It was like they drew energy from the Man.

During the five years he worked with Brown, Wesley learned about composing and arranging as well as leading a band for the sometimes difficult star. He remains mostly philosophical about the experience, writing in his autobiography: "His principles are not my principles, but he is true to what he is as I am true to what I am."

After leaving the James Brown band again, Wesley worked with, among others, Bootsy Collins and George Clinton in Parliament/Funkadelic, Count Basie and the JB Horns. He's composed and arranged for dozens of other artists, recorded albums of his own and conquered a drug problem. He even played with James Brown again. He's been called "one of the architects of funk," but said in a National Public Radio interview, "I'm a funky player who can play jazz." These days he travels the world, lecturing and playing with various bands.

Wesley has lived for many years in Manning, S.C. "I could live anywhere I wanted to live," he says, "but the people, the weather, the food and the convenience of South Carolina keep me here in the Carolinas."

~~~

Live From the Revival, It's James Brown!

BY JOHN GROOMS

Critics often accuse baby boomers of glorifying the era we grew up in, and sometimes I have to agree. I don't see how you can "glorify" a time that gave us the Vietnam War, Edsels, and Fruit Stripe Gum, but nevertheless, some people do it. Now, the music we grew up with, that's another matter entirely. Our era rocked—heck, we even invented the turn of phrase denoting that something "rocks"—and we don't mind telling anyone and everyone about it. One of the few real advantages of being a baby boomer is that we were able to see a slew of legendary musicians during our youth. The drawback is now we can't stay up late enough to catch shows by new artists, much less jump around to music for a couple of hours. But that's a trade-off I can live with, since we boomers were around when musical gods walked the earth. For many of us, that made all the difference in how we see the world.

The first big concert I ever attended was a show by James Brown and the Famous Flames. It was late 1963 or early '64, at the old Charlotte Coliseum on Independence Boulevard, or maybe it was at Park Center. I don't remember—a frequently heard phrase these days,

as the "classic rock" veterans step forcefully over the hill—but the show itself is something I'll never forget.

I was fourteen, meaning I had been a rock 'n' roll fan half of my life, ever since seeing Elvis Presley's first performance on *The Ed Sullivan Show* (which, contrary to legend, was definitely *not* filmed only from the waist up). I was also saddled with a protective mother, especially since her divorce two years earlier, so I have no idea how my best friend's twenty-year-old brother convinced Mom to let me go with the two of them to see James Brown. Thank God it happened, though, because it was one of the greatest eye-openers of my life.

We lived fifty miles from Charlotte in Gaffney, S.C. I was lucky to be part of a family that didn't bring the era's racial bigotry into our home, but legal segregation and Jim Crow customs had still kept me from knowing many black people other than as passing acquaintances. I escaped the stifling small-town atmosphere by reading books and, mostly, by listening to the radio and buying records. I knew who James Brown was. At the same time, I *didn't* know who James Brown was.

There may have been a hundred white people at

the Charlotte concert, but I doubt it. Probably more like fifty. The place was packed, the lines to buy a Coke were fifteen minutes long, and the atmosphere was electric, as if everyone there was ready to blast off. Then the show started, and they did.

Lights flashed onto the stage and reflected off the matching black-with-red-trim suits worn by members of Brown's churning band, the men moving in unison, their horns twirling around their index fingers simultaneously. After playing a couple of instrumental numbers, sharp horn riffs punctuating the songs and the bass and drums driving thousands of tapping feet, the band stopped. The inside of the building went completely dark. Screams split the air and I jerked upright, startled.

The band, their sound now coming out of the dark, started playing again for a couple of bars. A spotlight hit the stage, and the young James Brown strutted out in a blue sharkskin suit, grabbed the mike, twirled around and, in perfect time with the band, wailed, *"If you le-e-e-ave me, I'll go crazy . . ."* and the whole place went completely insane. A primal roar sent a charge through the building as women screamed at the tops of their lungs and a crowd of them rushed the stage. Before the first song was over, more than a dozen pairs of panties were scattered on the floor around a beaming James Brown.

It went on like that for about an hour and a half, the music and the crowd's passion building in intensity. Brown moved like someone possessed: dropping the mike stand, whirling around, and catching it before it hit the stage; dancing in place, and then sliding across the stage, away from and then back to the mike, as smoothly as if he were skiing across a lake. He took off his sweat-soaked jacket after a couple of songs, teased the audience by pretending to throw it into the front row, then handed it to an assistant who folded it carefully over a coat rack next to an amplifier. Brown and the band moved almost seamlessly from one song or medley to another, the crowd yelling more loudly by the minute. During wrenching ballads like "Lost Someone" and "Prisoner of Love," which Brown partly sang on his knees, he *was* that man in the song—the lonely, weak and aching lover—and the women around us, pained at the singer's agony, screamed their encouragement: "I'll love you, James! I love you, baby!"

Near the end of the show, Brown led the band through a full-tilt, dancing-fool, call-and-response version of "Night Train" that seemed to last ten minutes, and followed that with the final, cape-wielding melodrama of "Please Please Please."

The show left Brown and the audience satiated and exhausted, like we'd been through some kind of emotional orgy, or, more to the point, a revival meeting.

To say that I had never seen anything like it before hardly describes what I felt. I was like Alice, falling down the rabbit hole into a whole new world. The spectacle was spellbinding. The power of the music's hold over the audience was an exciting revelation. But more than any of that, simply being in the middle of that explosive, communal expression of black American joy was a thrill that took me completely by surprise— and wiped out any chance that I would succumb to my environment's racial ignorance.

I thought of that show and those days after James Brown died on Christmas Day 2006 and the accolades started pouring in. He was, the talking heads told us, an icon of American culture (which was true). A symbol of black pride (true again). The originator of Soul music (well, not really; that honor goes to Ray Charles, although J.B. did a lot to help the genre blossom). The praise that struck the truest chord, however, was that Brown was practically without peer as an influence on American, and thus, the world's, music.

They say the deaths of famous people come in threes. If so, the three Yuletide goners of late 2006—James Brown, Gerald Ford, and Saddam Hussein—have to be the oddest trio of celeb mortality on record. Only one of them, though, will have lasting significance.

A hundred years from now, the awful tyrant Hussein will be nothing more than a footnote in history.

Gerald Ford was praised, as all newly dead Presidents are, as a saintly statesman, even though he had been a banal politician who disillusioned millions of Americans when he pardoned Nixon. Ford, too, will be forgotten in a hundred years—heck, probably in one year.

But James Brown, the genius whose staggered beats and rhythms opened up spaces in American music that are still being filled—and who bowled over that Southern white kid forty-odd years ago—you can bet they'll know who he was a hundred years from now, and maybe longer.

~~~

James Taylor

BY DAVID PERLMUTT

As a boy, he'd whittle holes into a piece of his mother's garden hose and amaze his Chapel Hill neighbors by playing it like a flute.

At nine, he reluctantly took up the cello. Still, as a sixth-grader, there was Ike and Trudy Taylor's second-oldest child, James, performing with the North Carolina Symphony.

By fourteen, James Taylor was in an exclusive Massachusetts boarding school, battling depression and soothing his loneliness by picking a guitar. His junior year, he stayed home, enrolled at Chapel Hill High School and joined older brother Alex's dance band.

Years later, former members of the Fabulous Corsairs snicker at the thought he wasn't good enough to be lead singer. "James was so laid-back, so painfully shy," said Corsairs lead guitarist Steve Oakley, now of Durham. "His brother Alex was an out-front guy, so he was the obvious choice."

***

Born in Boston March 12, 1948, James Vernon Taylor's life in music began on thirty-two rolling acres of woodland and pasture near the University of North Carolina campus. There, in a house full of glass and sunlight, music and encouragement to try anything flowed freely.

His confessional songs provide glimpses of those abundant surroundings: from sunshine, geese in flight, and old friends in "Carolina in My Mind"; to Morgan Creek (which courses behind his old house), Hercules (the family dog who ate rocks), snakes and wood smoke in "Copperline."

Though he left North Carolina as a teenager, many longtimers—adopting the "Carolina" song as the state anthem—claim him as a native son. Taylor credits his North Carolina upbringing for molding his creativity. "Being Southern is a central part of my make-up, certainly in terms of my writing," he said in a 2000 interview shortly before his induction into the Rock and Roll Hall of Fame. "When I left North Carolina, I identified for a long time as being from a different culture that people didn't understand. But the South I knew was Chapel Hill, and there were brilliant people there who enthusiastically embraced the Civil Rights movement. I'd sit on my grandmother's porch in Morganton and feel that Faulknerian, defended, proud post-bellum Southern experience.

"Some of it was deeply tragic, but profound and resonant."

***

His parents were an unlikely union.

North Carolina native Isaac Taylor, with deep family roots in New Bern and Morganton, and New Englander Gertrude Woodard married in Salisbury during World War II.

Ike, with an M.D. from Harvard, was chief resident at Boston's Massachusetts General Hospital when he was offered a teaching job at the UNC medical school.

By then, he and Trudy had four children: Alex was born in 1947, James in '48, Kate a year later, and Livingston in '50. Ike jumped at the chance to return and become part of a flood of young physicians and medical researchers who arrived in Chapel Hill in the early 1950s. He moved his family into a rented farmhouse outside Chapel Hill in 1952. Soon a fifth child, Hugh, came along.

While Ike put in long hours at the med school, Trudy oversaw design and construction of an eleven-room house on Morgan Creek Road. In 1954, they moved in.

A year later, the Navy drafted Ike and assigned him to Operation Deepfreeze near the South Pole, where he was medical officer and conducted research. He spent eighteen months on the ice, with little opportunity to reach his family.

James was seven.

"His leaving for what to a young boy seemed like the moon reinforced this sense of being somehow different," James said. "I felt proud that my dad was a part of this small expeditionary force in the Antarctic; he hadn't just gone to Baltimore on business.

"But it was different, strange; he had left a wife new to the South and five young kids. It was hard on all of us; we felt very isolated."

***

In Chapel Hill, Trudy, trained as a soprano, held the family together and filled the house with music. Liv sang Tuberose snuff jingles in his high chair. Kate danced. And James blew on harmonicas, built tree houses and roamed the woods.

"What I remember most about Chapel Hill is the landscape," James said. "I tell my kids that we were pre-TV and there was a lot of empty time there—long uninterrupted time when you just walked into the woods and let your imagination grow. I believe that was an important part of whatever creative life I've had."

When Ike returned, the children had taken up the cello, violin and piano.

Evenings they gathered for "kitchen concerts."

Mary Gray White (Clarke then) of Chapel Hill taught James cello, or tried to: "The lad was not encouraged to practice. He was a sweet lad, but I think his heart was with the guitar."

Credit the oldest Taylor for that. By then, Alex was studying his masters—Ray Charles, Aretha Franklin and Otis Redding—and soon he and his siblings were picking and singing. "Mom tried to foster music in all of us when we were young," James said. "The cello felt like hard work to me. The guitar felt like the life-of-the-party kind of thing."

About that time, they saw less of their father, as he climbed the med school ranks. Still he provided materials for an idyllic childhood: a spare Briggs & Stratton engine to power go-karts, a cable car that crossed one of the pastures, jungle hammocks to sling between trees, bamboo poles to fish in Morgan Creek.

"My parents wanted things for us," James said. "Mom wanted us to be exposed to musical theater. Speak a foreign language. Go to environmental camp. Go to Jugtown, or to camp at the Black Mountain School.

"Both my parents were always pushing for these things to try to get us to lift off."

The Taylors spent each August on Martha's Vineyard off Massachusetts, in a house overlooking South Beach.

After they left for the Vineyard, their Chapel Hill neighborhood seemed ghostly empty. When they returned, you knew summer was over. Soon go-karts were buzzing down the street, Hercules giving chase.

Yet in the early 1960s, that began to change. Ike was appointed dean in 1964 and hit the road to expand the school's services to the state. He and Trudy grew apart. At fourteen, James was shipped off to Milton Academy near Boston. His parents wanted him to be more independent and get a better education. He didn't want to go and soon was engulfed by depression. "I felt alienated; I missed home terribly," he said. "I went for long stretches thinking about my family in North Carolina. I filled the loneliness by feeling bad and teaching myself to play my guitar. I knew how to isolate myself, and when I did, I turned to the guitar."

His parents sensed his depression and kept him home his junior year. Alex recruited James to play rhythm guitar for the Corsairs. He had no electric guitar, so Alex bought him a clunker, a Fender.

James made it wail.

Steve Oakley listened in wonderment. "I was playing lead guitar, and studying James the whole time," he said. "I was so embarrassed; I was nowhere near as good as him. He had such a feel for it."

***

His life in music and battles with depression and drugs after that are well chronicled. He returned to Milton, but grew suicidal and at seventeen checked into a mental hospital, where he finished high school and wrote songs.

He fled after nine months for New York and joined the Flying Machine band with Danny "Kootch" Kortchmar, an old Vineyard friend who James says was his greatest influence on guitar. Now James was the out-front guy; the band played his songs. But he slipped precipitously into drugs, escaping his internal desolation with heroin.

The fall of 1967, his father hauled him back home. "He heard in my voice that I was in trouble," James said. "I stayed there six months and got my strength back."

Before long, he left for London, where he sang on the streets and in cafés. "I couldn't see any future for my music in this country," he said. "I decided I couldn't be in North Carolina; I didn't belong there anymore."

In London, Kootch put James in touch with Peter Asher, scouting talent for the Beatles' new Apple label.

Asher invited him to cut a demo tape. Beatle Paul McCartney liked what he heard.

One night in early 1968 James called his parents in Chapel Hill. "Mother, the Beatles want to cut a record of my songs," he told Trudy. "They want to run it up the flagpole and see if anyone salutes." A few days later a pile of documents arrived in Chapel Hill for Ike and Trudy to sign. James was only nineteen; he'd become the first American to sign with Apple.

***

When *James Taylor* reached U.S. record stores in 1969, Chapel Hillians saluted. There was long-haired James on the cover, in a suit he'd bought for $1.50 in a London thrift shop.

It surprised his former bandmates. "It was almost disbelief," Oakley said. "We all knew he was certainly talented enough to do it. He just didn't show it off."

Over the next thirty-eight years, he's released eighteen more albums. He's won five Grammys. *Billboard* magazine awarded him its 1998 Century Award, and two years later he was inducted into the Rock and Roll and Songwriters halls of fame. In 2006, The National Academy of Recording Arts and Sciences honored Taylor as its MUSICARES Person of the Year.

He co-starred in a movie (*Two-lane Blacktop*), played Carnegie Hall and is a member of the North Carolina Hall of Fame. Two marriages ended in divorce; the first, to singer-songwriter Carly Simon, produced a daughter (Sally) and son (Ben).

In 2001, he married Boston Symphony Orchestra executive Kim Smedvig. They are raising twin boys, Henry and Rufus.

And now, like the images in his songs, his dark days have turned dramatically brighter: He's been drug-free and a fitness fiend for nearly twenty-five years. He says his drug addiction should have made him another rock 'n' roll casualty. Grateful for the second chance, he believes his drug use ultimately served a purpose.

"As dangerous as self-medication is, I think my problems are the reason I have something to offer," he said. "Yet I wouldn't recommend it to anyone and I think it was a waste of time."

Rarely does he perform near Chapel Hill and not stop by his old home and walk among the woods of his youth. When Alex died in 1993, James called the North Carolina relatives. When Ike died in 1996, the family descended on Chapel Hill for a memorial service. "I really believe we never left Chapel Hill," said his mother, who sold the house in 1974 after she and Ike divorced and she moved to their Vineyard home. "I warned the people who bought the house that 'on a quiet, still night, if you hear something, it's just us haunting the place.'"

3

THE BANDS

Hootie Comes Home

BY MICHAEL LEON MILLER

The air conditioner was cranked to the max, R.E.M. was blasting from the stereo, and I-20 stretched out ahead like an endless asphalt ribbon across the Deep South. It was late summer 1994, and Hootie and the Blowfish were headed home to Columbia, S.C. The four bleary-eyed pop rockers were crammed into their Ford Econoline van, and they were in a hurry.

Dean Felber was behind the wheel, the easygoing bass player with savvy business skills. Jim Sonefeld was riding shotgun, the drummer with long blonde hair and a cool sense of percolating rhythm. In the back sat Darius Rucker, the singer with a rich, resonating voice that could boom like a shotgun one second, soothe like a gospel lullaby the next. Mark Bryan, the curly-haired lead guitarist who usually had energy to burn, was trying to get some sleep.

If the back of the van wasn't crowded enough already, soundman Billy Huelin and guitar tech/T-shirt salesman Gary Greene were crammed in there as well.

For the past few weeks, the Hootie gang had been making a swing through clubs and colleges in Georgia, Alabama, Mississippi, and Louisiana, a circuit they'd come to know all too well. The Blowfish had been doing this sort of thing almost non-stop for the better part of five years. From town to town, show to show. Maybe a round of golf between gigs. Wash a load of clothes when they found the time. Four young musicians all in their late twenties had struck a perfect balance between partying and paying the bills.

But this road trip was different. The stakes were higher. The rooms were larger. The crowds more energized than ever. The Blowfish had even played a Democratic Party fundraiser where they'd met President Bill Clinton, had a nice chat with the Commander in Chief after the gig.

The breezy Blowfish lifestyle was rapidly becoming a whirlwind, and things were sure to get even more blustery in the weeks to come.

The first stiff breeze was felt ten months earlier when the Blowfish signed a major-label deal with Atlantic Records, one of the most hallowed names in the music business. The band's hard work had finally paid off. All those long hours on the highway. All the lugging of equipment into bandbox nightclubs. All the junk food and cheap motels. The Blowfish had paid their dues and were now ready to step onto a larger stage.

In February 1994, the band flew to Los Angeles and began work with noted producer Don Gehman on its debut for Atlantic Records. On July 5, just seven weeks before their mad dash for home along I-20, Hootie and the Blowfish released *Cracked Rear View*, an eleven-track disc that featured studio versions of several crowd favorites as well as some brand new songs.

Cracked Rear View debuted at No. 1 on *Billboard* magazine's "Heatseekers" chart, a guide to up-and-coming artists bubbling just under the radar. *Rolling Stone* magazine gave the album a three-and-a-half-star review, calling it a "hugely appealing major-label debut" and describing Rucker's voice as "Big and bluesy . . . a force of nature."

The first single from the album, "Hold My Hand," made nice inroads on *Billboard's* "Album Rock Tracks" chart, and the video for the song was garnering impressive airplay on the VH1 cable channel. But *Cracked Rear View* wasn't exactly roaring to the top of *Billboard's* Top 200 albums chart, languishing instead in the bottom half. After all their dreams, dedication, and hard work, would the Blowfish flounder halfway up the charts and disappear like so many other one-hit wonders?

Rock 'n' roll dreams can be fleeting, but sometimes a simple twist of fate can secure a place in pop history.

❋ ❋ ❋

On Monday afternoon, August 29, 1994, the phone rang in the band's business office in Five Points, the shopping-and-drinking village near the University of South Carolina campus where the band played its first gigs. Patti Conti from Atlantic Records had big news. Nancy Smith, their all-world office girl, took the

call and passed it along to the band's manager Rusty Harmon.

"David Letterman's people called," Conti told Harmon. "They want Hootie to play the show this Friday night."

Harmon was dumbfounded. It was the kind of call he dreamed of getting. This is it, he thought, the big time. No longer was he only dealing with club owners, regional concert promoters, and annoying reporters from the local newspaper. Now it was major-label promotions people and the staff from David Letterman's *The Late Show*.

Apparently, the wisecracking TV host had heard "Hold My Hand" on New York's WNEW-FM while driving home from work the previous Friday. When he got to his office the following Monday, he told his staff he had to have this band Hootie and the Blowfish on the show. Right away. As soon as possible.

Then another fortuitous twist occurred. The musical act for that Friday's *The Late Show* canceled, giving the Blowfish a highly prized opening.

There was a snag, however. A *big* snag. The band was scheduled to play a sold-out concert at Columbia's cozy old Township Auditorium that Friday night. All 3,200 tickets had been snapped up to celebrate the return of Columbia's hometown heroes. No way Harmon could cancel that gig.

"Well," Conti said. "They start taping the Letterman show at 4:30. Maybe you could catch an early flight, make it back to Columbia in time for the concert."

Harmon had a better idea. "Get us a private plane," he said.

Conti told him to fax a budget to the record label. Harmon got on the phone with Eagle Aviation at Columbia's Metropolitan Airport and secured a nice deal on a seven-seat Lear jet. The folks at Atlantic Records looked over the budget proposal and said, "Cool."

Harmon called his charges. They had played some golf after a gig in Baton Rouge, Louisiana, and were now in New Orleans, getting ready for a show that night in a club called Jimmy's.

"Letterman!" they gasped in unison. "No way!"

The Blowfish had been big fans of David Letterman's late-night show for years. They had more stops to make and more sets to play on their way home to Columbia, but those gigs paled in comparison to playing one of the coolest shows on television.

But they had to stay focused. Keep their eyes on the road and their hands upon the wheel. The Blowfish raced home, a trailer filled with amps, drums and sound equipment bouncing along behind their van. Connections had to be made to a gig that would not only change their lives, but also signal a surprising shift in American pop music.

When the Blowfish began to surface in the early 1990s, they found themselves in a sea of punk rock, grunge, and gangsta rap. Bands such as Nirvana, Green Day, Pearl Jam, and Soundgarden were critical darlings and big sellers. These bands made music that was edgy, loud, and angry, vastly different from the more melodic appeal of Hootie's rock 'n' roll.

The Blowfish had peppered early sets in their career with plenty of punk covers, but as they matured, they moved away from the faster, louder sounds of punk and new wave. The band brought a more classic-rock vibe and old-school R&B sensibility to its original songs. It was a refreshing change from all the angst on the radio, and pop-rock fans who heard tunes such as

"Time," "Hold My Hand," and "Only Wanna Be With You" were making the same kind of giddy connection David Letterman had made.

When the Blowfish arrived home in Columbia during the wee hours of September 2, 1994, they barely had time to shower and brush their teeth before meeting at the airport for the flight north to *The Late Show*. If they were road-weary, they didn't show it.

By late morning, they'd arrived at the Teterboro Airport in New Jersey where a limo was waiting to whisk Harmon and the band across the Hudson River and to the offices of Atlantic Records in Manhattan. The staff at Atlantic was excited to see the Blowfish, and they were all buzzing about the Letterman gig. The schedule was checked and re-checked, and after a quick lunch and a lot of high-fives and calls of "Good luck!" the Blowfish were back in the limo and headed for CBS Studios.

"We were nervous," Sonefeld said. "It was our first television gig and we didn't know what to expect."

The Blowfish needn't have worried. On arriving at the studio, they were greeted by veteran late-night musical director Paul Schaffer, who put the fellows at ease by telling them he'd do whatever they needed to make their performance a knockout.

The band was scheduled to play "Hold My Hand," a song that runs over four minutes on *Cracked Rear View*. But Schaffer told the band they'd have to play it in three minutes and thirty seconds on *The Late Show*. After a few rehearsals and some shrewd editing suggestions from Schaffer, the Blowfish were ready. At 5 P.M., Letterman introduced them as "my favorite new band," and the Blowfish launched into "Hold My Hand," Rucker in his Miami Dolphins baseball cap and Bryan bouncing around in his favorite black Rockafellas' T-shirt, a tribute to the Five Points music club in Columbia.

They nailed it, a flawless version of "Hold My Hand" that was filled with their trademark power pop and was right on the money, time-wise. After shaking hands with Letterman before the commercial break, the Blowfish were out the door and headed back to the limo.

"If nothing goes wrong, we should be back in Columbia by 9:30," Harmon said. "I'm allowing an hour for screw-ups."

❋ ❋ ❋

As the Blowfish jetted home in their private plane, dizzy from the rush of playing Letterman, the home folks at The Township awaited the band's return. Fans lined the sidewalks and gathered in the outside backstage area, while inside two other South Carolina bands, Columbia's Treadmill Trackstar and Greenville's Cravin' Melon, warmed up the packed house.

The Blowfish touched down at the Columbia airport at 10 P.M. and found another limo and two state-trooper patrol cars waiting to escort them to The Township. With the lights atop the patrol cars flashing, the caravan tore through the streets to the auditorium. When they turned into the backstage area, fans cheered and circled the limo, banging on the roof and windows.

"It was like *A Hard Day's Night*," Harmon said.

Everything was set up and ready onstage, so they had little time to linger in the dressing room. They walked straight onto the stage to a thundering ovation that didn't subside until Rucker walked up to his microphone.

"It's been a long, long day," he told the crowd. "This is the culmination of the biggest day in Hootie history."

With that, he and his bandmates kicked into the song "Hannah Jane," and The Township began to rock. When Rucker strummed the opening chords to "Hold My Hand" at fifteen minutes past midnight—almost the exact same time the *Late Show* performance was being televised nationwide—the fans roared as one, their arms outstretched over their heads as if they were indeed trying to hold Hootie's hand.

The Blowfish didn't let them down. Their ninety-minute concert was a supercharged affair, flushed with the fervor of a band that knew great things were ahead. Afterwards, the sweaty, happy Blowfish sipped beer and talked to fans backstage, trying to put it all in perspective.

"It's been amazing," Rucker said. "Sometimes I feel like I'm going to wake up and be in the back of the van, coming home from Birmingham."

It was indeed like a dream, one of those rock 'n' roll dreams that can be oh so fleeting. But for Hootie and the Blowfish, the events of that Friday in September of 1994 signaled that their dream was just beginning. After the Letterman show and the Township concert, the van gave way to a full-fledged tour bus; *Cracked Rear View* soared to the top of the charts; and songs such as "Only Wanna Be With You" and "Let Her Cry" became massive hits. The band would record four more studio albums, sell more than ten million records worldwide, and win two Grammy Awards.

Oh, and they played the David Letterman show twelve more times.

〜〜

In the Swing

BY MARK MCGRATH

Long before they became national basketball power-houses, the University of North Carolina at Chapel Hill and Duke University were known for producing some of the nation's most popular dance orchestras. Unknown to many, these two universities were hotbeds of musical talent from the 1920s through the 1940s, and a startling number of their alumni went on to become top bandleaders and musicians during the Big Band era.

The tradition began when a talented freshman named Hal Kemp arrived in Chapel Hill in the fall of 1922. Kemp was already an accomplished musician. As a child in Charlotte, he had worked at a theater where he played clarinet and player piano in tandem to accompany silent films. While a student at Central High School, he formed his first band, the Merrymakers Jazz Orchestra.

During his freshman year at Carolina, Kemp formed the Carolina Club Orchestra. An immediate hit, it became a fixture at college proms, society balls, and fraternity dances throughout the Southeast. In Kemp's sophomore year, he recruited three freshman musicians to his orchestra: Skinnay Ennis, Saxie Dowell, and John Scott Trotter.

Ennis, a drummer from Salisbury, N.C., sang on many of the orchestra's numbers and his distinctive, breathless singing style became one of the band's trademarks. Dowell, a Raleigh, N.C., native, became the orchestra's featured reed player. Trotter, who played piano and handled most of the band's arrangements, knew Kemp from his Charlotte days. He was a 1925 graduate of Central High, and they had played together in a Sunday school orchestra at Hawthorne Lane Methodist Church.

Together with most of his band, Kemp left Carolina in the mid-1920s to embark on a professional career. The Kemp Band, of course, would later become the most popular dance orchestra of the period, but the original foursome broke up in the last half of the 1930s. Trotter left in 1936 to become Bing Crosby's musical director and arranger, a relationship that lasted until Trotter's death in 1975. Ennis left in 1938 to lead the Bob Hope radio orchestra, and Dowell departed to front his own band about the same time. Kemp died in 1940 from injuries suffered in an automobile accident in Madera, California, a tragic end to a brilliant career. He was only thirty-six.

LEADER OF THE BAND

When Kemp left Chapel Hill in the 1920s to pursue his dreams, a jovial sophomore from Rocky Mount, N.C., stepped up and began to organize what soon became the leading orchestra on campus. Kay Kyser, previously the university's head cheerleader, had no musical training and couldn't play an instrument or read music.

Kyser, along with saxophonist and vocalist Sully Mason of Durham, experimented with several lineups during the band's formative years. By 1927, the roster had solidified, and by the time of his graduation in 1928, Kyser's band was recognized as the leading college orchestra in the Southeast. The young graduate took to the road as a professional bandleader, and after several years of relative obscurity, his orchestra took off in the early days of the Great Depression.

By the late 1930s the orchestra had a national reputation, ranked among the top in the country. Kyser's popularity crossed over into motion pictures as well, and his band was featured in more than a dozen movies in the 1940s.

Kyser is probably best remembered for his Wednesday night radio show, *The Kollege of Musical Knowledge*. Sponsored by Lucky Strike cigarettes, the program adopted a zany musical quiz show format and was one of America's most popular radio shows for more than a decade. In its prime, the program attracted as many as twenty million listeners each week.

CROONING HALFBACK

Down the road at Duke University in Durham, N.C., music was becoming an equally important part of campus life in the 1920s. The university's dance band tradi-

tion began with the arrival of George "Jelly" Leftwich in the mid-1920s as director of the school band and symphony orchestra. In his free time, the Wilmington, N.C., native organized a professional dance orchestra, recruiting talent from Duke's student body.

Known as the Duke University Orchestra, the Leftwich band became extremely popular, performing at ballrooms, country clubs, and resorts in Virginia, Tennessee and the Carolinas. During the early 1930s, the band became a featured act at the Lumina Pavilion on Wrightsville Beach, making nightly appearances there during the summer months.

The orchestra never truly made the big time, but it paved the way for those that followed. Under Leftwich's guidance several Duke underclassmen formed a student orchestra in 1931 that became known as the Blue Devils. The band's leader and vocalist was Nick Laney, who was also a star player on Wallace Wade's Duke football team. Tagged the "crooning halfback," the campus idol led the Blue Devils to statewide prominence in the early 1930s.

When Laney graduated in 1934, leadership of the Blue Devils passed to a graduate of the Ithaca Conservatory of Music named Les Brown, who later became one of the biggest names of the Big Band era. Les Brown and his "Band of Renown" toured frequently with Bob Hope in the 1940s but possibly was best known for launching the career of Doris Day. She joined the orchestra in 1940 at the age of seventeen.

SOUND BITES

The Blue Devils weren't the only orchestra on the Duke campus in the early 1930s. In 1931, a wavy-haired, left-handed violinist from Newell named Johnny Long enrolled for his freshman year and immediately organized the Duke Collegians. After a 1932 summer engagement at White Lake in Bladen County, the Collegians were known as one of the most polished dance bands in the Southeast.

During the school year, the Collegians and the Blue Devils played every night following dinner in the lobby of the Women's College Union and in the first floor lounge of the West Campus Union. The two bands alternated monthly between the two venues, a tradition remembered fondly by students of that era. The bands received free meals in exchange for their musical efforts.

Following their graduation in 1935, most of the Collegians remained together and formed the Johnny Long Orchestra. The band enjoyed considerable professional success playing at leading ballrooms and dance pavilions across the country, including New York's Paramount Theater. Its rendition of "In a Shanty in an Old Shanty Town" sold more than four million copies in the 1940s. The band was featured in the 1943 Abbott and Costello movie *Hit the Ice*, and Long appeared on the cover of *Billboard* magazine in 1944. There were many personnel changes over the years, but Long continued to perform until his untimely death in 1972.

It was a romantic time. Imagine students swaying to the music of these college orchestras at fraternity dances, perhaps at Chapel Hill's Tin Can or in the Duke Union ballroom. On autumn nights, the languid strains of saxophones and muted trumpets spilled through open windows and drifted across the campuses.

The era was as fleeting as it was remarkable. By 1940, the golden age of student orchestras had begun to wane. But this romantic period is still remembered wistfully by those who were part of it. "The dances and the music of those bands meant everything to us," recalls David Henderson, a 1935 graduate of Duke. "It was a wonderful time."

Carolina Chocolate Drops: The Kids Are All Right

BY LYNN FARRIS

For many of us, attending a contra dance wouldn't exactly be a life changing event, but for North Carolina native Rhiannon Giddens, a graduate of the prestigious Oberlin Conservatory of Music and professionally trained opera singer, it changed everything.

For it was at a contra dance where Giddens fell in love with string-band dance music and realized that performing opera might not be the path she was supposed to take. This change in direction would lead her down another musical road and to the formation of the Carolina Chocolate Drops.

Soon after that first contra dance, Giddens' interest in this old time music led her to Boone, N.C., for the Black Banjo Gathering in April of 2005, an event celebrating the banjo's African-American roots.

Also making a pilgrimage to this festival was Justin Robinson, another N.C. native and classically trained violinist. Robinson's musical background was a bit diverse as his mother sang opera but his *Hee-Haw* watching grandparents loved country music. He'd traded in his violin for a fiddle and become a fan of longtime black traditional string-band player, Joe Thompson, whose performance was to be one of the highlights of the festival.

Journeying the furthest was Dom Flemons, a street musician and solo artist, hailing from Arizona. Flemons had immersed himself in music early on, playing drums and percussion in his school band and taking on the guitar and harmonica as a teenager.

Giddens met both Flemons and Robinson at the Black Banjo Gathering, although the two fellows didn't meet until all three moved to Durham, N.C., which happened in the months after the festival.

Flemons later explained to one interviewer, "I decided after seeing all that talent—including Joe Thompson—I was moving to North Carolina."

During the summer of 2005, the three visited Thompson regularly, playing music together and soaking in everything they could from watching and listening to Thompson play. They've been under the master's tutelage ever since.

Robinson has said it was during these visits with Thompson where the trio clicked and developed their own sound, which eventually led to the creation of the Carolina Chocolate Drops. The band features unbelievable musicianship by way of the many different influences and resonates with an old-time sound. The Carolina Chocolate Drops have taken the stage in North

Carolina and beyond, including numerous trips to Canada for folk festivals, and playing most everywhere in between. In early 2008, they toured in the Midwest and Canada again before heading to shows in Ireland, England, Scotland and France.

In 2007, the Music Maker Relief Foundation, an organization dedicated to supporting elderly Southern musicians and preserving traditional roots music, declared the Chocolate Drops as the only young, black jug band currently in existence. And the band doesn't just spread their message by way of the stage or recordings (in 2007 the band released their debut record, *Dona Got A Ramblin' Mind*), Flemons schedules frequent appearances at inner-city schools and black community events.

The group's many accolades and accomplishments include a glowing album review in *Rolling Stone* and landing small roles in the 2007 film, *The Great Debaters*, produced by Oprah Winfrey and directed by and starring Denzel Washington. Music by the Drops was featured the soundtrack and on Oprah's show about the film.

In response to the band's achievements, their mentor Thompson laughingly told one interviewer, "They're all right," with much approval.

The Accelerators: Riding the Dream Train

BY BAKER MAULTSBY

Veterans of the Southeast's music scene will sometimes reminisce about the days when you could
see R.E.M in a small club, the Connells were hot
on the college circuit, and Jason and the Scorchers and
the Georgia Satellites were paving the way for later
"alternative country" acts.

Every so often, someone in the conversation
will think of the Accelerators—a band that hailed
from Raleigh, N.C., and before that South Carolina's
Upstate—and declare that, hands down, they were one
of the best groups of the era.

They remember the band's blaring guitars played
over the rock-steady groove of an impeccably tight
rhythm section. And they can still hum the crisp melodies of songs like "Boy and Girl," "(Why You) Hang Up
on Me," and "Regina."

And they might remember that while the Accelerators never sold a great many records, they garnered
a positive review in *Rolling Stone* and glowing praise
from *Billboard*.

One fan from those days was Cory Robbins, then a
partner in Profile Records. Profile released two albums
by the band—*The Accelerators* and *Dream Train*.

"Some would compare them to the Georgia Satellites or the Fabulous Thunderbirds. But, you know, I
liked them a lot better," says Robbins.

Indeed, while blues-based barroom rock was the
foundation of the Accelerators' sound, there was something that distinguished their songs from "Tough
Enough" or "Keep Your Hands to Yourself."

Music writers constantly look for pithy descrip-
tions of musical sounds. In the case of the Accelerators,
it's difficult to put a finger on.

There was a subtle sophistication: plenty of volume
and swagger, not unlike the Satellites or the Scorchers,
but also an element of cool restraint perhaps most com-
parable to Nick Lowe's work with Rockpile. And while
the lyrical content is in no way self-involved or gloomy,
there is often the perspective of an outsider and under-
dog as well as an earnest, blue-collar stance.

If you're looking to lead writer and singer Gerald
Duncan to pin it down for you, he doesn't offer much.
"It was mostly a matter of following your nose, basi-
cally," Duncan says, though he points to a few of the
sounds that shaped his musical awareness as a kid—
the Wilburn Brothers on TV, songs by Otis Blackwell,
hymns at the Southern Baptist church he attended.

As for his lyrical point of view, Duncan gives no

firm explanation—but a few hints: "My heroes were Martin Luther King and Muhammad Ali . . . people who were willing to stand up and take consequences for doing what was right. That was always pretty impressive to me."

✳ ✳ ✳

Duncan grew up in Taylors, at that time a growing community making the transition from back-road town to full-blown suburb of Greenville, S.C. Duncan was the first student body president of then-new Eastside High School. High school politics wasn't the only matter commanding his attention. Duncan was learning guitar and becoming a serious student of songcraft.

"I was serious about it always," he says. "Mostly, I started playing to write. I don't know. I had no choice."

✳ ✳ ✳

It was particularly hot time for local kids to be driven by musical ambitions. The area was in the throes of the Southern Rock heyday, with regional acts like Lynyrd Skynyrd and the Allman Brothers churning out hit after hit and the Marshall Tucker Band, just thirty miles away in Spartanburg, breaking through as well.

These groups spawned plenty of imitators. Duncan was not one of them. He quickly developed a sound that was decidedly Southern. . . . but not Southern Rock.

At a time when "extended" twin guitar solos were the goal for most local outfits (and bands whose goal was to make as much money as possible in local nightclubs played disco covers), Duncan was unusual. Other groups featured improvisational jams; Duncan wrote concise rock songs with an emphasis on lyrics.

He says, "Songs are not words and not music, they're music and words together. They're both part of the thing together."

It was a thing that quickly attracted attention.

"The great thing about Gerald was that it was about rock 'n' roll," says Gene Berger, owner of Greenville's Horizon Records and a longtime Upstate music honcho.

"He was a star," says record producer Dick Hodgin. "His songs were different. He was a very clever wordsmith, and he had a penchant for putting these quirky songs and wordsmanship to just balls-out rock songs."

Hodgin, who got to know Duncan in the 1970s, went on to work with artists ranging from Hootie and the Blowfish to Clay Aiken to the Flat Duo Jets. Until the early 1990s, he worked as the Accelerators' manager and lead producer. He and the band relocated from Greenville to Raleigh as a team in the early '80s. "Depending on which set of musicians [Duncan] had, the rock level went up or down," Hodgin says, "the rockabilly influence moved up or down, the pop sensibilities moved up or down."

The Accelerators' first album—*Leave My Heart*, released on the tiny Dolphin label—was recorded with production support from Don Dixon. The album features rockabilly-tinged pop songs that stand up alongside the work of contemporaries like Marshall Crenshaw, Nick Lowe, and Dixon.

Aside from Duncan's customary wit, there are lyrical surprises: a glimpse at interracial romance in the South ("Regina"), the grisly story of "Stiletto," and a tale of "Two Girls in Love."

After the album, bassist Keller Anderson and guitarist Chris Moran exited the band, to be replaced, respectively, by Mike Johns and Brad Rice. Rice and Johns brought a harder edge to Duncan's songs, while Johns contributed songs and lead vocals.

Johns' song, "Stayin' Up in the City," kicks off the band's self-titled 1987 release on Profile Records.

Profile's Cory Robbins had gotten a cassette tape in the mail of *Leave My Heart*. Don Dixon's name in the credits motivated Robbins to give it a serious listen, and he was sold. "They just had great songs, singing, and playing," he recalls.

Profile was best-known for breaking Run-DMC and advancing the commercial appeal of rap music. Reviews were positive, in some cases gushing, and the band continued to build a following on the club circuit, where rockers like "Radio" and "You're a Fool" as well as Johns' cover of "Black Slacks" were favorites. But widespread commercial success eluded the band.

"We worked it, but we never could get anything going on it," says Robbins. It didn't help that Robbins' partner at Profile "hated the band," an issue that contributed to the label's closing a few years later.

The Accelerators managed to get one more record out on Profile. *Dream Train* was perhaps the group's most polished recording, and Hodgin maintains that if the band and Profile had each been able to stick things out, the Accelerators' breakthrough may have been imminent.

Hodgin sent copies around, including one to WRDU, in Raleigh. He was somewhat surprised to hear the lead-off song, "Boy and Girl," blaring out of a friend's car stereo. "The program director told me, 'Man, I can't believe how much response we're getting

on this,'" Hodgin recalls. "All it would have taken was a little push."

But by then, Profile was breaking up. The band followed suit soon after.

The break-up ended an intensely creative period of Duncan's life marked by substantial accomplishment and equally major disappointment. He and his band had achieved what few even come near: They'd released albums with label backing. Their music attracted the praise of national publications. They made a living touring and playing music.

But when it was over, there was little money in the bank and no clear support structure. "Would I advise someone to do this? Not if you have any other choice. Not unless there was no other way," Duncan says now. "I had no choice. It's a really difficult life."

Mike Johns moved back to Greenville, S.C., and joined forces with Spartanburg-based singer-songwriter-rocker Matthew Knights in the short-lived Fluffy. Doug Welchel, the brilliant drummer who had been with Duncan from the start, played with Knights for a while, too, before dropping off the radar.

Brad Rice continued to expand his range as a guitarist, and is now one of the hottest sidemen on the Americana scene.

Duncan settled into a more workaday life in Raleigh, got married and plays occasional gigs with a new group of Accelerators.

✳ ✳ ✳

In 2000, the band released *Nearer*. This album was recorded without Hodgin at the soundboard, but once again, Duncan's songs captured the praise of reviewers.

Rockers like "Cry like a Baby" and "Waiting in Line," along with the introspective title cut, stand among his best work. But as an independent release with little touring support, the album was mostly picked up by longtime fans.

One of those fans is Jerker Emanuelson, a Swedish fellow with something of an obsessive streak when it comes to American music. He runs his own label, Sound Asleep Records, which has released albums by Bill Lloyd and Tim Carroll along with the well-received *Hit the Hay* compilation series.

Sound Asleep is planning to release a "best of" collection of Accelerators material. Emanuelson's projects have a way of making the rounds among rock 'n' roll fans with good ears. Perhaps the record will inspire critics and song publishers and others to take another look at the Accelerators catalog, bringing long-overdue financial rewards for Duncan. Perhaps it won't.

Either way, Duncan says he's determined to go back in the studio with Hodgin and make another album of original material.

And he's satisfied that he and his band-mates over the years have done the best they could. "We tried to do it for the music," Duncan says. "We tried to do good songs and to do them well. It is unto itself the goal."

Conquering the World, One Gig at a Time

BY COURTNEY DEVORES

Framed by clear blue sky and palm trees smack in the middle of Southern California's mountainous desert, the Avett Brothers aren't quite in their element. But you wouldn't know it by the way the trio bashes through its mid-afternoon set—in sweat-soaked suits. The Coachella Festival, staged on a grassy polo field in Indio, just outside ritzy Palm Springs, has become a taste-making event for the indie-rock crowd and ever-influential Hollywood. It's not quite where you'd expect to find banjo-ripping country boys from Concord, N.C. When the Avetts were one of a handful of acoustic Americana acts booked for the 2007 festival, it capped the trio's transition from jam, folk and bluegrass festivals to the not-quite-commercial but more mainstream indie-rock circuit.

Unlike their gigs in the Carolinas where they've been winning over crowds, most of the audience that day filed into the tent to satisfy their curiosity.

"We're proud to be invited to a festival of this magnitude," guitarist Seth Avett said after the show. That didn't mean that they altered their set to somehow appeal to the more rock and dance-friendly crowd. They didn't prepare a set list (in fact, they never do). As they hit the stage they simply went to work—all brash

emotion, attacking their instruments, delivering sometimes spot-on, sometimes off-kilter harmonies. They didn't even up the foot-stomping or scream-style singing. Instead, they relied on romantic songs, heavy-duty strumming, and brotherly harmonies that sound like they were put on this Earth to sing together ("We were each born with a built-in partner," Seth said). My best friend, a California native who hadn't heard of them, was there at my insistence. She was practically ready to propose to them after the set.

Like stops at MerleFest and Bonnaroo, the Avetts' appearance at Coachella was just another rung on an ever-extending ladder. When they released a second disc, *Carolina Jubilee,* on Ramseur Records in 2003, the Avetts set lofty, but not entirely unattainable, goals and have met them in what seems to an outsider like record time. The group first sold out the Neighborhood Theatre in Charlotte in fall 2003 (and continues to do so each New Year's Eve). They followed that with their first MerleFest, a particular feat for bassist Bob Crawford (not a biological Brother) who moved to North Carolina from New Jersey after attending the North Wilkesboro festival in the mid-1990s.

"I wanted to live in North Carolina, because I

thought every day was like MerleFest," Crawford said. "I fell in love with the music and the area."

From our first conversation in spring 2004, the Avetts credited manager and record-label owner Dolph Ramseur with a good portion of their success. Ramseur, a candid, down-home music lover and Concord native in his mid-thirties, worked as a tennis pro and in venture capital before launching the label with the Avetts as its flagship artist. His passion has served the Avetts well. I was skeptical when Ramseur told me in April 2007 that he wanted the Avetts' new album *Emotionalism* to crack *Billboard's* Top 200 upon release and to secure a spot for them on *Late Night with Conan O'Brien*. He'd accomplished both within a month.

The climb to *Billboard's* charts and New York City's Irving Plaza wasn't instantaneous as it sounds, considering that the prolific ensemble has released around eight CDs (including live albums and EPs) in five years. But for a genre-defying group with few sonically like-minded contemporaries to follow and no major label doling out cash, the gigs, sales, and exposure are impressive.

✳ ✳ ✳

When I met them in 2004, I didn't predict the Avetts' national success—at the time, I had not seen them live. Years earlier, I witnessed brothers Scott and Seth Avett's phenomenal stage presence while they were part of the hard-rock group Nemo. They sweated, screamed, and fell in a heap at the set's end like they were exorcising demons from the stage. "Wow," I thought, "I bet that's what it was like to see early Led Zeppelin." They just had this confident, sweaty swagger not easy to forget.

Despite watching rapt crowds sing along and hang on every lyric, I didn't quite get the same heart stopping feeling from the Avett Brothers until they headlined their own Festival Essex at Verizon Wireless Amphitheatre, Charlotte's largest outdoor venue, in August 2006. Three men with only an upright bass, banjo, and guitar put on one of the most moving performances I'd ever seen. They stood relatively still, but exhibited more emotion, skill, and originality than most national acts.

And what's more, the Avetts have been able to succeed so far on their own terms. Before the release of 2004's *Mignonette* the trio performed in boardrooms for Nashville A&R executives. Suits dubbed them the male Dixie Chicks but were anxious to make changes with which the group wasn't comfortable.

"We'd do a song and the deal-breaking questions were things like, 'You guys know you have to use [other] songwriters?'" recalled older brother, banjo player and lead vocalist Scott Avett.

"We have one hundred percent freedom with Dolph. We're way below our compromise threshold," Scott said. "We're not saying that's the way the business *is*, but those are some of the encounters we've had. There *are* truthful artists who have made it with big labels."

Truth has been a resounding theme since the Avetts' inception. It's a concept they put to music on *Mignonette's* "A Gift for Melody Anne." In a near-round, the trio sings ardently: *I just want my life to be true/ I just want my words to be true/I just want my heart to be true.* Everything about them *does* seem natural—the unrehearsed spontaneity of their live shows and honest and free-flowing songwriting.

That honesty translates to relatability in their songs. An intimate folk ballad like "Sixteen in July" from

2006's *Four Thieves Gone: The Robbinsville Sessions* romantically captures the summer between innocent adolescence and teen deviance: *"License in my hand/ And freedom on my mind."* Elsewhere it's often the tangible details that ring out, whether it's a musician asking his wife if she can watch the dog for three weeks or the insecurities of being seen in a swimsuit. It's those very true thoughts that fans remember.

The Avetts' integrity is also as much a part of its business model as is its songwriting. Their success is a testament to what four people—Scott, Seth, Bob, and Dolph—can accomplish. The Avetts have toured relentlessly, racking up festival spots at Bonnaroo, Wakarusa, and Floydfest, and gradually selling out larger venues across the states. Ramseur has pounded the pavement on their behalf, securing television spots, national magazine features, and prime bookings. Despite being on a small, independent hometown label or maybe because of it, the Avetts forged a path to national exposure and critical acclaim as a united front, defiantly independent with their diligent work ethic and Ramseur's strategic marketing.

Upon its release in May 2007, *Emotionalism* debuted at No. 134 on *Billboard's* Top 200. Also that May, Ramseur called to tell me that he'd finally secured the prized booking he'd been chasing for a couple of years—the Avetts as musical guest on NBC's *Late Night with Conan O'Brien*. In a way, the band's television debut not only rewarded years of hard work, but legitimized what Carolinians had been saying for years. The band stomped and strummed and sang and even won over O'Brien. As I'd told them at Coachella a few weeks before, they are, in a blue-collar way, living the rock-star dream, gradu-ally gaining notoriety and critical acclaim in the same way R.E.M. did in the 1980s.

Ramseur explained their appeal best: "They've got this thing that Johnny Cash had," he said. "No matter who you are, Johnny Cash is cool. That's the way they are. People respond to it."

〰〰

The Scream

BY STEVE STOECKEL

It's the last song of a hot, sticky Saturday night, and I feel like screaming. Actually, I don't just feel like it-the place and the moment demand it.

The place is the World Famous Double Door Inn, which is, despite its appearance, sacred ground. Eric Clapton once stood here, as did Stevie Ray Vaughan and hundreds of others whose photographs cram the rough, wooden walls.

One of those pictures has my face, or rather my face as it looked nearly thirty years ago. The three other musicians in that photo are on stage with me now, and I can almost feel indentations in the carpet from the hundreds of times I've stood on this duct-taped spot, staring out at people who, amazingly, agreed to meet us in this church of a sort to help us construct this illusion, this bit of ephemera that will vanish when the last note ends.

They are staring back at us now—the ones who stayed for the end of this night—and every face wears a smile. We're very much in the moment, as near to the present tense as I get when the crowd and the music click. The set has been up to this point a mixture of fast and slow songs: tension and release, the pulling of an invisible string between band and audience with each modifying the other.

It's exhilarating to have this much eye contact with so many people. I pinball my vision around the smoky room and see old friends next to total strangers: Becky stands a few rows back, clapping her hands and snapping her ponytail back and forth like a whip in time with the music, which has transformed her into a teenager. Bonny and Homonym Girl sit at a table beside the stage and giggle at my silly bass guitar antics whenever I turn to face them. Back near the mixing board, a Jack Black look-alike with unblinking eyes and a goblin grin pumps his fist and screams his approval at frequent intervals.

The song at present appears to be a wall of noise—absurdly loud, musical deconstruction built around one chord—but a lot is happening onstage. To my right, Pat stands perfectly straight, eyes closed, pulling out a guitar line that I've never heard, despite having played this tune with him hundreds of times. His solos are masterful, linear things of beauty, like all great improvisation a perfect blend of discipline and abandonment. He has the stance of a jazzman, a Coltrane-like dignity that contrasts with his guitar suddenly mimicking a passing ambulance that appears and vanishes within a measure. He opens his eyes for a second and gives me a glance, knowing I'm laughing.

Behind me, Rob has reduced his drumbeat to a simple foot-snare pattern with ride cymbal bashes, stripping the already simple tune down to its atavistic essence. Thinking of this causes me to flub a note on my bass, which gets me an extra "whack!" on the snare drum, a Rob reminder: Pay attention! I'm close enough to the bass drum to feel a puff of air hitting the back of my legs with each beat of his drum pedal.

Jamie is a sweaty mixture of movement and feeling on my left, swaying his body and guitar neck back and forth with a downward jerk on the start of every second bar of the tune. Jamie's solos are hotwired, taking-corners-on-two-wheels joyrides; at the moment, he's building a simple foundation for Pat's lead break.

It's actually quite crowded up here, but my band mates aren't aware of the other players who share the stage. Spock (the left, logical part of my brain) and Murray (the right, emotional half) are directing The Twins—my hands—and Victor, my voice.

The Twins are like a pair of golden retrievers, happy to be out playing anywhere, anytime. They're running on muscle memory, playing with this familiar tune like puppies with an old shoe. Commander Spock is content to let Murray have them on a long leash as they bound joyously toward the end of the song. My voice is the immediate problem demanding Spock's attention.

Victor sports a goatee, slicked back hair and a purple smoking jacket. Unlike the Twins, who can't wait to get to work, Victor doesn't always show up. Sometimes he's there for an entire night, hitting notes that astound even the unemotional Spock; other times he'll leave in the middle of a song, embarrassing the entire troupe. The air's too dry, the weather's too cold, he's not had his nap, he hasn't warmed up, the light's in his eyes, his knee hurts—the list is endless. The others inside my head snidely refer to Victor as "His Eminence" and detest the fact that his performance is what the audience often notices most.

Now Spock is uncharacteristically diplomatic, praising Victor for how well he's hit his notes on this song late at night, near the top of his range. Victor pouts a bit, knowing what's coming: The Scream.

I love to scream. Screaming is an improvisational art all its own, and I have my own favorite examples: Roger Daltrey in "Won't Get Fooled Again," McCartney at the end of "Hey Jude," Wilson Pickett in nearly anything—but for me, the God of Scream was James Brown.

I carry this mental image of James, all hair and teeth, sweat running like a river down the chiseled, mahogany face of an African king, in total command of the band and the crowd without so much as a glance toward either. He slaps the microphone stand away as though it's an insignificant, useless thing undeserving of his presence, then pirouettes and snatches it, pulls the chrome-grilled microphone to his lips, cradling it close and then the teeth flash white in a rictus of pain and longing and—out comes this *sound*, this animal noise that happens when all other means of communication fail. It starts low, "uh-ahhhhhh-hhhhhhh . . . ," climbs over the top note of the chord and keeps going up, up for two bars, then four, levels out with a bit of vibrato, and then it's gone. Another spin, a few grunts: "Huh!" and "Hey!" and he's leaning into the verse.

This is my benchmark, my aspiration, but it requires pushing Victor well past his comfort zone, even on a good night. A bad effort resembles not so much James Brown as it does the prom queen in a fright movie, something Victor (and everyone else) knows too well.

The moment is here. Pat gives me a quick glance, telling me he's pulling the solo back, giving me space. The Twins drop back to a single note bass guitar pattern while Spock and Murray recede, letting a darker, reptilian part of my brain emerge. There's no plan, merely a dim awareness of the beat and the key; I hear a sound emerge, a wordless wail that starts a bit below the chord—a tad too thin, so I push more from my diaphragm, deepening the tone a notch. Victor hesitates a second, but the dark part of my brain won't let him stop, and presses him ruthlessly upward past his highest note, then slides down the scale to his lowest and finally lets up. I realize afterward he has picked a variation on Robert Plant's ending to "Whole Lotta Love," which even Spock agrees to be a stellar choice.

I feel serene, as though I've been scraped clean inside. The Jack Black guy near the mixing board stops his fist pumping and gives me an openmouthed stare, then screams back his approval.

I get a final mental image, this one of an amused James Brown looking down at me, waggling his hand, palm down: "Not bad." Victor's smoking jacket is ripped, but he looks pleased, and the Twins snap the leash taut as piano wire, pulling us all to the finish line, where a cold Bass Pale Ale waits like a marathon trophy near the shabby dressing room sofa.

~~~

Southern Culture on the Skids

BY GRANT BRITT

Anybody can cook a chicken. But when it comes to the art of flinging fried yardbird, there's nobody better than Southern Culture on the Skids. Colonel Sanders might have 'em beat on a worldwide distribution level, but SCOTS' own hands-on distribution program can fill a room with greasy, flying cluck faster than you can say "eight-piece box."

It's become a glorious tradition for Chapel Hill, N.C.-based SCOTS to fling cluck at their shows, but founder/guitarist/frontman Rick Miller says the custom has an ignominious beginning. Back in the day when the band—Miller, bassist Mary Huff and drummer Dave Hartman—worked anywhere they could, they were playing to a Monday night crowd of five in a Mexican restaurant in Virginia. Four of the five attendees were male, in hot pursuit of the fifth, who was of the female persuasion, and nobody was paying any attention to the band. Things were so dull that the highlight of the evening was the bucket of Kentucky Fried Chicken the club owner had delivered and set by the side of the stage for the band's dinner. The band was in the middle of a number when a homeless guy walked in the front door, reached in the bucket and grabbed a piece of fried chicken with his grimy paw.

"Heyyy, that's the band's dinner!" Miller shouted. "And he goes, 'Well I'm hungry, too.' And I said, 'Okay, fine. We're working for our dinner. You can work a little bit, too. Come on up here and do a little dance for us.'

"It wasn't quite as glamorous as you might think, no scantily clad supermodels—just some homeless guy from Harrisonburg, Virginia, doing a little soft shoe," Miller says, laughing at the memory. "But those four guys at the bar that were cock-blocking each other trying to get that one chick, they all started to pay attention. So I thought, hunh—maybe you get a little more appetizing person with the chicken and it might be fun."

Nowadays, the custom has been upgraded a bit—Miller usually picks a pretty girl or three to dispense the cluck into the crowd while the band plays their signature chicken song, "Eight Piece Box." But the designated hurlers only initiate the fling. Once the chicken starts to fly, everybody gets into the act. Over the years, Miller has perfected the fine art of flinging and offers pointers on what flies best. "Drumsticks of course," Miller says. "Wings have too many pointed edges and breasts are just a little too weighty."

Chicken is not the only Southern foodstuff the

Skids are partial to. "Nanner puddin'" is a big fave as well. SCOTS has been known to offload fifty pounds of the stuff in the bottom of the Go-Go cage at Chapel Hill's Local 506 bar for Sleazefest. But closer to home, Miller is content to ingest nanner puddin' rather than dance in it. "Best banana puddin' I've ever had was at the Village Diner, in Hillsborough, North Carolina." He says he knows it's homemade 'cause it's sweet . . . and greasy. "I don't know what they use in their pudding for lubricant, but its got a lot," he laughs. "Whips nice."

But for some fans accustomed to the band's odes to food and the white trash lifestyle, SCOTS' 2007 release, *Countrypolitan Favorites,* was a real departure. An all-covers project, the band set out to cover '60s country pop. But SCOTS doesn't do anything straight, and the result was an off-the-charts romp that combined rare oldies with the band's own trademark exuberant "toe-suckin' geek rock" that horror meister Stephen King named one of his fave records for the year. It proved to be a tough job to retain the spirit of the originals and have it mesh with the liberties the band was taking. "We wanted to make everything quite danceable," Miller says. "So, it was almost like, how would Johnny Rivers do this?"

One of the most bizarre and interesting cuts on the record is Creedence Clearwater Revival's "Tombstone Shadow."

"You belt it out kinda like Wanda Jackson," Miller told Huff, "and we'll do bluegrass harmonies on it." The result is Huff wailing like a high and lonesome diva while Miller pursues her with a stinging guitar lead.

Miller says doing this country cover thing made him think about doing genre records. "It'd be fun to do a lysergic jug-band record. That would be our unplugged record," he says, laughing. "Or, I'm always up for just doing a good swamp-pop record."

But don't go looking for a complete SCOTS make-over—the evolution process does have its limits. "Then I think, why don't we just sing a song about living in N.C., like we have a lot," Miller muses. "It all comes out in the wash once you get started."

The Marshall Tucker Band

BY ANN WICKER

When I saw the Marshall Tucker Band and Lynyrd Skynyrd at the original Charlotte Coliseum in the summer of 1975, I thought the boys from Spartanburg, S.C., with their blistering opening set, stole the show from the headliners. Then poor Ronnie Van Zant, Skynyrd's late, much-lamented lead singer, fell during the first song of their set and was unable to finish the show. I seem to remember reading later that he took a header off the back of the stage and broke his collarbone, but it probably wasn't that serious. Skynyrd soldiered on playing a number of their hits, but "Sweet Home Alabama" as an instrumental just wasn't the same.

After a break, the guys in Marshall Tucker joined the rest of Skynyrd onstage and the guitar jams went to a whole new level—almost like a Southern rock orchestra. As the guitar players challenged each other, and the rest of the members of both bands pitched in, you hardly missed the vocals.

* * *

The Marshall Tucker Band's six original members were Toy and Tommy Caldwell, Paul Riddle, George McCorkle, Jerry Eubanks and Doug Gray. The Caldwell brothers had played with and led various bands in the Spartanburg area during the late 1960s, according to Peter Cooper's book, *Hub City Music Makers*. Marshall Tucker evolved mainly from Toy's band, The Toy Factory. The story goes that Marshall Tucker was a name on a key ring they found in their practice space in 1970; some sources indicate Marshall Tucker was a real person who'd previously rented the space.

They signed with Capricorn Records and recorded their first album in 1972 after barnstorming through the Southeast for a couple of years. Released in April 1973, the eponymous *The Marshall Tucker Band* went gold and reached No. 29 on *Billboard's* Album chart.

They toured almost nonstop for the next few years building a loyal fan following but had no hit singles until McCorkle's "Fire on the Mountain" went to No. 38. In 1975, *Searchin' For a Rainbow* hit No. 15 on the *Billboard* Album chart. Toy Caldwell's "Heard It in a Love Song" off their *Carolina Dreams* album went to No. 14 while the album hit No. 23.

* * *

Tragedy struck in 1980, when Tommy, the bass player, died from injuries sustained in a car accident. He was central to the band's music and spirit, and though they recorded three albums and continued to play to sold-out crowds, it just wasn't the same. In 1984, Toy Caldwell, Riddle and McCorkle decided to break up the band. However, Eubanks and Gray played on using the Marshall Tucker name. Gray bought out Eubanks in the mid-1990s and is the only original member who continues to perform with the band.

Toy Caldwell recorded a solo album but his health wasn't good, and he died of a heart attack in 1993. George McCorkle moved to the Nashville area and continued to write songs for other musicians. He died in June 2007.

The Marshall Tucker Band, along with Skynyrd and the Allman Brothers, personified the hard-livin', lovin', partyin' 1970s and early '80s and helped define the Southern rock genre.

~~~

How the West Won Us

BY BLAND SIMPSON

This is how we won the West, and how the West won us.

✳ ✳ ✳

Somewhere in the tawny rolling country east of Murdo, South Dakota, the van's headlights started running off the battery and quickly dimmed. Three out of five of us in the van were sleeping, and I have only the haziest recollection of Clay's piloting the craft into the sanctuary of the Murdo truck stop about two in the morning. Seeing that a mechanic came on duty at 7 A.M. and abjuring the stiff fee for a motel, Clay parked off to the side and we bivouacked: Clay, Tommy and I in the van's three beds, Jack and Chris in sleeping bags atop the van and U-Haul trailer, respectively.

The Red Clay Ramblers were westbound, out barnstorming in the old string-band tradition, hoping for a pot of gold in California if we could just get there. What was so unusual about the boys bunking under the stars? Already we had been billeted upstairs above a funeral home—though no one bothered to tell us. It only dawned on us as we left Beech Creek, Pennsylvania, and saw the mortuary sign out front, that when our hosts went downstairs to spend the night and gave us the upstairs rooms, they had disappeared into the world of corpses and coffins with nylon that chafes.

At exactly 7 A.M. Clay fired the old Dodge and drove into the open, waiting bay—with Jack and Chris still up top asleep. Clay stayed with the vehicle while the rest of us went to breakfast. The problem had to do with the fan belt, which had glazed to the point that it skidded and slid over the generator wheel and produced no volts. It was a new belt, too, bought and installed back in Chapel Hill for $35.

Playwright Sam Shepard has called Chapel Hill, N.C.'s Red Clay Ramblers "A great American band." The Ramblers are truly North Carolina's musical ambassadors, since for over thirty-five years they have toured widely, bringing the string band message to the world. They have also lent their considerable collective talents to a number of musicals, winning a Special Tony Award in 1999 along the way, and recording nearly twenty albums. Back in 1987, Ramblers Tommy Thompson, Clay Buckner, Jack Herrick, Chris Frank and Bland Simpson toured out west. This is an excerpt from Simpson's account of the trip, showing that, though you can take the boys out of North Carolina, you can't take the North Carolina out of the boys.

At 7:30 Clay walked into the truckstop diner and said, "All right, it's all done."

The rest of us were flabbergasted. We'd planned to spend half the day waiting for a new generator to get found and shipped in from some other remote location. We planned on touring Murdo's tourist attraction, Pioneer Village with Elvis Presley's motorcycle.

"Good Lord!"

"What's that set us back?"

"$17.49," said Clay. "Let's roll."

＊ ＊ ＊

"Watch how it changes," Ann Kindell, my future wife, told me before I ever left the South. She was speaking of the desert out West but she might have meant the Dakota Badlands as well.

Transfixed, I watched these worn, wind-and-water chiseled hills go from gray in the early light to a faint pink, saw a great reef of eroded rock lie long and violet between the yellowed green of the grass and the big pale blue sky. The cliffs I saw as we were coming into Wyoming were red for real, though, and bands of purplish red running through white clay road-cuts went streaking by.

Up a long broad shallow valley, Devil's Tower—that star of *Close Encounters*—was a tan thimble far off to the north of I-90, and there were antelopes everywhere, in tiny clutches of two or three, in herds ten times that size.

Past Big Timber, Montana, we headed into the big rocky hills, laughing and singing the Mills Brothers' "Up The Lazy River," through the dark night. Then down out of the mountains we came and Butte was there below us like a bright bed of diamonds. We bunked at a motel across from a prison in Deer Lodge, had a bite of breakfast next morning at the Nickelodeon Café. Then, filled with sentimental longings for the roughout snakeproof cowboy boots I'd bought out west twenty years before, I went shopping for a few minutes in a western wear store. A very few minutes. I studied the stock there in Deer Lodge and seeing nothing like the $20 pair I'd had, checked the price tag on some plain brown boots—$135. No wonder cowboys die with their boots on.

The day after a show at the dark, ornate Masonic Hall in Spokane, Washington, I tried again and found a better version of the Deer Lodge pair, these for the modestly outrageous fee of $80. When I got back from the saddle shop, our hostess—along with her husband, a transplanted North Carolinian—exclaimed over them:

"Good kicks! You got you some *good kicks*!"

On the way into the arid desert lands of eastern Montana we passed an old geezer driving a pickup with a camper shell, a stovepipe coming out the roof and a canoe strapped up there, too. The heat-blasted land was full of tumbleweeds and odd monuments: scalloped-sided mesas whose images shimmered and pulsed at us from twenty miles away, stacked square-rock outcropping beside the road. Before sunset we reached the grand Columbia River Gorge, and all of us stepped to its edge, stared at the chasm and spoke hardly at all. Forty-mile-an-hour winds were gusting and whipping up the 1,500-foot canyon walls, and there were whitecaps on the blue-green waters far below. When we crossed the great bridge that the gorge dwarfed. I looked back. Now the river was royal blue, and in another few moments, indigo.

Next morning, over coffee at the high-ceilinged Valley Café in Ellensburg, a waiter leaned forward on the counter and told us a tale of Yellowstone:

"My buddy and I were camped at 7,800 feet. It was really cold, so we didn't roll out till about nine. And I didn't have my contacts in—I wondered what this big brown thing was about twelve feet away, and when I came out of the tent, it snorted. It was a buffalo that had wandered in during the night and picked out our spot to sleep. Every time we tried to leave the tent, it snorted at us. Kept us in there about four hours before it got up and went away. See, they'd had a goring not long before. Some guy wanted a picture taken of himself with his hand on a buffalo's head. The buffalo spooked, knocked back at the guy and hooked the guy's arm with his horn."

❊ ❊ ❊

"Who's next? How 'bout you? Come on, come on, let's go."

The hucksters and goods-hawkers were shouting out and clapping their hands in the Pike Place Market, high up Seattle's harbor hill. They were pushing: gooey-duck clams, bivalves big as the biggest baking potato I ever saw; Uhu fish fresh in from Hawaii, their faces blue-laced as if with turquoise makeup; slender bunches of garlic with red and violet and yellow dried flowers woven in and among them, like beribboned mares' manes and tails at a fair; tiny bundles of "Tender Grass," the youngest asparagus imaginable, each shoot not more than six inches long and thinner than a pencil; Golden Mantle oysters with high-ripple shells; and in stalls and shops slung along a hundred yard walkway, a wide and wild variety of fruits, meats and gorgeous produce. The simple splendor of all this Thomas Wolfeian plentitude sent me reeling, longing for a kitchen to go to town in.

Tommy and I ducked into the Athenian Inn, an old alehouse and seafood bar there in the market. The mid-afternoon sun shone in molten gold off gray-blue Puget Sound below us. There was already mist low over the water beyond a head of land across the way, and the Olympic Mountains far past all that were hazy and gray-blue, too.

A ferryboat with a blue-striped stack was outward bound; others were coming in. An excursion boat with a jaunty blue-line design on its hull was just loading and leaving, and blue smoke trailed from the orange stack of a container ship. The sun was so bright we had to watch all this through a dark green window shade, and it was just fine.

There are moments for all of us when the wonderful spirits of endeavor and adventure merge in one's soul, and one hastens to raise a glass and toast all those heavenly hosts we sing of for the bounty and beauty of it all. Remember every bit of this, you tell yourself, for the joyful tellings and retellings to your kin, your friends, to the love of your life. Our western swing held many such moments, the sort that span innocent earnest orders you give others: "You have to go there—you really do."

Tommy Thompson had for years said these things to me about this place, this touchstone of full, good-hearted feeling far from our home, and he had overstated nothing. Now, with big bowls of steamers and Rainier beer in iced mugs set before us and with a small gesture of his upturned palm that excluded nothing, he said: "You like it?"

"Yes, Tommy," I said. "I like it."

This little share of time in Seattle would have been perfect if Tommy hadn't had his pocket picked over near the post office, before we entered the market. We had searched for the wallet on the busy sidewalk and failed. It upset him very much, I knew, but he refused to let it ruin my first visit to one of his favorite places in America, now one of mine, too. His character was rewarded though—when he called American Express to report the theft that night, Tommy learned that a man found the wallet intact there before him as he stepped off a city bus. He express-mailed it ahead of us, and all was well.

Seattle was still on my mind a few nights later as I hunkered down in Portland's East End Tavern for an open Irish music session that Jack and Clay and Chris were sitting in on. A half dozen women and two men cut vigorous Irish squares, dancing as the jigs and reels went flowing on into the Northwest night. Every heart, bar none, was filled with the good cheer and gaiety of the two accordions and the four fiddles, their bows drawn up and down in concert, like needles sewing melody into the air.

❋ ❋ ❋

We first saw the Pacific through a broad notch in the Oregon forest, and we kept expecting the ocean to be just over the next stretch of evergreen dunes as we went up, over and down. At long last we parked and ran over the sand in the gloaming, to the water's edge. My first time touching the Pacific I sent my right hand skimming atop the last reach of an old wave and scooped the water up to my face and mouth. I was baptized, but by no means as ready as John Hardy for my burying ground.

Later, in San Francisco at midday a fog bank was still obscuring the roadway and the bases of the Golden Gate Bridge. I zipped my jacket against the breeze and chill. From the esplanade at City Marina, I was watching the mothboats and sloops all sailing the bay when the enormous Dutch luxury liner *Noordam* announced itself, its big black brow emerging slowly, grandly from the fog.

After a half hour appearance on "West Coast Weekend," a public radio show, we hung around listening to the Lark Quartet—a scene from some off the wall sexual theater piece—and an extremely colorful zydeco man named Al Rapone. Al, sporting red shirt, green pants and a black flat-brimmed gaucho hat, explained to the audience there at the Fort Mason studio why it was so easy to dance to zydeco music, why there was no excuse not to: "We got something happening on every beat—you can't miss!"

Saturday evening was a hot night beneath a hot full moon, and we played a cantina at Davis, California, a corrugated metal building with two palms out front and with all its stage-lighting instruments gowned in spider webs. Sunday we were back into San Francisco, on the hottest day—100 degrees—ever recorded there, for a show at the Great American Music Hall, one of the old guilded-age Barbary Coast Clubs. There were friends from home, a table full of former Chapel Hillians, and there was a stomping spirit to that night. Afterwards we all repaired to Tommy's Joynt, a bistro pushing buffalo burgers and urging its imports on us with a sign that read: "Take a beer trip around the world." We settled for a domestic excursion on the Anchor Steam line.

*** *** ***

"All right, boys," said Tommy, who was driving now. "Everybody get your guns loaded—we'll be in L.A. in half an hour."

This suggestion was much on my mind a little later as I was buzzed into the dim lobby of a plain but unaccountably creepy stucco motel, and the door clicked shut behind me. Would I be able to get out? The team had sent me in to check rates, and I strode bravely over to a dark green window with a small aperture at the bottom, like a ticket taker's at the movies. I could just make out a woman in a white nightgown moving about some fifteen or twenty feet behind the glass. She moved quickly forward, shut off a light that made the glass go a fractured mirror-silver—so that now I could no longer see her—and shot her hand through the little opening, her red, red nails clutching at the air.

"May I help you?" she asked, her English inflected with non-western inscrutability.

No room at the inn, I told the band and we wound up instead at the modestly swanky Hotel Santa Monica. Our composer pal, Van Dyke Parks, came calling for Tommy and, when I picked up the phone in my room, said drolly, "Welcome to Los Angeles—city of to-morrow." After they had gone to dinner, the rest of us wandered down Pico Boulevard just missing out on a supper at a Rasta sushi joint, passing on a two-band club scene that featured the combos Down Boys Down and Celibate Boxer.

Next day, we lunched on the lawn at Van Dyke's 1917 white-shingled bungalow. Built and landscaped by a botanist with a judge for a husband, the place had a persimmon tree with baseball-sized fruit, a giant cactus with bulbous red flowers and an avocado tree big as a magnolia. He and his family were all at McCabe's—a guitar shop with a high-profile acoustic music center in back—for our show that night, and Van Dyke introduced us, warmly. On the walls were all sorts of guitars, mandolins and ukuleles. It was another warm and generous audience and we were happy in our work, which carried over to the next afternoon, on the beach at Venice. Jack and his brother had a Frisbee-like device called a ring, a flat plastic circle with a groove on its underside for lift. A quick wrist-flick would send it 600 feet. I was dressed exactly as I would have been on the Outer Banks, but the declination of the sun there must have had some other effect, for Jack laughed and said, "Kingfish, you're so *Cal'ed* out."

Perhaps I was. You don't spend a month riding the west in pursuit of music and remain the same. Who would wish it? In my head were a thousand new pictures and a million words, and on my feet I had eighty bucks worth of Acme bootwear. We lingered together after the final show at Riverside that night, lingering not because we didn't know our job was done but out of the sweet simple satisfaction of it. I thought of those glorious Cascades, the high half-forested hills that so moved a boy for whom Jockey's Ridge had once been the ultimate peak, which had made fresh tears of wonder come freely. Once again Jack was right, when he took my shoulder and shook my hand, smiling as he does, and said, "Life is sweet, Kingfish."

Despised By All The Right People

BY DON DIXON

One afternoon, in the early 1980s, my friend Mitch Easter called. He was in Winston-Salem at his Drive In studio; I was in my house outside of Chapel Hill working on a new song. A few years earlier, I had helped him get the Drive In together, and I liked recording there. We had known each other for a long time but had become close friends while he was a student at UNC. At this point, my band, Arrogance, had been signed to a major label recording contract, and I had more experience with "big time" record business having recorded in studios all over the country. Sometimes he would call looking for some advice.

"Do you remember Jefferson Holt?" Mitch said. "That guy from Greensboro that was in college with me in Chapel Hill? Well, he brought this band up from Athens, Georgia, last weekend to do some recording. Guitar, bass, drums and singer . . . the normal line up, but they're really interesting. The guitar player does arpeggiated parts, the bass player does these counterpoint lines instead of typical stuff and the drummer plays more like Al Jackson Jr. on speed than a new wave guy. The singer makes these amazing animal noises. The only problem is sorting it all out so that it sounds like a record. They're competing for a lot of the same aural space. Any suggestions?"

The combo was R.E.M.

I *always* have suggestions so we talked a bit and the next time I was at Mitch's studio, we put on their two-inch multi-track masters and listened to some of the recordings that became their EP, *Chronic Town*. I remember making a few stabs at mixing "Lower Wolves" and a couple of other songs. By this time, Mitch had things well in hand, and the stuff really appealed to me. Very fresh. Original in the best way. Music that made Toto fans furious. Music that eschewed the synthesizer and drum machines so popular in the sounds of the early '80s. Baffling lyrical content that sang well—I mean the sound of the words worked extremely well with the melody and attack of the vocal.

Back in the days before Michael Stipe was trying to "say" anything with his words, he was very gifted at the under-appreciated art of combining vowel sounds and the expletive consonants to create poetry that sings—whether it means anything or not. And of course, meaning can be relatively subjective. Intent versus Content versus Interpretation.

Since I wasn't directly involved in recording these songs and hadn't yet met the band, I was able to retain an objective point of view regarding their development. Now don't get me wrong, objectivity is highly overrated. Give me a passionately subjective point of view any time, but this slight distance was beneficial to me when I began working with them, for two reasons.

First, I was a stranger to them. The band thought of me as an old studio rat that had been in some horrid '70s coliseum rock outfit, not as a peer. This afforded me a kind of anonymity that allowed me to think clearly without any expectations on their part. Nothing to live up to. Second, they didn't realize how much experience with major label politics I already had, so it never occurred to them that I might have a secret agenda. And I did. Mitch and I both did.

We wanted them to survive these early sessions intact.

Let me explain. A label will find an exciting new band. They wine and dine them, trying to woo them into their fold. The band, while trying to maintain some sort of dignity, eventually falls into bed with the label, and like a sophomore in high school with a steady girl, the label immediately starts looking around for something new. Or trying to turn the band they just signed into some band they heard on the radio that has a hit. Or even worse, has a video that looks cool. The second-guessing begins.

By the time Mitch and I went into Reflection Sound Studios in Charlotte to begin recording *Murmur*, R.E.M. already had a zealous group of fans. Almost Deadheads in their blind enthusiasm. We recognized the fact that R.E.M. was despised by all the right people and loved by just the right people: college kids and music critic geeks. This bunch was eating out of the band's hand. Hanging on every word. Waiting for every new note. The band had a tangible audience to build on.

"Despised by all the right people," you say. "How can being despised be a good thing?"

This is how: Where would Madonna be if she hadn't courted controversy at every opportunity? Her enemies defined her audience for her. R.E.M. didn't need to find a controversy to be misunderstood and derided by the music store crowd. They weren't "musician's musicians." They were a product of the record store, the library, and the college classroom colliding with the ultimate counter-culture, nerd, dance, ambiguous sex party.

The perfect extension of The Velvet Underground and The Doors.

While we were working on *Murmur* at Reflection, a musician from the D.C. area dropped by to check out the facility. He listened for a few minutes, and at the end of a playback he asked, "What kind of music do you call that?"

I pondered his question for a moment then replied, "Alternative."

His answer was swift and condescending. "Alternative to what? Good?"

This is the kind of attitude held by many musicians of that time toward R.E.M. These players had been the children of Fusion. ELP, Yes, Asia, Toto. Even King Crimson and Zappa fans had trouble understanding this band. But guys and girls who read books got them. Kids new to their instruments sat in their dorm rooms and played along to the quirky, brooding tracks.

Most of the best popular music is easy to play along with. From country to rock, the art is in the creation of music that connects with a specific audience. It's supposed to speak to the people for whom it is intended and totally piss off everyone else. A hit song is seldom dependant on a virtuoso performance. Being "good" in this context means having a feel, a special sound, a point of view.

After R.E.M. began to make some retail noise, bands in college towns all over the country began to stand up and be counted. Our objective for R.E.M., our collective goal, was to get them to the top of the college charts and sell 100,000 records. No one was thinking beyond that, and our budgets reflected that goal.

R.E.M. was a guitar band in those early days, a throwback to a time that wasn't blinded by science. They weren't dedicated to *teaching* you anything but they weren't content to be the ultimate party band like their friends The B-52s, either. Intriguing intellectually, they were alternately light and dense. I loved them.

Please understand that bands don't sit around figuring all this out up front. I don't care what you read in books or magazines or see on *Behind The Music*. Bands are lucky if they can agree on where to eat on any given night. A band might talk about direction and what music they love (or hate), but when you're out playing night after night, you enter a survival mode that creates its own vortex with the van you're in, the town you're in, the motel you're in, the club you're in, at the center.

In this vortex, you lose some of your personal identity and in the best circumstances, a collective consciousness emerges that is "The Band." When everything is working right, this consciousness is quite independent of any band member but totally dependant on each band member. When the balance is disturbed, chaos can rule.

No band can maintain its balance forever. Or its innocence.

While touring in support of *Murmur*, R.E.M.

played a lot—clubs, small theaters—they even opened a bunch of shows for The Police. I went to one up in D.C. and to my astonishment, Michael wasn't the old Michael I'd seen at the Milestone Club but a shy, underachiever, barely looking at the audience and delivering his vocals in a particularly inarticulate manner.

When they came back to Charlotte to record *Reckoning*, their second full length LP, the tone of the band had changed. I don't recall any direct conversations about the situation, but my impression was that Michael was exhausted and confused about being a rock star.

We started the sessions without Mitch because the band had a very limited period of time set aside to record, and Mitch had previous commitments. The first few days were spent working on sounds and getting a few tracks down. We settled on a routine whereby we'd record tracks into the night, and around noon the next day Michael and I would come in to record some vocals. All by ourselves.

Singing in the studio can be nerve-wracking. Your bandmates and record company idiots stand on the other side of a huge pane of glass judging your every little grunt and whisper. Sometimes this can make a good singer great, but sometimes it can make a great singer choke. I call this "The Fishbowl Effect."

Reflection had a stairwell that went from the control room down to Studio A. From the very beginning, I'd set up the studio for Michael to have this stairwell space as his own little domain. A place where no one could see him and he'd feel free. Out of the Fishbowl.

One morning we were working on a vocal for "Seven Chinese Brothers." The track was this terrific, energetic beast that contained all of the little things I loved about the band, but Michael just wasn't into singing that day. He barely opened his mouth. Hardly made any sound at all. Where was the guy that made all those wonderful animal noises I heard on *Chronic Town* only a few years ago?

He was down in the stairwell.

I hit the talkback to let him know I was coming through to make an adjustment on the echo chamber, a large EMT plate housed in an attic over the stairwell. It was really just an excuse to get a look at him, see if I could figure out how to loosen him up a little. Actually, I needed to *wind* him up a little.

While I was up with the plate, I noticed a tumbled-over stack of old records that had been taken up there to die . . . old local R&B and gospel stuff mostly. I grabbed one off the top, and as I passed Michael on the way back to the control room, I tossed it to him at the bottom of the stairs. I thought he might be amused. I didn't expect him to be inspired.

When I fired up the track a few seconds later, Michael was singing, but he wasn't singing the lyrics to "Seven Chinese Brothers." He was singing the liner notes to the album I'd tossed him.

If you've ever heard "Voice of Harold," you'll notice how distorted the vocals are at the beginning. Michael was singing so much louder when he began to sing the liner notes, it took me a few seconds to roll the preamp level back. He made it all the way through the song, we had a chuckle as I rewound the tape and he proceeded to give me the beautiful, one-take vocal of the real words that you hear on *Reckoning*.

I would never dream of taking any credit for Michael's great singing on *Reckoning,* but I think this day was a bit of a breakthrough for him. He seemed more confident after this. The balance of the band seemed to be restored. Later, they shot the video for "So. Central Rain" in Studio A at Reflection with a live vocal from him. You must be very confident to do that. I was quite proud.

We had fun making these records. We even found time for some late night two-track recording, which found its way into the hands of the fans over the years. I believe the version of the song known as "Voice of Harold" appears on *Dead Letter Office* along with all those fantastic recordings from the Drive In that make up *Chronic Town.*

Bands like this don't come along every day. I was lucky enough to be around when the fates came together and put all things in order so the world could have R.E.M.

Lucky indeed.

〜〜〜

4

MUSIC EXPERIENCES

Catching Smoke

BY KEVIN WINCHESTER

If you have a choice between music and becoming a heroin addict, pick the smack, it's healthier. Once the music monkey gets on your back, it'll cut a wide path. It'll break your heart, tempt you, tease you, make you miserable and will probably destroy everything around you not related to the music. But ohhh, when it's right. When you rake that chord or hit the G run, when the day draws down and a note rings crystal clear as the October air; when the band's sweaty, all lathered up and funky, and the crowd, no matter if it's one or a hundred, is right there with you... it all comes together and you close your eyes and just feel it and you're gone. Transported, free, sailing above it all, and even if you're not religious, in that moment you know what God is. There are no words to describe it, but it's as real and beautiful and right as anything could be. It's that golden spike in the vein, chasing the dragon, nirvana. It's catching smoke in your hand, and once you've been there, the rest of your life is spent reaching.

* * *

In any collection of stories or essays about music, we writers try to get beneath the surface, to somehow bring the canvas behind the art into focus. To get at that *thing*, that underlying thread which will hopefully explain it all, tie together the talent, the stars, the songs, the inspiration maybe, into something tangible. Explainable. There are thousands of stories to go along with the Carolina musical history, and each is as unique and colorful as the musicians and fans who have created—are creating—our musical heritage. Each a brush stroke, vivid splashes of color, an on-going mural open to a wide range of interpretation. But underneath this musical painting lies the canvas: stretched, seldom considered, maybe a bit frayed, but never swaying from the task at hand. There's a sustaining strength in such a tightly woven fabric; a constant foundation without which there'd be no masterpiece.

It's like my grandmother, who taught me my first simple songs, once said: "If the music's in you, it'll come bubbling up sooner or later. And if it's in you deep, they ain't no stopping it. They's times you'll want to, but it's no use. You'll come back and the music will always be there, it'll never leave you."

Forty plus years later she's more right than ever. I've played my entire life, professionally, part-time, or just to amuse myself. I've tried to quit a couple times, but she was right, it's no use. Never made any real money at it, and I long ago stopped thinking about how much money I've spent. My first paying gig was in the house band at a bar that'll remain nameless for now. It was a low-slung building with a massage parlor downstairs. We weren't old enough to get in, but that wasn't an issue with the manager. His only requirement was we kept playing all night, *no matter what,* and if he came out from behind the bar with "Ol' Betsy," we best try to stay out of his line of fire. *But don't stop playing.* "Ain't shot no guitar picker, yet," he promised.

While everybody else spent Friday night going all rah-rah at the football game, or Saturday night at the movies trying to cop a feel, I was playing music and getting *paid* for it. In a *bar.* With *liquor.* And *hookers* who'd come upstairs when business was slow. What more could a seventeen-year-old guy want?

Since then I've played festivals and clubs, mall openings and weddings. Reunions, proms, Holiday Inns, as the opening act for a cattle auction once. I've played cover tunes and originals, standards and P.D. numbers. Played rockabilly, funk, gospel, country (the real stuff, not the crap that's out there these days), blues, Top 40, punk, bluegrass, and of course—saw-your-dog-in-half rock 'n' roll. I've played "Free Bird" 1,328,496 times and "Wonderful Tonight" twice that.

I've quit jobs, lost jobs, avoided jobs, to play music. Been kicked out of my house (the parents found out about the gig at the massage parlor bar), apartments, friends' houses, a couple of ex-wives' houses, and a car I was living in, all because of music. Spent years working for booking agents—you know the ones, Miles and Associates; who called a Wednesday night in Salisbury, a Thursday night in Topeka, Kansas, and Friday night at the VFW back in Waxhaw, a *tour.* Lost friends, broken relationships, pawned gear. Frustrated,

jaded and older than your years—it's a messy wake left behind.

But I'm still at it. At least my current wife is understanding. She knows if the house catches fire to grab the dog and get out on her own, and to tell the firemen I've gone back in the music room yet again to try and rescue another guitar, or mandolin, *or God knows whatever else kind of instrument he's blown our savings on...*

✳ ✳ ✳

No, it's not just me. It's the *fabric,* the canvas that holds this thing we call our musical heritage together. It's the one thing we share, not just the stars, not the familiar names, but anyone and everyone that *knows.* For every big name who plays The Orange Peel in Asheville, The Palm Room in Wilmington, The Neighborhood Theater in Charlotte, Ziggy's in Winston-Salem, or Walnut Creek in Raleigh, there are a hundred, a thousand more around the Carolinas who know *exactly* what I'm talking about. They're the ones bowing a fiddle on the back porch, the thunder rumbling down the valley as accompaniment. Strumming a guitar in time to the waves easing onto the sand. Around campfires, in living rooms, festival parking lots. They're the wives, mothers, brothers, friends new and old, who listen, not for perfection or ability or even talent, but because the music touches something in them they can't name.

✳ ✳ ✳

The reality of it hit me a few years ago. I had the opportunity to play bass for Bill Price. Bill was born in Union County, N.C. and lived there most of his life. His claim to fame was being one of Bill Monroe's Blue Grass Boys back in the '50s until, as he put it, "that damn Presley kid came along and everybody took to screaming and wiggling their ass." He went on to play with several of the bluegrass legends, even won a gold record for his version of "Pretty Polly." He'd been out of the business for a while due to health problems and he called because he was *putting something together for one more shot.*

It was a nice gig—we played all the larger bluegrass festivals in the Southeast and I got to meet several of the legends before they passed away. Unfortunately, Bill's cancer returned as we were working on his new release. Near the end, his wife called and asked me to come by once more. He was in and out and barely knew I was there. At one point, he opened his eyes, looked at me and said: "I think this record's gonna be the one. We'll finish it when I'm feeling better." He drifted away again and I started to leave. As I stood, he spoke once more. "Would you bring me my guitar?" he whispered.

And there it was. Catching smoke in your hand.

~~~

The Last Waltz Blues Jam

BY BOB MARGOLIN

The more blues-driven musicians commandeered the instruments at the jam, and played some old favorite songs together, mostly Robert Johnson's. This sounds like a common scene at open-mike jams at blues clubs, where more experienced blues players sometimes conspire to sit in together. But this jam happened at about 7 A.M., the morning *after* The Band's Last Waltz concert on Thanksgiving, 1976. The Band had hired the entire Miyako Hotel in San Francisco to accommodate their guests. The banquet room, which had been used for rehearsal before the show, was now the party room, and musicians had been jamming in random combinations since the concert ended, many hours before. But unlike your local blues jam, every blues player that morning was a rock star.

Except me. I was there with Muddy Waters, who had been invited to perform two songs at The Last Waltz. Muddy had recorded his Grammy-winning *The Muddy Waters Woodstock Album* the year before with Levon Helm and Garth Hudson from The Band, but The Band itself was an unknown quantity to him. He brought Pinetop Perkins and me from his own band to accompany him, so that he would have someone familiar to play with, in addition to The Band and Paul Butterfield on harp. Muddy also felt I was good at explaining what he wanted onstage to musicians he hadn't worked with, though many years later, I still find myself wishing I knew more about what Muddy wanted.

* * *

Muddy, Pinetop, and I checked into the hotel the day before the show and went to the restaurant. I saw a few familiar faces from the rock world, and some came over to say hello and pay respects to Muddy. I remember this surreal encounter: Kinky Friedman approached our

Award-winning bluesman Bob Margolin played guitar in the legendary Muddy Waters' band from 1973 to 1980. In 1976, Margolin accompanied Muddy to San Francisco to participate in The Band's Last Waltz concert event. He says, in part in an introduction to the story on his website, "I wrote this story for *Blues Revue* magazine in 2002. Since I always get asked, "What was it like to be in . . . ?" here's the long answer. The short answer is: "There were so many rock stars around, it was like walking through a living *Rolling Stone* magazine." Massachusetts-native Margolin moved to Greensboro, N.C., in 1989. He continues to tour all over the world as well as record and produce work for himself and others.

table. I knew that he was a Texas Jewboy (his band's name) musical comedian. The Kinkster sported Texas attire complemented by a white satin smoking jacket accented with blue Jewish stars, an Israeli flag motif. Embroidered along the hem were scenes of the crucifixion. Mr. Friedman exercises his ethnicity in provocative ways, in fashion, in his music, and in his mystery novels (recommended!). He was a Kosher cowboy *mensch* as he introduced himself to Muddy, assuring him that "people of the Jewish persuasion appreciate the blues, too." Muddy, used to folks stranger than Kinky saying weird shit to him, just smiled and thanked him. Didn't bat an eye.

That night, as Pinetop, Muddy, and I rehearsed our songs for the show, I didn't realize that some of those blues-oriented rock stars must have been in the room to watch Muddy.

The next night, at the concert, Muddy, Pinetop, and I waited backstage to perform. Pinetop told me he heard one of The Beatles was there, not realizing that Ringo Starr was sitting next to him. Born in 1913, Pinetop knew as much about The Beatles as I know about The Backstreet Boys. Joni Mitchell, looking impossibly beautiful, introduced herself to Muddy. He didn't know who she was and just saw her as a young, pretty woman, his favorite dish. He flirted but she didn't respond.

I'm told that there was a backstage cocaine room, with a glass table and a "sniff-sniff" tape playing, but I never saw it. I did, however, see through Rolling Stone Ron Wood's nearly-transparent prominent proboscis in profile. In the "green room," while a joint was being passed around, Neil Young smiled and said, "We're all old hippies here." Though I was twenty-seven, some-

thing about "old hippies" resonated with me. Young was older than me by a few years and even had a couple of gray hairs then, but I remember thinking that nobody in that room was old yet except for Muddy and Pinetop. Now, I'm certainly an old hippie, though Pinetop (going strong now at ninety-four) is neither.

When it was our turn to play, Muddy and Pinetop sang the light, swinging "Caledonia" as they had for *The Woodstock Album*. In hindsight, I think Muddy could have presented himself more strongly with a deep slow blues like "Long Distance Call" which would feature his almighty slide guitar. But nobody could argue with his second song choice—"Mannish Boy" was always a showstopper. It was preserved in full in *The Last Waltz* movie, which was released in 1978. Harp player tip: Muddy loved the way Butterfield played on that song, setting up a warble that "holds my voice up" rather than just playing the song's signature lick.

Fatefully, only one camera was operating during our song, zooming on Muddy, but not changing angle. Standing close to Muddy, I was in every frame. Pinetop, at the piano way off to the side, unfortunately, was never seen in the film. But as Muddy hollers "I'm a MAN!" and we shout, "Yeah!" to answer, as we always did in that song, you can hear Pinetop also yelling, "Wahoo!" That was a line from a politically incorrect joke that Pine had heard on the road and was fond of telling over and over in 1976.

Now, whenever *The Last Waltz* is shown on TV, a few people at my gigs tell me, "I saw you on TV!" and how I looked—happy or mad or scared or bored. I think they just project how they would feel. I was simply concentrating on playing, and particularly enjoying

Muddy's powerful shouting, Butterfield's warbling-tension harp, Levon's deep groove, and Robbie Robertson's fiery guitar fills.

Eric Clapton followed us, and as he began his first solo, his guitar strap unfastened, and he nearly dropped his Stratocaster. In the movie, his lips distinctly mouth, "Fuck!" and as he refastens the strap, Robbie picks up the solo and runs away with it.

Muddy and Pinetop went to their rooms after our set, but I went down to jam back at the hotel after the concert. That's when I realized some of those blues-oriented rock stars had watched me rehearsing with Muddy and been impressed that I was playing old-school Chicago blues in his road band and helping to arrange the songs for our performance. I also had a very cool blues guitar with me—my late-'50s Gibson ES-150 arch-top, which I also cradle on the cover of my album, *Hold Me To It*. Bob Dylan approached me and said he hoped we'd get to jam together. Then he disappeared. I did play "Hideaway" and some slow blues with Eric Clapton, whom I met that night. Dr. John sat at the piano for hours and played along with everyone. My piano-pickin' sister Sherry, who lived nearby and was hanging out, sat near him, eyes glued to his "fonky fangers."

Around dawn, I put my old guitar back in its case and started to leave. Dylan caught me in the hall and said, "I thought we were going to jam..." I decided to stay awake a little longer. We had Dr. John on piano, Ron Wood on bass, Levon on drums, Butterfield on harp; and Clapton, Dylan, and myself playing guitars. There were no vocal microphones, and we all played softly enough to hear Dylan sing "Kind Hearted Woman" and a few other well-known blues songs. His

trademark vocal eccentricities sounded outlandish in the blues, but he did make them his own. Generally, the blues we played that morning were not remarkable, but I was honored to be jamming with these fine musicians.

When I read Levon Helm's inside story of *The Last Waltz* in his autobiography, *This Wheel's On Fire* (recommended!), I was shocked to find that because of time and budget constraints and Band politics, Muddy was nearly bumped from the show. Levon fought bitterly behind the scenes and prevailed to not only keep Muddy in, but to indulge him with me and Pinetop, too. We were treated as honored guests at The Last Waltz and I enjoyed the once-in-a-lifetime jam afterwards, but Levon never told us about making a stand for us. He just made us welcome. Ultimately, this gracious, classy, and tough gentleman was responsible for my good time there.

~~~

Roger Burt: Sunday Serenade

BY LORI K. TATE

As a boy growing up in Michigan, Roger Burt stayed up past his bedtime listening to the *Hillbilly Jamboree* on WCKY. Unbeknownst to his mother, Burt hooked up headphones to a table radio so he could listen to the show being broadcast from Kentucky. "I was a country music guy as a kid," says the sixty-nine-year-old who now lives in Stanley, N.C.

Although Burt still likes his country-western tunes, his favorite kind of music is big band from the 1930s, '40s, and early '50s. Nothing makes him happier than sharing his knowledge of this genre on his radio show, *Roger on Your Radio*. From 2 P.M. to 6 P.M. every Sunday afternoon on Gaston College's WSGE (91.7 FM) Burt plays the music of G.I. Jill, Guy Lombardo, Sammy Kaye, Glenn Miller, Artie Shaw and more while intermittently sharing stories about these big band legends.

LABOR OF LASTING LOVE

Burt's was the first voice heard on the air at WSGE when the station began in October 1980. When Ken Quick, the man who ran the broadcast program at the time, asked Burt to kick the station off, he failed to mention that the room would be filled with press, the mayor of Gastonia, and various members of Congress.

"Here I am doing my very first show, boy was I nervous. I had been on the air amateur radio-wise since 1954. I've been doing radio for over fifty-two years, but there's a difference," Burt explains. "When you're talking to somebody on amateur radio you're talking to one person, and that's how I finally came to grips with this. I just imagine I am talking to one person, and that's how I treat each show."

Ever since that October day, Burt has been a volunteer DJ for the Dallas station that operates on 7,500 watts and has only three paid employees. "I've probably spent somewhere between $2,000 and $3,000 out of my own pocket in twenty-six years just for the gas," says Burt, who lives eight miles from the station with his wife, Joyce. "Two different station managers and the old general manager have said, 'If we ever get any money you are going to be the first person that ever gets paid.'"

Payment isn't that important to Burt, who is a U.S. Coast Guard retiree. What is important to him is keeping the music from the big band era alive, and he envisions himself as an ambassador of sorts for the genre. "Nobody else does it so it's my job to keep this genre alive," he says. "I've always been a history buff, too, so it's like the old Mary Poppins' song, 'A Spoonful of Sugar.' That's how I look at my show. I'm playing the music, and at the same time a little sugar helps the medicine go down as hopefully people learn."

LOVE AT FIRST LISTEN

Burt's fascination with big band started after his father, James, passed away in 1974. "Mom said, 'Well, take anything you want of his.' One thing was a six-record set of *Reader's Digest* big band music, and that was the start," recalls Burt. "My first show is what we call in the business, MOR, middle of the road. I played some of those [*Reader's Digest* records], and every time I would play one people would call in and say, 'Play more, play more,' and I started to buy more."

A few months later Burt's show morphed into a big band-only format, and his interest in the music grew along with his following. He found a big band collection priced at $1,250. A listener/friend volunteered to buy it for his show. "That's the point where I said, 'Now I am ready to go,' " recalls Burt.

"I have at least 90 percent of the charted songs recorded in the '30s, '40s, and early '50s. I have every song that charted from 1955 through 2006 on *Billboard*," says Burt—more than 60,000 songs.

Burt has read books such as *The Big Band Almanac* by Leo Walker and *Pop Hits 1940–1954* by Joel Whitburn to learn the stories behind the music. One listener gave him a copy of *Moonlight Serenade* by John Flower,

which lists every gig Glenn Miller played and features photographs and his pay records. More recently he's been doing research on the Internet.

"I have a great memory so when I read something and I'm playing a song years after I buy it, that information pops into my head," says Burt. "People say, 'How in the world do you know that? You've got to have a cheat sheet.' All I have is this play list here."

That's the truth. As he broadcasts his show from the station's studio, he stands before the microphone wearing jeans and a WSGE T-shirt while holding a list of the seventy or so songs he's going to play during the show. "I don't know what I'm going to say until I say it," says Burt.

A LOYAL FOLLOWING

Listeners appreciate his commentary as much as they appreciate the music. "Roger is so knowledgeable. It's almost as if he lived through those times and knew those people personally," says Lewis Jenkins of North Wilkesboro. "I've tried him on everybody that I could think of from the way backs, and I've made a list of music that I've enjoyed that goes back into the '20s and he's familiar with every bit of it and the people who played it."

In his early eighties, Jenkins has been listening to Burt's show for ten years and owns Jenkins Restorations in North Wilkesboro and the Jenkins Automotive Museum in Wilkesboro, where he stores Glenn Miller's wife's 1941 Cadillac convertible. "Roger and I have gotten to be friends because of our mutual interest in big band music and all the personalities involved in it," he says. "I followed the big bands all through my life and my career and I met a lot of them in person and knew them and enjoyed their music."

Burt occasionally comes to Jenkins' museum and tells guests which music was popular during certain eras. "I just enjoy the information along with the music, and he's the only one that does it," says Jenkins.

Frank Deason, business manager of The Stardusters Big Band in Gastonia, agrees. "Roger knows more than anyone about every one of the old time, big band people," says Deason. "He tells stories about things that happened with some of the old timers, big bands. It's real interesting. He's real good at what he does."

The Stardusters have four dances a year at the Adult Recreation Center in Gastonia, and Burt tries to attend whenever he can. "We're always glad to have him," says Deason.

The Stardusters modeled their band after the bands of Tommy Dorsey and Glenn Miller. Miller just happens to be one of Burt's favorite big band artists. "I like him because he does everything. He does swing. He does sweet [a softer style of music]. It's a complete cross section," says Burt. "Many of the band leaders didn't do their own announcing very much, but he did. So I've got hundreds of hours of Glenn Miller telling you what you're about to listen to, and I like that."

Benny Goodman and Artie Shaw rank pretty high on his list as well, but for Burt it's the overall sound of big band that he loves so much. Now that the WSGE is broadcasting over the Internet, people all over the world can enjoy the sound of big band with Burt. He's already had listeners contact him from Australia and Germany.

"Many people say, 'I love your music but what I really like are your stories,' " says Burt. " I just love the fact that there will be more people out there that can listen to the stories. I love that."

The Chords That Bind: Traditional Music in the South

BY SI KAHN

I go through life humming to myself. On a clear day, you can hear me before you can see me. Even when by sheer mental effort I succeed in sealing my lips, if you look deep into my eyes you can see the notes silently making their way along the staff.

Where did all this music come from? What is a nice Jewish boy doing singing in a place like this?

When I was growing up—not here in the South, but in the Deep North—our family sang together. On the Sabbath and on holidays, we would stay at the dinner table long after the food and dishes had been cleared, and we would sing. Because musical instruments were not allowed on the Sabbath, we sang without instrumentation—but not without accompaniment. From my grandfather, Gabriel Kahn, I learned the fine points of creating a rhythm section, using only two basic variations (closed fist and open palm) of the basic hand-on-table technique. From my parents, Rosalind and Benjamin Kahn, I learned—once my sister and I had the basic tunes down well enough not to be distracted—the rudiments of high and low harmony, made up as you go along.

The songs we sang were mostly prayers, composed thousands of years ago in Hebrew. There were different prayers for different holidays, for different phases of the moon, for the Sabbath, and for various combinations thereof. Naturally, over that many years, melodies had changed. My mother's side of the family was convinced that my father's side had changed them, accidentally or deliberately, and vice versa. The preferred method for settling these disagreements was to sing as loudly as possible. Whichever side of the family was able to overwhelm the other was generally conceded to have history on its side, along with the correct version of the melody.

We sang a little bit in Yiddish, too, folk and story songs from the Old Country, which in this case meant almost any place in Europe. Hebrew had been the language of prayer for the Jews of Europe, but Yiddish was the language of everyday life. In our house, except for the songs, it had been reduced to the language of secrets, which our parents used when they wanted to communicate with each other privately in front of us. Despite this incentive to learn Yiddish, I never did, beyond the few phrases known to anyone who has lived in New York, regardless of race, color, creed, or national origin.

So the truth of the matter is that although I learned many songs and am still amazed at how many I still know by heart, I never understood most of what I was singing. What's amazing is that it never seemed to matter. I understood quite well what the songs really meant to us as Jews, as a family, as people in the world. They were our bond, our unity, our affirmation, our courage. They were our way of claiming our rhythmic and harmonic relation with each other and with our community. Our songs reinforced our solidarity, our sense that we could overcome the obstacles in our path. They helped us feel proud of the side we were on.

That, of course, is what all this personal history has to do with the songs of Southern struggle. Because that is what these songs do, not just for Southerners, permanent or temporary, but for all kinds of people who have never set foot or voice in the South. They reach us in a deep and personal way, even though they are in a sense a language we do not completely understand, a language which can only be translated by the heart.

✳ ✳ ✳

Like all prayers, the political songs of the South connect us in time. Who can stand swaying with arms linked in a circle singing, "We Shall Overcome," and not be taken back in time? Yet we hear with different hearts, according to when the song first came to us. Blacks, women, trade unionists, peace activists each hear the song with the ears of their own movement, because the song has been a part of each of these and others. Though we can trace the genealogy of the song, what matters when we close our eyes and link arms is the images that float before us: of picket lines, marches, demonstrations, vigils, jails. We hear the places we have been, ourselves and others like us, in the songs.

We hear the people we want to be. We hear, too, those who are *not* like us, the segregationists and gun thugs and sheriffs who so often blocked the way. They,

too, are immortalized in the songs, frozen in time, caught as if by a camera in a fast moving moment of history. If it were not for Florence Reece's wonderful song, "Which Side Are You On?" who would ever remember Bloody Harlan's Sheriff Blair? Yet as our singing voices build the song, we swear again that we will *not* thug for J.H. Blair, in Kentucky or anywhere else, because we *are* for the union, we *know* which side *we* are on.

We hear also the people we have been. There is Ralph Chaplin, organizer and songwriter for the Industrial Workers of the World, just back from the West Virginia mine wars at the beginning of the twentieth century. What was it Mother Jones said that affected him so deeply? "You don't need the vote to raise hell"? "The Lord God Almighty made the women and the Rockefeller gang of thieves made the ladies"? That you should "Pray for the dead and fight like hell for the living"? What was it about the South and Southern workers that tears out of Ohio-born organizer Chaplin his wonderful lines:

> In our hands is placed a power greater than
>   their hoarded gold
> Greater than the might of armies magnified a
>   thousand-fold
> We can bring to birth a new world from the
>   ashes of the old
> For the union makes us strong.

He's right, you know. The union *does* make us strong. The truth *will* make us free. We *shall* live in peace.
And we *shall* overcome.

A Country Music Moment

BY FRYE GAILLARD

For those of us worried about the colorless flow of the country music mainstream, you cling to the occasional moments of hope—and for me at least one of them came on an October evening just a few years ago. There was an overflow crowd at the Bluebird Café, a listening room on the south side of Nashville, where the dark hills rise against the Tennessee sky, and the picker-poets gather on a Saturday night.

The star of the show this time was Marshall Chapman, a country-rocker from South Carolina who came to Nashville as a student at Vanderbilt, majored in French, then set out to become a country star. She never quite made it. But along the way, she established herself as one of the finest songwriters in the town, and she was appearing at the Bluebird with Matraca Berg, a country music diva with a storyteller's eye, equally gifted as a singer and a writer.

On this particular night, there was an unexpected twist. The two songwriters were sharing the stage with a pair of Carolina novelists, Lee Smith and Jill McCorkle, whose stories seemed to fit with a good country song. Even the audience was cluttered with stars, songwriters Kim Carnes and Rodney Crowell, and a handful of authors passing through the city for the annual South-ern Festival of Books. They cheered the stories interspersed with the songs, a rollicking interplay of comedy and poignance, but the mood turned serious near the end of the show when Marshall Chapman sang a signature ballad.

"Good-bye Little Rock and Roller," which would soon become the title of her songwriter's memoir, told the story of a girl and her dreams and a life on the road in a rock 'n' roll band:

> *"Every night was now or never, the road just*
> *seemed to go forever."*

But after a while, it came full circle, and the woman was married with a daughter of her own, and she could feel her hopes giving way to her child's.

That was not literally Marshall Chapman's own story—not quite, at least. In the 1950s and '60s, she had grown up wealthy in Spartanburg, and a life of privilege was laid out before her. But then one night Elvis Presley came to town. Chapman was only seven years old, and Presley was on a package show out of Nashville, the opening act on a tour of country stars. According to one version of the story, the Chapman family's babysitter and maid, Lula Mae Moore, took little Marshall by the hand, and led her down to the Carolina Theater. They climbed the back stairs to the all-colored balcony, steamy and packed, to catch a glimpse of this picker from Memphis who sang country music as if he were black.

"When he came on, it was like an explosion," Chapman said years later. "The whole place just shook."

Such was her personal discovery of the music—the power it had to cross old barriers, and touch something basic about people's lives. For a while she was drawn to the adrenaline rush, as she grew up listening to early rock 'n' roll—to Elvis, of course, and the black singers, too: Jackie Wilson, Maurice Williams and all the rest. When she graduated from college in 1971, and began her own career as a singer, she cut quite a figure in the music clubs of Nashville. She was six feet tall with flowing blond hair and a rock 'n' roller's swagger as she leaned toward the mike. She cut a few albums for Epic records, including the country-flavored "Me, I'm Feelin' Free," and she was writing songs for a wide range of artists, from Joe Cocker to Dion DiMucci, Conway Twitty to Emmylou Harris.

Looking back on it now, she knows the early years got a little bit wild. There were too many boyfriends and too much booze, but over time as she began to mellow out, she began to think more about what Emmylou called "the literature of music." She and Harris were friends, contemporaries with Carolina roots (Harris got her musical start as a college student singing in the folk clubs of Greensboro), and they were inclined to reflect on the meaning of the craft.

"People know how hard life is," Harris told an interviewer. "They have feelings. They need music that will give them a voice."

Chapman came to share that view, particularly as she read the great southern novelists, including Lee Smith of Hillsborough, N.C., whose 1992 book, *The Devil's Dream*, was set against the backdrop of country music. Chapman felt a connection to that kind of writing, just as Smith felt connected to the music. And now, a decade later, here they were together at the Bluebird, sharing the stage with their stories and songs, making people laugh or making them cry, bearing witness to the power of a good country song.

They closed the show with one of Chapman's finest, the ballad of a rock 'n' roller growing older, wistful in the wake of her new understandings, the subtle interplay of wisdom and loss. For Marshall herself, soon to be married and comfortable in a life of writing her songs, it was one of those magical moments when the music takes flight and nothing else matters. And for those of us in the crowd that night, it was more than a fleeting moment of escape. It was a night when the music did what it should, what it has done at least since the days of Hank Williams—touching people's feelings and giving them a voice, somehow making them easier to bear.

Drinking, Dogs, and Darlin' Corey

BY MARJORIE HUDSON

Thirty years ago, in my café days in D.C., there was a singer/songwriter I loved to watch play. He could wail out a tune and draw you into a different world, a world far away from the city. I loved it when he sang "Darlin' Corey," a high lonesome old-timey song about revenuers and whiskey stills that spoke of some wild place I yearned to go to, if only in my bartending dreams.

> Wake up wake up darlin' Corey
> What makes you sleep so sound
> The revenue officers are coming
> They're gonna tear your still-house down.

That song and a dog I named for it took me down a path to a life in North Carolina.

✳ ✳ ✳

The pup had wild black and white hair that spritzed out over her eyes, muzzle, and paws, and snappy, humorous black eyes. My boyfriend brought her home to our city apartment—claimed he'd found her living in an old refrigerator in a trash heap in the Virginia woods (I knew he'd been checking his cash crop of marijuana).

I took one look at her and said, "Mine."

I took her into the bathroom put her in the tub and scrubbed out the briars and ticks. I went out for drinks to celebrate, tying her inside the fenced yard of the bar. She pulled out of her collar and leash, leaped the fence, and trotted in right behind me. I turned and saw that crazy face, that laughing mouth, that determined gaze that was part rat terrier and part border-collie-hypnotizing-the-sheep.

Her eyes said, *Don't you ever leave me behind again.*

✳ ✳ ✳

She was perfectly trained right away, except for a tendency to prefer my boyfriend's new Oriental rug when I overslept after a late shift. She could sit and stay and jump as high as my shoulder, and I was working on the "treat on the nose" trick. I called her "Puppy," waiting for the right name to come along. The name had to be something smart, and worthy of her. During my cook shift at the bar I mulled the spice shelves, thinking how she was a spicy pup, and I ought to be able to find something that fit her there. I settled on "Coriander Pepper," a kind of AKC-sounding name, and tried it out on her. I swear, I actually saw her laugh at my city-girl pretension.

One day my musician friend was singing "Darlin' Corey" as I sneaked past the stage with the puppy tucked inside my denim jacket.

Well the first time I seen darlin' Corey
She was sitting by the banks of the sea
Had a forty-four around her body
And a five-string on her knee.

Corey was the perfect name for a dog rescued from a trash heap in the woods outside the city. She was an outlaw dog who'd been God-knows-where doing God-knows-what.

I had to ditch the boyfriend. He made me choose.

* * *

Corey went everywhere with me after that. I got a car so she could hang her head out the window in the seat beside me. Various boyfriends fought her for bed space, and one of them laughed when I said she was my alter ego. "Alter ego?" he hooted. "She's *just like* you." I took that as a compliment.

Like the mountain gal in the song, Corey was funny, tough, smart, and brave. I watched, agape, as she attempted to out-alpha a female timber wolf at the dog park in my neighborhood. I stood, frozen, on the median strip, as she herded four lanes of Connecticut Avenue rush hour traffic up the hill. I woke in the night to her growling, then furious barking, when a burglar tried to pry my window. She surfed waves in the bow of my whitewater canoe. She warned of invading raccoons in my apartment. She made me laugh. She saved my life.

I sang her the "Darlin' Corey" song from time to time, and the high lonesome sound of it made me want to be someplace else. What was I doing living in the city? Corey was a country dog. In my heart, I was a country girl.

I'd rather drink muddy water,
Sleep in a hollow log,
Than live there in your city
And get treated like a dirty dog.

My musician friend would throw in lines from time to time that were exactly how I felt: I'd rather drink muddy water than stay here any longer.

I moved to North Carolina, and Corey became a wild country dog complete with briars and ticks stuck in her fur and an ecstatic grin on her face.

* * *

Unlike where I came from, here in North Carolina the "Darlin' Corey" song came on the radio with great frequency. I learned that the "muddy water" lyric was from an old blues song, and that "Darlin' Cora" was a "white blues" song that went back in music time to the nineteenth century, recorded as early as 1927 by B.F. Shelton. The song is sometimes rendered as "Little Maggie" or "Little Lulie," and there are more than forty-six recordings and versions of the song, including those by Doc Watson, Bill Monroe and His Blue Grass Boys, Pete Seeger, Harry Belafonte, Flatt and Scruggs, and the Monroe Brothers.

The song had been traditional in western North Carolina and east Tennessee for generations. Every bluegrass band around claimed some version of that outlaw love song and spun it out live in performance at street fairs and music fests, and on Friday nights on WUNC-FM's *Back Porch Music*.

I had followed my song to the place where it was born. Me and Corey both, we were country girls now.

After seventeen years, she died in my arms.

Dig a hole dig a hole in the meadow
Dig a hole in the cold damp ground
Dig a hole dig a hole in the meadow
We're gonna lay darlin' Corey down.

✳ ✳ ✳

It's been thirteen years since we buried darlin' Corey. We've been through our share of "new dogs" since then. Our most recent was Oz, a fierce mutt with bowlegs, sweet eyes, and the body of a harbor seal. After we buried him in the meadow this spring, we went to the Fish Place for dinner, feeling a little lonesome. Turned out our friend Tommy Edwards was playing. I requested "Darlin' Corey," and he played the "Little Maggie" version.

It was a high lonesome sound, and it felt just like home.

~~~

Tom Dooley: Bound to Die

BY SHARYN MCCRUMB

"Why do they still make such a big deal about Tom Dooley?" David asks me. "I mean, nobody ever sings 'Hang down your head, Ted Bundy.'"

When I told my writer friends that I was heading to Wilkes County, N.C., to research that old murder case, their response was a collective shrug, and the comment: "Ann did it."

But David McPherson, my old friend from grade school, had no preconceived notions at all beyond the suspicion that novelists lead more interesting lives than computer executives, so he agreed to meet me in Statesville one summer morning to visit the scenes of the crime.

Armed with a camera and a copy of *Lift Up Your Head, Tom Dooley*, an account of the case by North Carolina historian John Foster West, David and I head north on I-77, to the US 421 exit west towards Wilkesboro—past the great stone mansion of NASCAR legend Junior Johnson, visible from the road; past the old Wilkesboro Speedway where he once raced against the like of Ralph Earnhardt. We take Exit 256 off 421 onto N.C. 268, down past the turn-off for Kerr Lake, and straight into the other branch of Wilkes County legend—the inspiration for the folk song "Tom Dooley."

"It was the first love-triangle murder case to become national news," I tell David as we ride toward Ferguson, where it all happened. "If your information comes from the folk song, then almost everything you know about the story is wrong—beginning with the culprit's name, which was spelled Dula, not Dooley."

"So he wasn't hanged from a white oak tree?"

"Nope. From a post near the train depot in Statesville in May 1868. From the back of a cart."

"Okay, but he did kill his sweetheart, right?"

"Well . . . I wouldn't bet on it."

***

In the spring of 1865, when twenty-year-old Pvt. Tom Dula of the 42nd North Carolina Infantry, released from a Union prison camp, returned to his mother's house in the Reedy Branch section of Wilkes County, near the Yadkin River, he rekindled his affair with Ann Melton. The two had been lovers before the war—"Back when Tom was fifteen?" says David.

"Yes. Even then Ann was married to James Melton, a local farmer. According to court testimony Tom used to bed down with Ann while James slept alone a few feet away."

"How old was James Melton? Ninety?"

"Early thirties, I think. He remarried afterward."

Just before the Yadkin River bridge, we turn left on to Tom Dula Road in search of Tom Dula's grave. His modern-looking granite tombstone, half-chiseled away by souvenir-hunters, sits in a small, manicured meadow on private land, less than a mile from the crossroads, not visible from the road.

As we walk back to the car, I resume the tale. "On March 1st, 1866, Ann's cousin Pauline Foster arrived in Reedy Branch, and began working as the Meltons' maid while she was being treated for syphilis. In court she testified that Ann had told her have sex with Tom in the barn so that people would not suspect that Ann herself was involved with him."

David nods. "Just another farm chore. So Tom got syphilis from Pauline, and then I suppose he gave it to Ann?"

"Yes, and then to Laura Foster, another cousin of theirs, who was also sleeping with Tom."

"Jerry Springer, call your office," mutters David.

※ ※ ※

Farther along Tom Dula Road we come to a chicken farm, whose cylindrical metal buildings are decorated with cartoons warning of the necessity of good hygiene. One sign reads, "Disease Kills!"

David nods knowingly at the cartoon. "How apt. So who got murdered?"

"Laura Foster."

"Not my first choice. Any idea why?"

"Well, people have always said that Tom blamed Laura for giving him syphilis."

"But—but—"

"I know. But maybe he really was that dumb. Or maybe the traditional story is wrong. What we know is that on May 25, 1866, Laura Foster stole her father's horse, and she told a passing neighbor that she was eloping to Tennessee. Except that she had ridden five miles east to Reedy Branch, and thus away from Tennessee. She was never seen again. Her father said he didn't care if he ever saw Laura again, but he wanted his horse back."

"Wish granted?"

"Yes, a couple of days later, the horse returned with a broken rein, as if it had escaped being tethered."

"So they started to search for Laura's body?"

"Three months later, yes. Rumors flew around all summer, fueled by Pauline, who offered to find Mr. Foster's horse in exchange for a quart of whiskey, and who then accused Tom and Ann of having killed her. She was drunk at the time and said she had been joking. When the gossip forced Tom to leave the county, he and Ann clung together weeping at the thought of being separated. Wilkes County issued a warrant for his arrest, and he was captured near the state line by James Grayson."

"'If it hadn't been for Grayson, I'd a been in Tennessee.'"

"He hardly merits a mention in the song, does he? Laura isn't mentioned. She figures in the Doc Watson version of the tune, though."

※ ※ ※

By now we are back on 268, heading west until we reach a historical marker commemorating the grave of Laura

Foster, located in a white fenced enclosure a hundred yards back from the road, in a meadow bordered by woods and set against a backdrop of green hills.

"How did they find her body?" asks David.

"They arrested Pauline, who promptly turned state's evidence, and led them to a clearing where she claimed that Ann had told her the body was buried. When the searchers found the shallow grave under some bushes, they arrested Ann as Tom's accomplice. By the way, Tom Dula was about five feet, ten inches; and Laura Foster was tiny—about five feet tall, maybe ninety pounds."

"Was she strangled? Beaten to death?"

"Stabbed once through the heart."

"So they think a big strapping Confederate veteran stabbed a tiny frail girl? Was she pregnant?"

"The autopsy did not say so."

David thinks it over. "It doesn't make sense," he says.

"I know. Let me finish. Tom's trial dragged on for two years, while Ann waited in the Wilkes County jail for her turn. He was found guilty and sentenced to hang. After his appeals were exhausted and an escape attempt foiled, he seemed to realize that his death was inevitable, so on that last night, he wrote out a confession, saying that he had acted alone in the killing of Laura Foster. Ann was set free, but she died in a fever two years later, raving about seeing demon cats around her bed."

"Maybe Pauline did it," says David hopefully.

"But why would she? She didn't care about Tom. And can you see Ann or Tom not denouncing her if she had done it? Nobody likes Pauline, including us."

David has to concede this point. "Okay, suppose Tom really loved Laura, and he was eloping with her, so Ann got jealous and killed her."

"But if Ann had killed the woman Tom loved, then why would he spend his last night on earth writing a confession that would free Ann?"

"What if James Melton killed Laura in order to frame Tom for the crime?"

I sigh. "Do you see anybody in this story capable of that amount of subtlety or complex planning? Especially him?"

"Well, somebody killed her. She didn't commit suicide and bury herself in a shallow grave."

"Maybe Ann thought Laura was eloping with Tom, and overreacted out of jealousy, but Laura was really eloping with somebody else."

"Who?"

"They say she got around."

＊＊＊

We spend the rest of the afternoon driving the Wilkes County back roads, finding the clearing where Laura's body was found, the cabin sites, and Ann's grave. We keep envisioning possible scenarios, but nothing seems to justify the murder of Laura Foster. A century of romanticism has transformed her into a beautiful, doomed maiden, but in reality she seems to have been little loved and scarcely missed. Why would anybody bother to kill her, we wonder.

At dusk in downtown Wilkesboro, after examining the old brick jail behind the courthouse on North Bridge Street, where Tom and Ann had been imprisoned, we can't resist ending the day with dinner at Dooley's Tavern, opposite the courthouse at 102 E. Main Street.

The rest room hallway at Dooley's is decorated with three romanticized portraits of Tom Dula, Laura Foster and Ann Melton, but the door of the ladies room bears a reminder of Wilkes County's other obsession: a life-sized photo of NASCAR driver Dale Earnhardt, Jr.

When the waitress brings our sandwiches, David cannot resist asking her, "Do you know anything about the case of Tom Dula?"

The dark-haired young woman sets down our plates, and shrugs. "Ann did it."

Whoever did it, we decide that the Tom Dula case is a sordid tale without any heroes, and but for the catchy folk tune commemorating the incident, the story would have been forgotten long ago. Who did it? *Who cares?*

~~~

Heavy Rebels

BY ED SOUTHERN

Around quittin' time, on a Friday near the Fourth of July, they start walking the streets of downtown Winston-Salem. They walk past all the people driving home from work who can't help but turn to stare. Even after seven years, the good townsfolk of Winston still don't know what to make of them.

Many of the townsfolk might think they are, in the words of one observer, "the most lowest vilest crew breathing . . . their living and behavior as rude or more so than the savages."

Now, this observer—strictly speaking—was not referring to the tattooed crew who walk through Winston-Salem every year near the Fourth of July. The Reverend Charles Woodmason was referring to the eighteenth-century settlers of the Carolina backcountry, America's first white trash, the poor pioneers who risked everything to find a little freedom, a little room to move, in the Carolina wilderness.

The tattooed crew who comes to Winston-Salem every Fourth of July for the Heavy Rebel Weekender is descended from that long-ago crew, spiritually if not biologically.

Heavy Rebel is a three-day (five-day, if you count the Thursday-night pre-party and the Monday recovery) music festival. Though Heavy Rebel also includes a car show, mud wrestling, a beer drinking contest, a banana pudding eating contest, a wet-wifebeater contest (you don't want the details, but I assure you no wives are harmed), the Crossroads Guitar Contest, and a bass slap-off (no basses are harmed, either), people come for the music. About seventy bands play on three stages over the course of the weekend.

Though many bands are from the Carolinas—Winston-Salem's Bo-Stevens, Charlotte's Hick'ry Hawkins, and Rock Hill's Truckstop Preachers come to mind—some come from as far away as France and Australia. None of them play reels or jigs, and none of them dress in buckskin and linen hunting shirts. But just as Bob Dylan did more for American folk by electrifying it than a thousand stale strumming folkies, the Heavy Rebel bands and those who come to hear them honor the spirit of the backcountry white trash more than the most devout re-enactors toting muskets and powder horns.

✳ ✳ ✳

Mike Martin and Dave Quick held the first Heavy Rebel in 2001. Both had produced shows ranging from one-night concerts to Quick's two-day ElvisFest in Chapel Hill. They wanted to produce a festival, "an amazing party where everyone felt like friends," according to their website. They tossed around a few names, until Quick suggested Heavy Rebel, "like all the Heaviest Rebels of Rock 'n' Roll": Elvis, Gene Vincent, Chuck Berry, Johnny Cash, musicians who took the post-World War II collision of city and country, black and white, Old South and new, and changed the world.

The first HRW had forty-five bands; about 500 people came to hear them. More than 2,000 came in 2007, filling room blocks in three hotels.

"Most people hear about it from word of mouth," Martin said. "At first it was all from me talking about it online, and from bands talking about it. We really rely on friends to spread the gospel."

The bands play all sorts of music—rockabilly, honky-tonk country, psychobilly, punk, borderline heavy metal, even something that would be close to power pop if the bands slowed down just a bit. Slowing down isn't really part of Heavy Rebel, though; the one constant among all the bands is energy, lots of energy, a friendly sort of aggression. The highest praise the Heavy Rebel crowd can give a band is to throw empty beer cans at them in the middle of their set.

Martin and Quick both feel that being in North Carolina helps Heavy Rebel. "HRW does not have any sort of snobbery and we don't want it," Quick said. "Folks that come to HRW from elsewhere have often mentioned everyone being very friendly here. I don't think they get that experience at other festivals.

"Then there's the barbecue and hush puppies. Yankees freak over that."

Some of them save money all year long to make the Heavy Rebel trip, the way most people save for an overseas vacation. Some keep their calendars and count the years by the Weekender, ignoring New Year's Day. Andy from Boston rode a bus eighteen hours to make the 2006 Weekender; he arrived at the Winston-Salem terminal (conveniently across Fifth Street from the Millenium Center, which hosts HRW) with no ride and no place to stay, knowing no one except one of the bands. He had the clothes on his back, a change of pants and socks, and some pomade for his hair. He camped, without a tent or blanket, in some nearby woods, where he got run off one night by a drunk and awakened one morning by a rottweiler. He posted his story online "so people know that you should go to this event no matter what, 'cause it's worth it."

Here's a little secret about those beer-can throwing fans, that "lowest vilest sort of crew," a secret some of them probably don't want me to share: they're not really white trash. They might call themselves white trash, and some of them have thrown themselves into a pre-Reagan form of white-trash culture, but they work all kinds of jobs, earn all kinds of salaries, hold all manner of degrees and professional licenses.

So what are they doing there, year after year, with their tattoos and black clothes and pomaded hair, scaring the daylights out of the good townsfolk of Winston-Salem? What is it about Heavy Rebel and its music that brings them—us—back every year, and every year in larger numbers? What is it about that music, particularly the rockabilly and honky-tonk, musical forms that had peaked before most of the crowd at Heavy Rebel was even born?

"Once upon a time," Joe Queenan wrote in the British newspaper *The Guardian*, "rock 'n' roll was an idiom that enabled young people from humble circumstances to escape poverty and make a name for themselves. This was before scions of the landed gentry, masquerading as outcasts, began forming bands like the Wallflowers and the Strokes, producing a brand of music best described as plutocrap: cute, but extraneous."

The music at Heavy Rebel is not cute or extraneous. The Heavy Rebel bands who play honky-tonk and rockabilly aren't hipsters, parodying old forms with an ironic wink. They play, and the crowd at Heavy Rebel listens, with a sincere love for the music and a passionate conviction that it is not dead.

People who complain that contemporary country music is inauthentic, that today's country stars can't compare with greats like Johnny Cash, miss the point: the fault lies not in the stars, but in their fans. The same holds true for most contemporary rock. When Johnny Cash sang "Five Feet High and Rising," he sang to a vast audience that could relate to losing your farm to a flood. Nowadays, that audience's children and grandchildren live in new suburbs, in houses made from processed plastics, with two cars and a Ranger bass boat parked in the driveway. A song like "Five Feet High and Rising" does not speak to them or their experience. They will have their crises, their ups and downs, but they likely will never have to watch that bitch Mother Nature slowly and surely take everything they own.

Neither, I hope, will anyone at Heavy Rebel, but the spirit of those songs—the toughness, the realness, the lust for life (all of which was passed down into punk, and is what rock 'n' roll is supposed to be about in the first place)—appeals to them more than whatever passes for spirit in most radio-ready songs today. I have known a lot of people who come to Heavy Rebel, and I have known a lot of historians, and I do declare that a good many of the Heavy Rebel folks have a stronger and more personal sense of history than most of the professional students. The folks at Heavy Rebel, by and large, know where they came from. I know that I'm just a generation or two removed from farming or laying brick or hauling timber for a living, and I don't ever want to get so accustomed to no-hassle credit cards, health benefits, and cheap imports that I forget that.

"I feel that the rockabilly/honky-tonk music captures the spirit, a sense of pride, that so many people feel has been lost," Martin said.

Quick said, "The HRW crowd knows that it has to play by the rules of society, ultimately. They have regular jobs, children, and mortgages, but they're just not satisfied with *American Idol* for entertainment. They reject all that claptrap.

"I think rockabilly has so many appealing things about it, including that it is real music, made by real people like all of us. They all liked to go out and raise hell and so do we, just in a more fun and less dangerous way than, say, Elvis shooting out TV sets.

"I like other kinds of music, as do other people (at Heavy Rebel), but there's something explosive, sexual, fun, cool, and dangerous all at once about rockabilly music. There's also an element of perfectionism."

∗ ∗ ∗

Around quittin' time, on a Friday near the Fourth of July, we come back to Heavy Rebel. The rest of the year, we live in a world where nothing much is made to last, where "being yourself" boils down to whether you buy your clothes at Hot Topic or the Gap, where even the bars on Beale Street play Top 40 hits. At Heavy Rebel, we find an escape from that. We're willing to take some risks to find a little room to move, and the right kind of music to move to.

~~~

Hotel Charlotte

BY LEW HERMAN

One of the best-kept musical secrets of Charlotte, N.C., is the once-glorious, then faded, then imploded Hotel Charlotte. All that's left are the hundreds if not thousands of recordings made in the West Trade Street hotel's upper floors during the 1930s and 1940s, during the heyday of the hotel and a corresponding golden age of American country, blues and gospel recordings.

In the 1930s, Charlotte was a major recording center for country, blues and gospel. Hundreds of sides were waxed in a suite of rooms on the Hotel Charlotte's tenth floor. According to historian Tom Hanchett's "Recording in the Charlotte Area 1927–1939": "It is possible that the Charlotte area was America's busiest recording center during the years immediately before World War II."

By 1937, recording sessions in Charlotte were so frequent that RCA Victor needed a permanent studio. They took over three top-floor rooms of Charlotte's most exclusive hotel. They knocked out walls and partitions, draped walls with heavy curtains and created one large recording area out of Rooms 1050, 1052 and 1054 at the rear south corner of the hotel. Though primitive by today's standards, it was a step up from Charlotte's temporary warehouse studios of previous decades.

In 1936, the Monroe Brothers —Bill and Charlie— had already recorded their first songs, "Roll in My Sweet Baby's Arms" and "What Would You Give in Exchange For Your Soul?" and had their first major country hit records. In 1937 and early 1938, they recorded additional songs at the Hotel Charlotte studios—the last recordings they made as the Monroe Brothers. Later in 1938, when the Monroe Brothers split up, Bill Monroe formed his now-famous Blue Grass Boys and became known as the Father of Bluegrass.

Many other well-known groups of the day also recorded at the hotel, conveniently down the street from the old train station. A partial list includes the Delmore Brothers, known for their harmonizing duets (Doc Watson often performs their "Deep River Blues"), J.E. Mainer's Mountaineers and their various family offshoot bands and the Blue Sky Boys ("Are You from Dixie?" "I'm Just Here to Get My Baby Out of Jail"). Banjo star-of-the-day Uncle Dave Macon (with his Fruit Jar Drinkers) made his last recordings here at the Hotel Charlotte, as did the era's most influential fiddle player, Fiddlin' Arthur Smith (no relation to Charlotte's Arthur "Guitar Boogie" Smith of "Duelin' Banjos" fame). The Georgia Yellow Hammers, a well-known out-of-state string band, also recorded here, as did the Dixon Brothers. The Dixons' "I Didn't Hear Nobody Pray" became a monster smash for Roy Acuff retitled as "Wreck on the Highway." Even the Carter Family, in Charlotte for their radio show on WBT, recorded at the hotel.

Charlotte stars such as Homer Sherrill and brothers Wiley and Zeke Morris recorded at the hotel, as did Homer Briarhopper, Fred Kirby, Cliff and Bill Carlisle and various versions of the Briarhoppers, who were created by WBT radio's Charles Crutchfield. Also recorded at the hotel were the big-band sounds of Bob Pope's Hotel Charlotte Orchestra as well as numerous amateur and part-time musicians. As late as 1945, RCA Victor recorded Cecil Campbell's Tennessee Ramblers and Claude Casey at the hotel studios.

One particular session from the Hotel Charlotte in August, 1937, remains a pivotal point of the early country-music era. According to Hanchett, J. E. Mainer's session with Cleveland County (N.C.) banjo player DeWitt "Snuffy" Jenkins led directly to today's bluegrass banjo sound, popularized by Cleveland County legend Earl Scruggs. These sessions featured for the first time Snuffy's characteristic three-fingered banjo playing, which influenced Bill Monroe's Blue Grass Boys and, of course, Flatt and Scruggs and all else that followed.

Black gospel groups were heavily recorded at the Hotel Charlotte. The most influential and widely copied group, the Golden Gate Quartet, began their recording careers at an August 1937 RCA session. The following year they played New York's Carnegie Hall as part of the significant "Spirituals to Swing Concert." This legendary event combined big band stars of the 1930s—Count Basie, Benny Goodman, Sidney Bechet, Meade "Lux" Lewis—with blues and gospel musicians. It also led directly to the folk-music revival, rhythm 'n' blues and the birth of rock decades later. Another popular gospel group recorded at the hotel was the Heavenly Gospel Singers, an a cappella quartet rivaling the Monroe Brothers in record sales.

More than twenty years ago, Hanchett wrote, "This historic [Hotel Charlotte] studio survives today, untouched . . . some metal component racks and microphone cables remain in place and there are bits of electronic debris—knobs, tubes, broken switches in the corners." But the building was imploded in 1988 and a new skyscraper built on the site.

There were only a few other permanent recording studios in the South in the 1920s and 1930s in places like New Orleans, San Antonio and Atlanta. Most have been demolished long since. That the Hotel Charlotte survived so long—until the 1980s—suggests that it was considered by many to be of unique historical importance.

All that is left today of Charlotte's other early recording sites is a plaque commemorating the demolished Southern Radio Corporation building at 208 South Tryon Street. This was an earlier, temporary studio where Bill Monroe recorded his first hits and where other country, blues and gospel performers first recorded in Charlotte.

A few pieces of the old hotel remain in a bar and restaurant on South Sharon Amity Road called the

Hotel Charlotte Restaurant, where they've incorporated some original doors and still use half the hotel's original old bar. The elevator cage is stored in the basement along with other bits of memorabilia, like an old menu showing hamburgers at fifteen cents. But like the earlier temporary studios, the Hotel Charlotte finally disappeared into dust and little remains but the outstanding music recorded there.

The Man In Black Has Left the Building

BY FRED MILLS

One morning in 2003, coffee brewing in the kitchen, I went into my den and, as is always part of my morning ritual, turned on the radio. A Johnny Cash song was playing—possibly "Ring of Fire," maybe something more recent from his *American* series—and as Cash's voice came over the airwaves, I was hit by an odd chill, like a flash of intuition. And in that moment I also caught a whiff of a sense memory, too.

✳ ✳ ✳

I met Johnny Cash once, back in January of 1990. At the time I was living in Charlotte, N.C., working as the music editor for local newsweekly *Creative Loafing*. For a couple of months the Tom Cruise race car flick *Days Of Thunder* had been filming at the Charlotte (now Lowe's) Motor Speedway and in and around town. Now, with shooting finally completed, it was time for the traditional cast/crew wrap party. Cruise put out a call for some live entertainment for his bash, to be held at the track's Speedway Club overlooking the racetrack, and local roots-rock kingpins the Belmont Playboys got the nod.

Sensing a choice publicity angle to be exploited, the band decided to smuggle my wife and me in to the party under the guise of "roadies," thinking I could

report on the event and possibly even finagle a quote from Cruise about them for their press kit. There had been a near-complete media blackout during the filming, so for a writer from the lowly alternative paper to obtain this type of access when the large daily had consistently been thwarted in its efforts also amounted to no small coup for *Loafing*.

And while I would get my Cruise quote, pithy in its succinctness ("Man, they [the Playboys] were rockin'!"), we all got a *lot* more than we had bargained for.

Just before the Playboys' first set at 9 P.M., who should walk in but Cruise's co-star, Robert Duvall, accompanied by an entourage of Johnny Cash, June Carter Cash, Waylon Jennings and Jessi Colter. Jaws dropped. People gawked. Once they were all settled in at their table I had to go speak to them.

I first approached Duvall. Shaking his hand, I told him I enjoyed his singing in *Tender Mercies*, the 1983 film in which he played an alcoholic, down-and-out country musician. He grinned and pointed at Cash. "Well thanks, but there's the *real* king right there." I asked him how the Cashes and the Jennings wound up here this evening. "They're friends of mine, so I invited 'em, figured we'd have some fun."

I went over to Cash. I shook his hand and, improvising, offered, "Mr. Cash, I think you're gonna like this band that's fixing to play." In that unmistakable, indelible deep baritone of his he replied, "Thank you son, I'm sure I will." His wife smiled graciously at me and accepted my handshake as well.

The Playboys opened the show with a lively version of "Shake, Rattle and Roll," and by the third number Duvall was out on the boards making some sharp turns with a female companion. Not long after that the band plowed into "Rock 'n' Roll Ruby," an old, somewhat obscure rockabilly tune of Cash's. Sneaking a look in his direction, I saw Cash standing beside Jennings, both of them smiling and nodding their heads.

Between songs Cash walked over to the band to thank them, saying, "I just wanted to express my appreciation to you for doing my song. You guys sound great, just like we did forty years ago!" Jennings introduced himself as well, and before anyone realized what was happening both men were onstage, guitarist Jake Berger handing his instrument to Cash, bandleader Mike Hendrix passing his to Jennings. After a quick conference with the band the pair launched into "Folsom Prison Blues," followed by "Mamas, Don't Let Your Babies Grow Up To Be Cowboys" and several other tunes.

By now the room was pure electricity, the dance floor crowded with enthusiastic hoofers—Cruise, grinning his million-buck Pepsodent grin, included. June Carter Cash soon came up to harmonize with her husband and Jennings, then prefaced a song of her own by quipping, "We'd like to thank Tom for having us here. We went to [one of his movies] this afternoon so we wouldn't feel too ignorant," drawing laughs from Cruise. She and Johnny next dueted on an upbeat version of "Jackson," followed by Jennings singing "a new song I just wrote about my wife, Jessi Colter," and that

was followed by Colter getting up to sing a song of *hers*. After much coaxing, Duvall, too, joined the Cashes, the Jenningses and the Playboys onstage. As the set made its way to its conclusion, Duvall took a solo turn with "I Overlooked A Rose" and led the entire room in an arm-waving group sing-along of "Will the Circle Be Unbroken."

It was a night to tell the grandchildren about.

As the Playboys' Mike Hendrix deadpanned afterwards, "It's not every day you get to get up onstage with Johnny Cash and Waylon Jennings."

Among my memories of the party, one in particular stands out. Tom Cruise is on the dance floor a few feet away from me, while just beyond him, on the bandstand and standing side-by-side, are Johnny and June. She's clutching the mike, a huge, radiant smile on her face; he's brandishing one of the Playboys' Telecasters and casting an adoring sideways glance at her.

I'd like to think it was a night *they* told *their* grandchildren about, too.

✳ ✳ ✳

Back to that morning in 2003—September 12, to be exact. Sometimes, if you're a true music fan, you just *know* without anyone telling you. All those years of loving rock 'n' roll, and the artists who create it, gives you something akin to a sixth sense. And the instant I flicked on the radio and heard that Johnny Cash song, I *knew*.

Four months after the death of his beloved June Carter, the Man In Black had left the building.

The New Old MerleFest Shuffle

BY RICK CORNELL

How to keep the current customers happy while also attracting newcomers? It's a bit unflattering and unfair to think of MerleFest as a product and its attendees as customers, but the MerleFest moniker certainly has strong brand-name recognition, and its organizers do face the challenge of ensuring that the "regulars" keep returning year after year while at the same time attracting fresh faces.

The inaugural MerleFest took place in April 1988, a little more than two years after Merle Watson, son of acoustic-music legend Doc Watson (and, like his father, one of the best finger-picking guitarists on the planet), died in a tractor accident. The idea to raise money for a memorial garden to honor Merle evolved into a plan for a multi-day festival showcasing the kind of music loved by the Watsons, and this led to the first MerleFest. Four thousand acoustic-music lovers, many of them undoubtedly fans of, even friends of, Doc and Merle Watson, watched New Grass Revival and other blue-grass and traditional acts perform on the stage of the John A. Walker Center on the campus of Wilkes Community College and on the deck of two flatbed trucks.

From those humble roots, an honest-to-goodness musical juggernaut has sprung (although, granted, the words "roots music" and "juggernaut" go together about like "heavy metal" and "pickin' circle"). A couple of trucks and one indoor stage have turned into more than a dozen outdoor stages; crowds are now close to twenty times the size of that initial gathering of 4000. In contrast to 1988's handful of performers, the 2003 roster numbered 99, a roll call that included Ralph Stanley & the Clinch Mountain Boys, Ricky Skaggs & Kentucky Thunder, Donna the Buffalo, Asleep At the Wheel and, as always, Arthel "Doc" Watson. The 2008 line-up included the Avett Brothers, the Carolina Chocolate Drops, Levon Helm & The Midnight Ramble, Peter Rowan, Tony Rice; and Bruce Hornsby joined Ricky Skaggs & Kentucky Thunder.

✳ ✳ ✳

Former MerleFest Director Jim Barrow witnessed the phenomenal growth of the festival. Among other things, the staff is responsible for keeping the faithful satisfied and bringing fresh faces to the grounds of Wilkes Community College come late April. When asked about the unenviable task of properly blending a little bit of the new with a lot of the time-tested, Barrow explained in a 2003 interview, "We look at what our festival attendees are asking for on the MerleFest Talk Page and in our surveys," referencing the discussion board available on the MerleFest website and questionnaires for concert-goers. "We keep our ear to the ground by reading the trade publications and seeing live music as often as possible. We talk to other professionals in the music business and get their opinions on what's new and fresh, and we watch the radio charts."

I don't press that last point, so I can only guess that, based on most years' line-ups, Barrow and company watch the radio charts and then pick primarily what's not getting played on commercial country stations. (Believe me, that's not a criticism.) That said, a few years back festival organizers did draw plenty of complaints for bringing an exceptionally rock-chart-friendly act to MerleFest: Hootie and the Blowfish.

"We sometimes like to throw a wildcard like Hootie and the Blowfish into the mix to keep things interesting. Whatever reaction we get from our attendees is a good reaction," Barrow said. It was a move that met the goal of drawing some people who were not previously familiar with MerleFest, and it also allowed detractors to see the mega-selling Blowfish in a different light. "Many of those who initially complained came back after the festival admitting that they were wrong," recalled Barrow. "It worked here. It was an acoustic set with Doc Watson, Chris Thile and Pete Wernick joining the band in a jam," referring to Merle's finger-picking father, the mandolin whiz kid from Nickel Creek and the banjo master, respectively.

* * *

Is MerleFest typically on target? Durham's Mark O'Donnell, a veteran of a number of MerleFests, thinks so. "What keeps me coming back, in spite of the larger and larger crowds that might otherwise be off-putting?" he asked himself on cue. "The chance to discover new talent I'd never heard before like Steve Earle at my first MerleFest, and rediscover old talent that I had mistakenly written off like Chris Smither. The chance to see old heroes like Jesse Winchester and new heroes like Gillian Welch and David Rawlings."

Jim McKelvey of Hillsborough agreed. Thanks to MerleFest, he's discovered such performers as Welch, Iris Dement, Holly and Barry Tashian, Pat Alger, Martin Simpson and Darrell Scott, often rather early in their careers. And McKelvey is a one-man testament to MerleFest's ability to keep the regulars happy and also bring in new folks. "I started going to MerleFest alone and sleeping in my car in 1993," he reminisced in 2003. "Slowly, friends and relatives started to come with me. This year we have fifteen reserved seats and are renting six motel rooms."

An Orchestra is Born

BY MEG FREEMAN WHALEN

How the Charlotte Symphony Orchestra got started remains a mystery. In some accounts, Charlotteans vacationing in Cuba in the early days of the Great Depression met a dashing Spanish violinist, Guillermo S. de Roxlo, and convinced him to immigrate to the Queen City and start an orchestra. De Roxlo said in a 1938 interview for the *Charlotte News* that the orchestra was his idea from the start. Having come to Charlotte in 1931 to teach violin, his first question upon arrival, he said, was, "Where is the Charlotte Symphony Orchestra playing?" When told there was none, de Roxlo replied, "All right. That is my place."

Regardless of whose head hatched the idea, the Charlotte Symphony was indeed de Roxlo's place. Described by journalist Dorothy Knox as having "the courage of a crusader, the infinite capacity for taking pains of a genius, the mind of a scholar, and the soul of a great musician," de Roxlo was a composer and conductor as well as a violinist, and in his new homeland was traveling as far as Hickory to teach budding musicians. In the fall of 1931, he ran an announcement in the newspapers inviting anyone interested in starting an orchestra to meet at Central High School. Twenty-five showed up, but de Roxlo scrounged around, gathered another thirty or so, and rehearsals began in December.

Three months later, on March 20, 1932 at 3:15 P.M., the Charlotte Symphony Orchestra made its debut. It was not the first band to take that name. In 1920, a Charlotte Symphony Orchestra of some thirty men and one woman had organized for a brief time. But this new crowd of fifty-seven musicians (nearly half of whom were women) would prove to have staying power.

The skies were cloudy and the weather was cool on that Palm Sunday afternoon, as hundreds of curious Charlotteans crowded into the Carolina Theatre on Tryon Street to hear their new orchestra. The free concert was sponsored by the Charlotte Parks and Recreation Commission. Later that week, the 1,450-seat theater would present Clark Gable's latest film, *Polly of the Circus,* and a recital by the movie house's new organist. But this day was devoted to orchestral music.

The program, more than two hours long, opened with Mozart's Overture to *The Marriage of Figaro,*

Founded in 1932, the Charlotte Symphony is the oldest continuously performing orchestra in the Carolinas. —MEG FREEMAN WHALEN

Debussy's *Reverie*, Wagner's Prelude to *Lohengrin*, and selections from Grieg's *Peer Gynt Suite*. Those shorter works were balanced by the premiere of de Roxlo's own long-winded *Symphony in F*. The next day, a review by Hazel Mizelle confirmed the show's success: It was, she wrote, "a presentation that brought splendid applause from the music lovers gathered at the concert."

With the support of the Charlotte Music Club, the Junior League, and the Charlotte Charity League, the orchestra was able to give two more concerts that season. Another indoor performance in the Little Theatre Auditorium of the College Apartments building at College and Ninth Streets took place on April 24, followed by an outdoor concert in July at Independence Park, featuring Beethoven's *Fifth Symphony*.

For the next two seasons, the Charlotte Symphony performed in the Little Theatre Auditorium, an old wooden building near the railroad track. Every evening around 9:15, a freight train would roar by, adding a percussive element to the music not called for in the scores. And the budget—a meager $60 the first full season and $300 the second—was tight. Neither de Roxlo nor the musicians, a hard-working group of music teachers, high school and college students, and members of most every professional field, were paid. Lacking money for sheet music, the conductor had to copy out orchestra parts by hand. But coffee was served in china cups at intermission.

By 1934, the group had moved into the 500-seat Alexander Graham Junior High School Auditorium and formed its first board. Principal flutist J. Spencer Bell, an attorney who would later become a state senator and a U.S. Circuit Court judge, was named president. Season subscriptions of five dollars per couple bought tickets to all five programs. Attendance averaged 250 for each concert.

＊ ＊ ＊

"The First Hundred Years Are the Hardest," announced an article in the *Charlotte News,* as the orchestra prepared to celebrate its tenth season. "The symphony has had to fight for its very existence… Its growth has been consistent, but not spectacular." But, while the paper lamented the orchestra's lack of an endowment, it recognized the Charlotte Symphony's accomplishments. Season subscriptions were up to 400. Wagnerian tenor Lauritz Melchior had become the orchestra's first big-name guest in 1938. De Roxlo had started a conservatory for young music students in 1940. Under the direction of the "sharp-eyed, fiery" Spaniard, the band's playing had improved.

In spite of American involvement in World War II, which called players away from Charlotte, the orchestra continued to thrive. The last concert of the 1941-42 season boasted the highest attendance ever. Later that year, on Sunday afternoon, December 13, 1942, the Charlotte Symphony presented its first concert for children. And de Roxlo was taking his ensemble on the road, performing concerts in nearby towns in both North and South Carolina.

But de Roxlo would himself be hitting the trail soon.

The handsome musician had arrived in Charlotte more than a dozen years before with his wife, Kitty. But the couple divorced, and Kitty de Roxlo moved to Florida. One evening in late 1944, musicians arriving for rehearsal got a big surprise. As they approached the door of the rehearsal room, they found an envelope taped to the door with a key and a note from de Roxlo inside. It read, "Owen Thomas (a violinist and former secretary for the orchestra) and I have eloped, and I will not be back." That was the last anyone heard from him.

It was not, however, the last they heard of Kitty de Roxlo. The next year, Spencer Bell, once a confirmed bachelor, returned from the army with his new wife—Kitty Bell.

~~~

Mount Airy Confidential

BY KENT PRIESTLEY

There is something indescribably moving about the sound of scores of fiddles, banjos, and guitars being played in close figure, scattered along a hillside after dark. It is the sound of a young America, or some vital part of it, shades of Thomas Hart Benton and Aaron Copland, oil lamp and twist tobacco, coal camp and cotton field, Antietam and Bull Run. And it's especially moving when the listener happens to be drunk and soaked to the bone.

It had been a pleasant, unremarkable early June day when I left Roanoke Island, in Eastern North Carolina, for the six-hour drive west to the 2002 Mount Airy Bluegrass and Old-Time Fiddler's Convention. But somewhere near Greensboro, things began to turn. The occasional clouds fused to make something bigger, and in time the sky became a fearful and boiling thing. *This*, I thought, as the first, fat drops smacked my windshield, *is not good.*

At length downtown Mount Airy loomed up, its red brick buildings gray in the rainy evening light. After a few wrong turns, I wound out of downtown, crossed the Ararat River, and passed through the gates of the Mount Airy Veterans Memorial Park. Near the back of the park and part-way up a hill was the friend I planned to camp with, Tim Wells. He'd arrived hours before and was already set up, with the top of his Volkswagen bus expanded and a tarp lashed to its gutters and staked out at the far side. Out of ten or more acres of grass and hills and sheltering oak groves, Tim had chosen to camp beside a row of port-o-lets.

"I prefer to call them 'comfort stations,'" he said. "Some people might call it a liability, being so close to these things. But the way I live, I consider it a necessity." He cleared his throat. "Care for a beer?"

We sat in the dark on folding chairs, sipped beer after beer and listened to the music being made around us. Tim pulled his banjo from its case and began replacing a broken tuning peg. Up and down the hill musicians huddled under tarps, lamp-lit, warming up for an evening of tunes. Others moved past us in a steady parade, instrument cases in hand, occasionally tripping over a tent stake or getting snagged on a guy line. They were anonymous in their raincoats and hoods, off to join other circles of players.

Despite the wind and rain, the show seemed determined to go on. The air was filled with the plinking of strings and first tentative bow-strokes from fiddles, the strum of guitars and the rubbery plunk of old-time banjos. The group of musicians nearest to us launched into a number; the bass-player, a dark-haired woman with a build like an egret, shouted verses:

> Have you ever seen a muskrat, Sally Ann?
> Pickin' on a banjo, Sally Ann
> Draggin' his slick tail through the sand
> I'm goin' home with Sally Ann . . .

Aside from this nearest group, the rest of the music in the park rolled into one big ambient pulse. "People talk about this thing called the 'D din,'" Tim offered by way of explanation. "At any given moment there are so many people playing in the key of D around here that it makes this weird hum. The air vibrates with it." Above us, the tarp flapped. Evidently, the gods didn't care much for the "D din."

"Did you bring any whiskey?" I asked, thinking that it might make things better.

"No," he said, raising his shoulders in an apologetic shrug.

A gust of wind came down the hill. The slender bamboo poles holding the tarp wavered and fell, sending the whole works down on top of us. Tim whistled through his teeth, a shrill descending figure. "Shoo," he said. "We're in it now, buddy."

* * *

By daybreak Saturday the music had trailed off, leaving only the sound of the rain. I awoke late with a headache (having violated the sacred beer-before-liquor rule sometime in the night). Tim was gone. A group of musicians from Chapel Hill offered me some of their leftovers, a little cold bacon and scrambled eggs. I set off down the hill to the main grounds to have a look at the rest of the convention goings-on, slipping on the rain-moistened grass and clay.

The performance stage sat empty and covered with a film of water; banners that read WPAQ, the call letters of the local AM radio station, hung loosely above. The weather had forced the 11 a.m. "traditional song competition" inside, into a room adjoining the park bathrooms, all part of the same low-slung, cement-block building. I stepped inside. The emcee worked down a list of competitors, introduced each singer or pair of singers, and added where they were from. The audience was small, maybe fifteen or twenty people on folding chairs, staring blankly ahead.

A girl and her father got up and moved to the front of the room. The emcee announced that the two were from somewhere in Virginia with a name along the lines of Leaning Cedar or Coal Tipple. The girl was no older than nine or ten and was yoked to an antique Gibson guitar nearly as big as her. The father played a mandolin. Her eyes were closed and her voice was high and quavering, full of soul-weariness beyond her years. She sang:

> I never will marry, or be no man's wife
> I expect to live single all the days of my life
> The shells in the ocean shall be my death-bed
> The fish in deep water swim over my head.

It was a tragic song, and, given the girl's age, a little odd. To gauge by the applause, it was also a crowd favorite.

Up to perform next were Tim and a friend of his named Ed from Chapel Hill. For the first time I noticed

Tim was dressed in a fuchsia-colored muscle shirt with a scattershot of holes in it and high-cut nylon running shorts. His feet were shod in all-terrain sandals. Inexplicably, there was nail-polish on his right hand. He played a knockabout banjo and Ed, a small-bodied guitar. Their entry in the competition was a cowboy song, and they yodeled each chorus in high harmony:

> *I-dee-o-dee-lay-hee-ee-oo, ay-ee-hoo, oh-de-*
> *lay-hee-ee-oo*
> *I-dee-o-dee-lay-he-ee-oo, I-ee-o-ee-hooooooooo . . .*

The audience looked stunned. I decided to leave before it got any worse.

Outside, at a food concession run by the local Kiwanis or Rotary club, white-haired men were already serving up lunch from a row of deep-fat fryers. They did a brisk trade in onion rings and chicken fingers, sweet tea and Pepsi Cola, all paid for and served through a sagging screen. There were a handful of picnic tables and lounging on them, apparently indifferent to the rain, were several young couples. The boys all had that intimidating brand of rural self-possession about them, a quality that makes pale, desk-bound people like me give them a wide berth. They wore sleeveless T-shirts and camouflaged hats whose brims they'd rolled to an almost half-round shape; the girls were dressed in tight jeans and shirts with warnings like HEARTBREAKER or NO ANGEL spelled out in glitter. Between their feet or off to one side were their instruments: mandolin, fiddle and guitar cases with C.F. MARTIN stenciled on them.

Aside from the food concession and a few stalls selling CDs, instruments, picks, strings, and a whole tent dedicated to someone named Fiddlin' Jake Krack, there was a blissful lack of consumerism at the convention.

I drifted through a livestock-judging barn with steep bleachers. There, a banjo competition was in progress; on stage, a teenage girl was seated on a folding chair and hunched over her instrument, playing a melody without words.

Next stop, bluegrass country. The central field was ringed with RVs, drawing power from electric services and discharging waste to the Mount Airy municipal sewerage system. (A friend of mine characterized the difference between bluegrass and old-time culture this way: "Bluegrass is like an electric bug-zapper and old-time is like a citronella candle.") The set-ups were elaborate, with custom awnings extended and indoor-outdoor carpets rolled out and strings of party lights draped here and there.

Under the dripping eaves of a green funeral home tent, a several bluegrass pickers were fully involved in their art. They had a quality about them of seeming more authentic than most of the old-time players, of actually being *of* the South, not just evoking it in song or melody. Their belts supported a conspicuous number of pagers and cell phones, the suggestion being that in their daily lives they were members of their local fire and rescue squads. A dobro player made spooky little *zings* and *wangs* on his instrument, while behind him, a heavy-set man in overalls played the bass. A banjoist propped his instrument on a considerable stomach, attacking the strings with a mechanical, crawling motion. The musicians would lean in closer during each chorus of the song, the verses of which were full of images of a dying mother and mossy graveyards and such. Each time, the sound of their instruments fell away to a murmur as they sang:

I've just seen the Rock of Ages
Jacob's Ladder hangin' down
I've just crossed the River of Jordan
Oh my son I'm homeward bound.

❋ ❋ ❋

Sunday morning felt like the end of a long siege. The sky above was the color of dishwater and a weak sun was probing through. Moisture rose from the ground in waves. There wasn't much lingering going on; instead, it seemed that pretty much everyone was striking camp and heading home. I couldn't blame them; they'd paid their dues several times over. The port-o-lets had taken on a life of their own, so I decided to trek down to the park bathroom and clean up. A mistake—the bathroom was a horror-story of mud, strewn toilet paper and bad smells.

I walked along the bank of the Ararat River on my way back to camp. Swollen from rain and the color of chocolate milk, it seemed reasonable to believe that if I waited long enough, I might see a bloated cow or two pass by, carried seaward on the flood.

Back at camp, I sat down with Tim and Ed, who were eating breakfast burritos in the shade of the tarp, swatting at flies.

"Like your shoes," said Tim.

"Thanks," I said, looking down. My sneakers had been mint on Friday, made of clean, black suede. Now they were unrecognizable, covered in slick red clay and swollen to nearly twice their original size. They looked like something that might be used as a building material in, say, Benin. Our interest shifted from my shoes to a septic pumping truck making the rounds of the camp, emptying the port-o-lets. Headed up the hill toward us, its six wheels slipped helplessly in the exposed clay. The wheels whined, spun and rained soil.

"Oh, this is good," said Ed.

The driver was making no progress. Eventually he climbed out and made a call on his two-way radio before lighting up a cigarette. We were rapt. If he noticed our scrutiny, though, he didn't give any indication. Several minutes passed before a big, industrial forklift with knobby tires appeared. The operator attached a stout chain to the septic truck's front bumper, the driver climbed back in and engaged the truck and the forklift, with considerable effort and slinging of mud, started up the hill, balking all the way. The truck driver gestured wildly as it did, another cigarette bobbing between his lips. It seemed the perfect coda to an unforgettable weekend.

"Now *that*," said Tim, pointing at the scene with a forkful of scrambled eggs, "is old-timey."

Beach Music: Heart & Soles

BY REV. BILLY C. WIRTZ

"Beach Music?"

To anyone outside the Carolinas it could mean anything from The Beach Boys to Jimmy Buffett to Bob Marley.

In the Carolinas, beach music means something completely different. For starters: Its national anthem is a fifty-year-old song about sixty-minute sex.

The music is a style of smooth rhythm and blues that generations of Carolinians have listened, danced and fallen in love to. There are entire music stores (The Wax Museum in Charlotte, N.C.; Judy's House Of Oldies in North Myrtle Beach, S.C.) devoted to selling it. It has made small fortunes for bands virtually unknown outside a four-state region, such as The Shakers, The Embers and The Chairmen of the Board. It has been around since the 1940s. There are over two hundred clubs that revolve around the music and a dance known as the shag.

This "Beach Music" is virtually unknown south of Brunswick, Georgia, or north of Richmond, Virginia, yet down here, its popularity rivals that of vinegar cole slaw and Rick Flair. The shag is the official state dance of South Carolina and is taught in public schools. It all happened by accident.

SPRING, 1948

The war had been over for three years. The baby boom was on, and folks were settling in and trying to get back to life as they knew it. The war had changed America forever. In the South, segregation and many of the old ways still held on, but young men and women from Hickory and Red Oak had been to faraway places like Copenhagen and Tangiers, seen and done things no one could mention back in Burke County, and slowly but surely, old walls were beginning to crumble.

Down in Carolina Beach, N.C., a couple of enterprising young merchant marines had opened up a little beer joint. The place wasn't very big, certainly no different from hundreds of other hole-in-the-wall beach bars catering to returning servicemen, ne'er-do-wells, and locals out for a little fun.

I wrote this a couple of years back. Since then, Mr. Hicks has passed on to that great dance floor in the sky. May he rest in peace and know that in the words of beach music's national anthem, "It Will Stand." Special thanks to Harry Turner, Judy's House Of Oldies and, especially, Professor John Hook. —REV. BILLY C. WIRTZ

The Tijuana Inn would change the culture of the Carolinas forever.

Jim Hanna and Chicken Hicks were frustrated; they were having fun running a beer joint but getting tired of the music that the local jukebox distributor was putting in their club.

"They were some lame records," says Hanna.

Chicken was a self-proclaimed "Hepcat" who flaunted the prevailing attitudes of the day. He made frequent trips over to Seabreeze, the black section of town, and he started making a list of the records that everyone danced to. He suggested to Hanna that they put some of the new tunes with that "crazy beat" he had been hearing over at Seabreeze on the jukebox. Songs like "Hey Bop A Ree Bop" by Lionel Hampton, "The Honeydripper" by Joe Liggins and "'Round The Clock" by Johnny Otis.

Hanna agreed, they put the records on the box, and all hell broke loose.

According to Hanna, "You couldn't get in the place. The people just loved that music." They not only loved the music, but they loved the dances that went with it: the Big Apple, the jitterbug, and a dance that would one day be known as the shag.

Hanna and company went on to convert an old bowling alley across the street into a dance hall, and the legendary Bop City was born.

Bop City was where black Pied Piper Paul Williams and his band would parade down the segregated boardwalk, and lead a crowd of over a hundred white kids back up the stairs of the club to Hucklebuck all night long.

Bop City was where Jimmy Cavallo and his high-octane band would blast out the latest bop tunes and have the dancers "Jumpin' From Six To Six."

Bop City got them all run out of Carolina Beach.

If the Carolina Beach scene had been an isolated occurrence, it might have left nothing but a few carefully edited stories to pass on to future generations, but more than 600 miles away in Nashville, Tennessee, WLAC radio was blanketing the South with a 50,000-watt signal. In between ads for hair pomade and "two dozen live baby chicks"—and seven years before Alan Freed used the term "rock 'n' roll" to disguise the fact that he was playing black music for white teen-agers— DJs like Gene Nobles and "Hossman" Allen were spinning the latest "Harlem" hits by Wynonie Harris and Billy Ward and The Dominoes for a small but ever-growing following.

Although this music began to show up on the pop charts around 1954, it was still virtually unknown to mainstream America. It was so far out of the mix, considered so lewd and suggestive, that the only place whites could hear it—before WLAC—was at one of the beach places.

Thanks to WLAC, thirty-five years before Snoop Dogg, the sons and daughters of "good families" from the South were listening to transistor radios stashed under their pillows, hearing Wynonie encouraging his baby to "Keep On Churnin' Till the Butter Comes" and counting the days till summer.

* * *

Jim Hanna packed his bags and headed for Florida. But the music that had rocked Carolina Beach had begun to spread. Bop music began to show up on jukeboxes all along the coast, but it found a permanent home around the North Myrtle Beach area. Unlike many of the other areas, North Myrtle was unincorporated, and therefore exempt from certain blue laws. This meant that the kids did not have to stop dancing at midnight on Saturday, and so young Carolinians danced the nights away to the forbidden music that they could only listen to far from home. By this time they no longer called it bop, now it was simply "Beach Music."

Over the next couple of decades, beach music became an accepted and integral part of summer life for generations of Carolinians. Such landmarks as the Pad, the OD (Ocean Drive) Pavilion, and dozens of other places along the "Grand Strand" of Myrtle Beach ensured its permanence in the culture. By the early 1980s some of the original shaggers and their sons and daughters had formed SOS (Society Of Stranders), and by the millennium, SOS weekends were highlights of the season for North Myrtle Beach with over 20,000 dancers arriving for the twice yearly event.

TUESDAYS WITH HAROLD

Brenda Rosser has tended bar at Fat Harold's in North Myrtle Beach for twenty-five years. On a rainy Tuesday night in April 2005, she simultaneously pours drinks, makes change, sings along with the music, and fires a non-stop series of verbal shots at a big man wearing rectangular glasses. The object of her taunts and comments is a man she refers to as "A legend in his own mind." His name is Harold Bessent, AKA Fat Harold. Harold is indeed a bigger-than-life personality, a great storyteller, a club owner, a father figure, a good drinkin' buddy, a beach music historian, and at seventy-two years old, a very happy man. He loves the music, the dance and the people.

He can't retire.

The club is his home, the customers and employees his family. The walls of the club tell a thousand stories. They are covered with plaques, pictures, newsletters, newspaper clippings and awards. The names and faces of legendary shaggers like Shad and Brenda Alberty, Harry Driver, Jackie Mcghee, and dozens of others are everywhere. Under the neon glow of beer signs and bar clocks, from the pool tables in the small front bar, to the walls of the cavernous main room, there is the history of a place and its people.

Harold's is by no means just a museum. It's also a great club, with a huge dance floor, and state of the art sound. On any given night the DJ will play everything from fifty-year-old classics to the latest blues and R&B, as long as it has that relaxed shag beat, or as Harold calls it: "The Rhythm of the Heart."

Harold's is open year-round, and along with such other legendary clubs as Ducks and The Spanish Galleon, it is one of the main destinations for SOS weekend. The cards and letters on the walls tell the story. People come from Memphis, London, and Barnwell, S.C., to dance, drink and swap lies with the man from Little River. He's been doing this for fifty-one years, and swears that he will keep doing it, "As long as there is a breath left in my body."

Harold's club sits at the end of the Main Street corridor in North Myrtle Beach. Much like Harold's, the rest of this small area is still the way it has been for several decades. Although big corporate hotels and national food chains are advancing daily, this little strip still has the old feel to it. There is Hoskins, a home-cooking restaurant, where the menu and some of the waitresses have been around since the days of Chicken

Hicks. There's no reason to change; home cooking doesn't get any better, anywhere.

Across the street from Hoskins is Judy's House of Oldies. If you want to take home the music you hear in the clubs, Judy will have it. She will also sell you shag instructional videos, beach music books and even fit you in a pair of dancing shoes for your next visit to North Myrtle.

IT WILL STAND

Beach music has survived and is thriving.

Which begs one question: How come, outside of the Carolinas, Georgia and parts of Virginia, virtually no one, including music writers, musicians and die-hard R&B fans, has ever heard of it?

Maybe for a few of the following reasons:

A. It was a jukebox phenomenon. Unless you went to Myrtle Beach as a youth, or heard it from a secondary source, you'd never make the important connection between the songs, the dance and the place.

B. The music and the shag are associated, in modern times, somewhat correctly with middle-aged, conservative white Southerners.

C. With the exception of the early years, it doesn't have a particularly colorful, sordid history that makes for great retelling on VH-1 specials.

Maybe some day the world will discover beach music and give it the exposure it deserves. Then again, maybe a little too much exposure would ruin it.

You can buy "Carolina Bar-B-Que" all over the country, but away from Lexington, it loses something. You can listen to beach music almost anywhere in the Carolinas, but at Fat Harold's, you don't just hear it, you feel it, it gets inside you. You begin to understand what Harold means, when he taps out a beat on his ample chest and says: "When I die, my heart will be doing this."

～～～

The New Southern Rock

BY MARK KEMP

On a hot summer day in 2005, Juan Miguel Marin stood on the front steps of the Film Foundry in Charlotte, smiling radiantly and shaking people's hands as they filed in the doors. His band, La Rúa, was about to premiere its first video, a narrative clip for the group's regional single, "El Chanchito," which translates in Spanish as "The Piggybank." La Rúa, a five-piece rock band made up of young Venezuelans and Ecuadorians, made history that day. In their music—and in the video for "El Chanchito," in particular—Juan Miguel and his friends documented the evolving story of the *new* New South.

"El Chanchito" is high-energy *rock en español*—rock 'n' roll sung in Spanish—in which Juan Miguel sings of a young Latin American immigrant named Samuel, who works multiple jobs to save money for his girlfriend Marta to come across the border and be with him in the United States. Samuel isn't a grape-picker in California or a *ranchero* in Texas—he washes dishes in a Southern greasy spoon, loads trucks at a warehouse and sweats on construction jobs in North Carolina's fastest-growing metropolis. The images in La Rúa's video are quintessentially Southern: hot rural roads, rich green grass and trees, deep red dirt, dusty construction sites and a gritty pool-hall parking lot filled with people in jeans and T-shirts, dancing and singing.

These are images of the South in which I grew up during the 1970s—beautiful, simple, soulful—but the people in the frames look very different from the young people of my generation. They're not just black or white; they're multiple shades in between. And they don't speak just English; most of them also speak Spanish. In historically Hispanic-heavy areas of the U.S., such as New York City, Miami, Texas or the West Coast, these images wouldn't seem particularly new or noteworthy. But for those of us who grew up in the black-and-white South, the Latinization of this region is nothing short of amazing. Our old Andy Griffith main drags and Sanford & Son junkyards are transforming into a colorful mosaic of new languages, new cuisines, new visual arts and, perhaps most exciting of all, new styles of music. When a pickup truck rumbles up next to your car at a stoplight in today's South, it's not necessarily Bubba behind the wheel with a rifle rack and hunting dogs behind him, rocking to Lynyrd Skynyrd or swaying to the sweet country moan of Randy Travis. It may be José and a handful of his buddies, blasting the latest album by Mexican rockers Maná or *norteño* kings Los Tigres del Norte.

* * *

During the 1990s, the South experienced an unprecedented Hispanic population explosion. In the Carolinas, the number of Spanish-speaking residents more than tripled. In 1990, North Carolina's Hispanic population was 76,726. By 2004, it had reached 600,913. In South Carolina during the '90s, the Hispanic population increased from 30,551 to 96,178.

The growing presence of Latino culture has changed the landscape of the Carolinas dramatically, rendering the racial dynamics of the Old South much more complicated than in earlier times. These days, some blue-collar African Americans complain as loudly of Latinos taking jobs as some blue-collar whites did of blacks in the post-Civil Rights years. And just as the Civil Rights era led to the blend of country, blues and gospel that were the raw ingredients of rock 'n' roll, the Latinization of the South is reconfiguring the recipe once again. It's doing so not just by bringing immigration issues into the Spanish lyrics of rock songs like La Rúa's "El Chanchito," but also by blending the various rhythms of traditional Latin musical styles into the soundtrack of our daily lives. On the streets, at outdoor festivals and in nightclubs across the Carolinas, you can hear Mexican-related genres such as *mariachi*, *tejano*, *norteño* and *musica ranchera*, as well as Caribbean and Central and South American styles like *bachata*, *cumbia*, *merengue* and *vallenato*.

In the past, in Southern California, Texas and New York City, the blending of Latin musical styles with American styles led to genres such as *Chicano rock*, *conjunto* and *salsa*. "It might take a few generations for the same thing to happen here," says David Garcia, an ethnomusicologist at the University of North Carolina in Chapel Hill. "Based on these past examples in other parts of the country, more than likely something is going to happen."

Indeed, in the past five years, bands performing *rock en español* in the Carolinas have begun to cross over to Anglo and African-American audiences, particularly in Charlotte, says Tony Arreaza, the former La Rúa guitarist who now plays in the electronic-rock band Eva Fina. "Charlotte is a real hot spot for the whole *rock en español* movement in the South," says Arreaza, who also heads up Carlotan Rock, an annual festival of *rock en español* that's brought international acts like the Venezuelan dance-rock band Los Amigos Invisibles. The festival also features regional Latin rock acts such as the Charlotte-based ska band Bakalao Stars, punk rockers Dorian Gris, the Fort Mill, S.C.-based reggaetón artist Buay Calito and the mainstream rock band Baco, from Winston-Salem. Carlotan Rock Productions also promotes big rock concerts throughout the year and is responsible for bringing to the Carolinas such internationally known artists as the critically acclaimed Mexican experimental rock band Café Tacuba and Spanish *rock en español* pioneers Hombres G. "These bands now see Charlotte as a must-stop city on their tours," says Arreaza.

Latino festivals in the Triad and Triangle areas of North Carolina, and in cities like Charlotte and Charleston often feature performances by homegrown acts that specialize in more traditional Latin styles. Some of the notable trad-Latin acts are Charanga Carolina, a UNC-sponsored student ensemble in Chapel Hill that performs Cuban and *salsa* music; Son de Cuba, a Charlotte-based family band that plays a mix of *son* and *salsa*; Durham's Samecumba, which blends *salsa* with *merengue* and *cumbia*; Leydy Bonilla, a Dominican singer based in Charlotte who sings pop *merengue* and *bachata*; Charleston-based singer Leah Suarez, who sprinkles Spanish and Portuguese into her eclectic playlist of Latin jazz styles; and Los Viajeros, a Mexican *mariachi* band from Greensboro.

✳ ✳ ✳

In 2006, a six-piece Raleigh band whose members sport cowboy hats and boots, jeans and well-pressed button-down shirts went into a recording studio to lay down a love song to the city they call home. From their well-scrubbed look to their good manners and love of this part of the South, you'd think the guys were just another area country band with a patriotic streak. *"Beneath your blessed sky, my life changed / Now I can live as I had come to dream,"* they sing. The words could have been written by the Wilmington-born Southern rocker Charlie Daniels, except that Fred Huerta wrote them in Spanish and sings them over the familiar oom-pah beat of norteño, the country music of northern Mexico. His band, Rey Norteño, consists of the genre's typical lineup: accordions, guitars, drums and the six-string bass known as a *bajo sexto*.

"Raleigh, Norte Carolina, te llevo en mi corazon,"

they sing *a cappella*, their r's rolling beautifully on the first two words, before the accordions and drums kick in. In English, the words translate as, *"Raleigh, North Carolina, you are in my heart."* Later in the song, the lyrics lament having to leave the town temporarily: *"Raleigh, I know that I owe you a lot . . . and I know that when I can, I'll be back."* Where the song differs from other music this area has produced is the longing Huerta expresses in another line for his *other* home, thousands of miles away. It's the classic immigrant's dilemma, and Rey Norteño expresses it with utter respect and integrity: *"How can I forget you (Raleigh) when I've poured my sweat into your land, working for my people, who wait for me in my nation."*

As songs like "El Chanchito" and "Raleigh" insinuate themselves into the cultural fabric of the Carolinas, all of the area's music eventually will be influenced by it—from country and rock to blues, R&B and hip-hop—just as all music was affected by the intermingling of the predominantly African-American and white styles of the '40s and '50s—blues, gospel, country and bluegrass. That mix, which led to rock 'n' roll, happened when young whites and young blacks began crossing the racial divide after hearing each other's music on regional radio stations. Today, young whites and blacks can hear norteño and other Latin styles across the AM radio spectrum, as well as the myriad of web radio stations and TV channels such as Univision. Those young white, black and Latino musicians curious about each others' musical styles are sure to begin experimenting together, blending it all into a new kind of Southern popular music.

Garcia points to Orquesta GarDel, a nine-piece

salsa group, directed by former students of his who are not just Latino but also Anglo and African-American. The non-Latino members, he says, "have adopted Latin music just as the Allman Brothers did with African-American blues in the late 1960s. So even though a new genre of music hasn't happened organically yet, more than likely something will. This is a continuing story."

~~~

One Night at the Gaston

BY DAVID CHILDERS

I grew up in Mount Holly, N.C., a place whose geographical location still survives while the town I knew, like so many of the people I knew, has left this earth forever. Cross the Catawba River now and you will find a neatly groomed little city with a couple of restaurants and bars, a coffee shop, a couple of banks, and lots of churches. It is safe, quiet, and boring with few people on the streets, and many abandoned buildings looking for a new wave of prosperity to put occupants into them. The town has recently benefited from younger, more progressive leadership. New people are moving in. The U.S. National Whitewater Center opened just across the river, and the city has hopes of becoming an eco-tourism location, even as its ecology is ruined, as the forests and fields, the farms and estates that once buffered the town from Charlotte continue to feed the developers' maw. In the midst of this, like the descendants of Troy, we live and grow on top of the graves of the past, all the while digging our own.

* * *

My memories of the old town begin in the mid-1950s. It was a rough place to live. If you were a boy, you had to be ready to fight every time you left your house. I always hated it, but that was how it was. Still, we could roam the town, and the creek and riverbanks that ran through it, staying out into the night if we wanted to. There were not so many lost, creepy types lurking about. People were more connected because they did not hide behind televisions and computers, or escape into cell phone conversations, shutting out the rest of life. There were crowds on the streets, especially on Saturdays, when people came in from the country to buy supplies, when blind guitar players with harmonica racks filled the air with carnival-like music, and legless men sold pencils on the curb. There were clothing stores, groceries, car dealerships, hardware stores, drug stores that also sold books and magazines, and boardinghouses and hotels. As I look back, there was still much of the nineteenth century left around then—the places, the people, the customs.

In the center of it all stood the Gaston Theater, the whites-only movie-house where we white kids learned of another, bigger world. Open every day, even Sundays, the Gaston was a cultural center of sorts. Movies shown varied from lots of black-and-white B and C-grade westerns, war and horror movies, to blockbusters like *The Ten Commandments* or *The Bridge on the River Kwai*. And they weren't the first run, rather they made their second, third, or later rounds of the small towns, after the cities had shown them. There would also be some movies that we kids were not supposed to see: *Never on Sunday*, an Italian movie that I remember in particular, and about which I argued with the theater manager, dogging him hard about why I could not see this movie that promised lots of naked women and other good stuff in its preview. I never did see it.

The things I did see inside that damp, cinderblock building left lifelong impressions. It was where the fifty-foot woman first walked, and where Moby Dick wreaked havoc on the *Pequod*. I met Dracula there, Elvis, and John Wayne. I saw the incredible shrinking man become small enough to climb through the holes in a window screen into a treacherous and frightening nuclear age. It was where God wrote the Ten Commandments on a block of stone. It was where the Red Sea parted then closed again on Pharaoh's wicked army. And yes, Christ was crucified within those walls.

Sometimes there would be live performers, like Fred Kirby, Saturday-morning *Little Rascals Show* hero, yodeler, horse rider, guitar-banging cowboy. For several years in the '50s, a stage horror and magic show came through every summer, a guy named Kira Kum, who wore a turban and performed magic tricks for the crowd.

As I grew older, I grew cynical, harder to please, harder to fool with fakery and theatrics. I lost the child's ability to believe the unbelievable. I became serious and observant, thus mercilessly critical. Such was I, on a balmy spring evening in 1965, standing in my parents' front yard watching the mess that is our world

pass by, when my friend Shannon Williams walked up and told me that there was a movie with Chuck Berry in it playing at the Gaston. Now, that was something I liked. I had bought Chuck's greatest hits that past Christmas. It was a piece of magic. A black vinyl disc with the Chess logo. The first time I ever played it, when the pumping chords of "Nadine" had pushed out into the dusty light of my attic room, I had realized that if music could make me feel what Chuck Berry's music did, life could end up being a lot of fun. So hell yes, let us go forth and see this thing.

The theater was less than half a mile from my house. Within minutes we bought our tickets, sat down, and found ourselves watching *The TAMI Show*. Filmed in black and white, *The TAMI Show* was a rock 'n' roll concert staged in Santa Monica, California. The lineup included Chuck Berry, James Brown, the Rolling Stones, the Supremes, Gerry and the Pacemakers, Smokey Robinson and the Miracles, Marvin Gaye with the Blossoms, Lesley Gore, Billy J. Kramer and the Dakotas, the Barbarians, the Beach Boys, and others. We knew little more than that. I was there because of Chuck Berry, who to me will always be the King.

Chuck did play and he did not disappoint. Yet, as has often happened in my fortunate life, having come to see Chuck, I came away with more. I met the genius of James Brown. I had never heard of him until that evening, but I will never forget the way he moved around onstage as if unseen forces controlled him. This was a black man with a kind of power I had only seen in spiritual leaders like Daddy Grace or Father Divine. He came off as more than an entertainer, more than a dancing, singing crazy man. He was shamanistic, although I did not know or use such words then. He was like a witch doctor, summoning forces from the unnatural world, somewhat as Kira Kum had done in that same theater, but more convincingly. The spirits were in my body, my feet moving, my eyes fastened on his motion and my ears singing back with an unknown tongue that said *yeahhhh*. Watching this man tear it up onstage and drive the racially mixed on-screen audience into a frenzy was beyond anything I had ever seen. All of the rules of singing, dancing, performing were being broken before my eyes, and reassembled into something wonderful, more amazing than the Red Sea parting. I do not remember much of the other performances, even Chuck's. The Rolling Stones had the task of following James, and they did not look comfortable or confident. Easily understood.

It was common back then, if you liked a movie enough, or if you were having too good a time to leave, that you could stay for reruns. I did that Thursday. I went back to the theater the following Saturday for more. Unbeknown to me, and without any big deal being made of it, that Saturday was the first night that black people were ever allowed into the Gaston. Mount Holly had another theater, the Holly. It was strictly for blacks, just as the Gaston was for whites. The Holly sat across the railroad tracks and the highways that split the town. I am not sure what movies showed there. Probably the same stuff we saw, but later. I was white and I never went.

* * *

I never understood the racial thing. The few black people I knew were good people. When I heard others speak hatefully and angrily of niggers, I thought of these good people, and would usually offer an argument against that kind of thinking. I was branded a nigger-lover. Here on this Saturday night were more black people than I had ever seen except for a night several years earlier watching the Harlem Globetrotters and Meadowlark Lemon at the original Charlotte Coliseum (now Cricket Arena), or when driving through the heart of old Charlotte, down the old Independence Avenue that ran through long rows of houses and widely meandering streets.

In 1965 the Ku Klux Klan was very visible in our community. Rallies held in fields outside of town drew hundreds. Bizarre, crudely drawn, and slimy-feeling pamphlets and posters would spread from these rallies into the community. Blacks were portrayed as apes clutching terrified and beautiful white women in their hairy claws. Science was invoked to explain white superiority and the animal, subhuman nature of the black. Even teachers and coaches at the local high school supported and espoused the Klan's all-white version of America. It was natural, generational.

Where was all the hatred on this night? Where was the resistance to integration? Where was our little Governor Wallace standing in the schoolhouse door, or our Lester Maddox chasing blacks away from his restaurant with an ax handle? From my vantage, and perhaps just because I wanted it this way, there was a mutual respect and a harmony among the young people who shared the theater that night. It was a vastly younger audience than might have normally been there, so maybe our prejudices, fears, hatreds were not as fully entrenched and developed as our elders'. It is also an inescapable conclusion in my worldview that rock 'n' roll had the potential to cure us of the great ancestral curse of racism. Maybe I did not see the bad stuff, if it happened at all: fights in the alleyways, slurs in the bathrooms, insults in the back row. Not that night.

As the music proceeded on the big screen, a good and powerful energy built up. A youthful, celebratory exuberance took over the place. Walls had fallen and we knew it. At first, the black audience was quiet, shy, unsure; but as the show went on, they became very expressive and louder than we whites. Then, it was all one big hollering and yowling, big smiles, wild dancing, people of both races blissfully strutting and swaggering.

I do not know what had gone on at the Holly, but having grown up going to the Gaston, I, and all the white kids, knew that the manager had a crew of duck-tailed tough guys only too willing to rough up smaller kids as they ousted them for various offenses: yakking, laughing too loud, running up and down the aisles. But this night, there were so many people, both black and white, dancing, hollering, having fun, that I realized I would probably not get caught. Then another thought hit me: What the hell if I do?! It felt good to hoot and cheer as the acts on the screen rocked the joint. It felt like the sack of Troy, or the wild worshipping of Bael by the wayward Israelites, except there was no Moses, no need for one, to hurl nuclear-tipped God-engraved stone tablets into our midst. This was a feeling I have since felt a number of others times in my life when I chose to defy authority: civil disobedience at its most enjoyable.

The high point of that wild and liberated feeling came during Saturday night's last showing. James Brown was the instigator. Here he came again, just like he had during the other showings, wiggling and sliding and screaming and singing in a rich, far-ranging voice, riding the night train through Charlotte, begging, pleading, please, please! Falling and rising! I remember that the noise from the audience drowned out the music, that I turned around and looked behind me and I saw the writhing, dancing silhouettes of people—their race, their shading, their ancestry blurred and indistinguishable in the blue falling light from the projection booth. I felt a great, exhilarating hopefulness. We could get along. We could share rock 'n' roll. We could share America. We could share our towns, our lives to come, our history, our goodness. A powerful alchemy was brewing up. This particular movie actually became a part of our immediate life, and we became a part of its immediate life, and the life of a nation as it began to slouch toward its destiny.

It goes without saying that I was overly optimistic, the way idealists and dreamers can be. What I saw as hopeful and good, a proud moment in the life of my town, was seen by most others as a sign of impending damnation. Racism has never died. In many ways it is worse than ever. We can all share the facilities, but we still have our hatreds, our irrational fears, and our rational fears based on bad experiences with each other. Yet, in that moment, as James Brown left the stage, and the Gaston shook with our exuberance, the fights and race riots of later days, the hatred I would later encounter in blacks toward whites, the enduring motivations of racism in our politics and in our social functioning did not seem possible. I walked home that night knowing that I had seen the future and it was good. Evil would not triumph.

～～～

Acknowledgments

An anthology like *Making Notes* is truly a cooperative endeavor.

First and foremost, thanks to Amy Rogers, who liked my idea and worked tirelessly to see it through, and to Frye Gaillard of the Novello Festival Press Board, who also lent his talents as a writer to this effort. Special thanks, too, to Lisa Kline for all the research and Betsy Thorpe for her support.

I am very grateful to each and every person who submitted an essay or article—without the contributors, there would be no collection. Sincere thanks to Steve Stoeckel for the title and to Woody Mitchell, my guitar-playing knight. I must also thank Sharyn McCrumb, John Stanfield, Rev. Billy C. Wirtz, John Grooms and Fred Mills for their inspiration and support.

For always being there to help me tweak my writing efforts, I thank Terry Hoover, Cathy Anderson, Paula Connolly, Dana Griffith and Nancy Northcott. For support above and beyond, I thank Linda Luise Brown, David Walters, Donna Campbell, Georgann Eubanks, Dr. Tony Abbott and the Davidson Braintrust. For suggestions, connections and research, I am grateful to Dr. Tom Hanchett, Carole Thompson, Richard Thurmond and Sara June Goldstein of the South Carolina Arts Commission.

Thanks to my mom, Opal Wicker, for buying records for me and for letting me go see the Monkees (with opener Jimi Hendrix) when I was twelve.

Special thanks to the Spongetones for their music and their friendship: Jamie Hoover, Pat Walters, Steve Stoeckel and Rob Thorne, and to my Spongesisters, their wives: Linda Dennehy, Carol Koball, Linda Hutchinson and Donna Gamble-Thorne. And I can't forget to thank Ellen Adams Griffin, Amanda Sullivan and Bonny Frain for their companionship at many a show with additional thanks to Amanda and Tony Dagnall for my photos.

I also need to mention those who inspired me and who are with us in spirit: Rick Miller, Stuart Grasberg, Loonis McGlohon, Chip Crawford and my mother- and father-in-law, Joy and Bob Williams.

I would never have attempted this project if not for the support of my ever-patient husband and soulmate, Mark Williams.

List of Contributors

MALCOLM BAUMGART works with Mick Patrick, and they are consultants for Ace Records of London, England, for whom they compile the *Where the Girls Are* CD series.

CHARLES BLACKBURN JR. has written about North Carolina history, people and places for a number of publications. He received the 2008 Sam Ragan Fine Arts Award in Literature from St. Andrews Presbyterian College. Charles lives in Raleigh with his wife and daughter.

JERRY BLEDSOE is the author of twenty-two books, including several national bestsellers. He has been a columnist for the *Charlotte Observer* and *Greensboro News & Record* and a contributing editor of *Esquire*. He lives in Randolph County, N.C.

SAM BOYKIN worked as a reporter for Charlotte's alternative weekly *Creative Loafing* from 1998 to 2005. He's won sixteen journalism awards, including first place for Enterprise News Reporting and Feature Writing from the N.C. Press Association. Now a full-time freelance writer, he contributes to a number of local and national publications.

GRANT BRITT had decades of dirty jobs 'rassling jack hammers, unloading railroad cars, slinging groceries from hot dogs to French cuisine in joints from Key West to the Carolinas, to sustain his true love—writing. He thanks *Creative Loafing*, *Greensboro Daily News* and *NC Boating Lifestyle* for currently keeping him clean.

PHILLIP BROWN has worked with Rock and Roll Hall-of-Famers Martha Reeves & the Vandellas, Ben E. King, The Original Family Stone, The Four Tops, The Temptations, The Miracles, George Clinton & Parliament Funkadelic, Tito Jackson and Freda Payne. These and other acts have benefited immeasurably from Brown's public relations and marketing strategies and concepts.

DAVID CHILDERS lives and writes in Mt. Holly, N.C.

PETER COOPER is a senior music writer for the *Tennessean* newspaper in Nashville.

RICK CORNELL lives in Hillsborough, N.C., with his wife, son, daughter, dog, cat, and—as far as those five are concerned—way too many CDs and records. He is a regular contributor to *No Depression* and *The Independent Weekly*.

STEVE CRUMP is a reporter for WBTV and an independent documentary producer for WTVI, both in Charlotte. A winner of several regional Emmys, he's also won four National Headliner Awards and been named the NAACP Legal Defense Fund Humanitarian of the Year. The Smithsonian and others have showcased his documentaries.

TIMOTHY C. DAVIS, a native of Charlotte, has written for *Saveur, The Christian Science Monitor, Gastronomica, Mother Jones, Harp* and *Salon.com*, among other outlets. He's also an associate editor for *Gravy*, the official newsletter of the Southern Foodways Alliance. He's currently co-authoring a book celebrating the ten years of the SFA.

CLAIR DELUNE, a writer, researcher and professor of music history, chose Columbia, S.C., as home after living in seventeen states—none of which were despair. Since 1990, DeLune has produced and hosted the popular Blues Moon radio show ("Tuesday is Bluesday from 8 until late" at http://wusc.sc.edu).

JOE DEPRIEST is a reporter/columnist for the *Charlotte Observer*. A native of Shelby, N.C., he graduated from the University of North Carolina at Chapel Hill School of Journalism and has spent more than forty years as a Carolina journalist.

COURTNEY DEVORES has written about entertainment for thirteen years. She's been a regular freelance music writer for the *Charlotte Observer* for five years and has been published in *Non-Sport Update, Charlotte* and *No Depression,* among others. She lives in Charlotte with her husband, two dogs and three cats.

JACK DILLARD has been a professional writer in Charlotte for more than twenty-five years and is a published songwriter whose songs, co-written with Craig Fulton and Tom Dillard, were covered by Tommy Faile, Billy Scott, Carlton Moody & the Moody Brothers and The Filibusters.

DON DIXON has devoted his life to the popular song as a singer, songwriter, musician, producer and occasional actor.

MATT EHLERS writes feature stories for the *News & Observer* in Raleigh.

LYNN FARRIS is a Charlotte native, wife, mother and self-proclaimed concert addict, who spent most of her childhood at the original Charlotte Coliseum where her dad worked. She's written about music for local publications for almost twenty years, including five years at *Creative Loafing,* where she is still a regular contributor.

FRYE GAILLARD, a Charlotte journalist for more than thirty years, is now writer in residence at the University of South Alabama. He is the author of *Watermelon Wine: Remembering the Golden Years of Country Music.*

RICHARD GARRISON is a visual artist and lover of jazz whose work, including many paintings of jazz musicians, can be found in private and corporate collections worldwide. He lives in Raleigh with his wife, Van, and Spencer the dog.

JOHN GROOMS is an award-winning journalist and freelance editor and writer who lives in Charlotte.

DR. TOM HANCHETT has hosted roots music radio on WFAE Charlotte and WUNC Chapel Hill, written a history of Charlotte called *Sorting Out the New South City,* and curated the award-winning permanent exhibit *Cotton Fields to Skyscrapers* at Levine Museum of the New South, where he is staff historian.

JANET HARTMAN is a freelance writer of both nonfiction and fiction. A resident of North Carolina, she is best known for her articles about boating and life on the East Coast.

LEW HERMAN has lived in Charlotte since 1978. Creator of the Public Library's Charlotte Music Archive, he also started FireAntMusic.com, a widely distributed label of ethnic and regional music. His music and travel articles have appeared in *Creative Loafing* and elsewhere. He works as reference services librarian at Queens University of Charlotte.

PETER HOLSAPPLE is a songwriter and musician who lives in Durham. He's eternally grateful that he has never been a member of a terrible band. Yet.

MARJORIE HUDSON is author of *Searching for Virginia Dare,* a personal journey into North Carolina history. She was 2005 Artist in Residence at Headlands Center for the Arts in Sausalito, Calif. In a previous life, she booked musical acts, including such artists as Magpie, Tift Merritt, Robin and Linda Williams and Jeff Deitchman.

DAN HUNTLEY is a Charlotte native and columnist for the *Charlotte Observer,* where he has worked since 1982. He is the co-author of *Extreme Barbecue* (Chronicle Books). www.extremebarbecuethebook.com

JOHN JETER's novel, *The Plunder Room,* will be published by St. Martin's Press. A former newspaperman, Jeter holds a master's degree from Columbia University's journalism school. He co-owns The Handlebar, an award-winning concert hall; has appeared on Oprah; has traveled the world; and had a kidney transplant in 1984.

SI KAHN (www.sikahn.com) is executive director of Grassroots Leadership (www.grassrootsleadership.org), an organization working to abolish for-profit private prisons and to help establish a just and humane criminal justice/prison system. He has released fifteen CDs of his original songs and has been composer/lyricist for musicals at the Berkeley, Milwaukee and Tennessee Repertory Theatres, among others.

MARK KEMP, author of *Dixie Lullaby: A Story of Music, Race and New Beginnings in a New South* (Free Press, 2004), has served as music editor of *Rolling Stone*, vice president of music editorial at MTV Networks and entertainment editor at *The Charlotte Observer*. Kemp is a free-lance writer based in Charlotte.

BOB MARGOLIN is a blues guitarist and leads his own band. From 1975 to 1980, he played guitar in Muddy Waters' band and appeared with him at The Last Waltz, The Band's farewell concert, in 1976.

BAKER MAULTSBY is a freelance writer in Spartanburg, S.C. He also works in the marketing and communications office at Wofford College.

SHARYN MCCRUMB, a *New York Times* best-selling author, won a 2006 Library of Virginia Award and AWA Book of the Year for *St. Dale*. A 2008 "Virginia Women in History" honoree, McCrumb is known for her Ballad novels, including *She Walks These Hills*. A film of *The Rosewood Casket* is in production.

MARK MCGRATH is an attorney and freelance writer living in Chapel Hill. He writes for local magazines about subjects ranging from North Carolina history and culture to local sports. *North Carolina Lawyers Weekly* features his bi-monthly column, "The Practical Litigator." Mark is a founding partner of Jensen McGrath Podgorny, P.A.

BRENDAN MCKENNEDY lives with his wife and son in Charlotte. He plays clawhammer banjo, guitar, harmonica, and a bunch of other instruments, but he's a better dancer than he is an architect.

MICHAEL LEON MILLER was a writer for *The State* in Columbia, from 1986 to 2003. His book, *Hootie! How the Blowfish Put Pop Back Into Pop Rock* was published in 1997. A 2007 South Carolina Fiction Project winner, he's currently working on a collection of short stories.

FRED MILLS is the managing editor of *Harp* magazine as well as a contributor to scores of music-related publications, including *No Depression, Magnet* and *Stereophile*. A Tarheel by birth, he currently lives in Asheville, N.C. His seven-year-old son Eli's favorite singer is Johnny Cash.

WOODY MITCHELL is a retired copy editor/music writer for the *Charlotte Observer* and a guitarist who's played in bands since 1972 (Woody & the Wingnuts, Loafer's Glory, Stragglers, Lunatic Fringe and Maurice Williams & the Zodiacs). He and his wife, Rhonda, published *Synergy*, a monthly tabloid, in the 1990s.

MICK PATRICK works with Malcolm Baumgart, and they are consultants for Ace Records of London, England, for whom they compile the *Where the Girls Are* CD series.

DAVID PERLMUTT has been a journalist and profiled Carolinians for thirty years, the last twenty-six of those years at the *Charlotte Observer*. He has won numerous awards for his work.

KENT PRIESTLEY is the author, with Jon Elliston, of *North Carolina Curiosities* (Globe Pequot, 2007). He is a staff writer at the weekly paper, *Mountain Xpress*. He lives in Asheville with his cat, Peachy, and his dog, Russell.

K. MICHAEL PRINCE, born and raised in Greenville, S.C., attended Clemson University and later, the University of Virginia and the University of Munich. He currently lives with his family in Munich, Germany, where he writes and translates. His published works include *Rally 'Round the Flag, Boys! South Carolina and the Confederate Flag.*

SHEILA SAINTS received her MFA in Creative Writing from Queens University of Charlotte. An award-winning broadcast journalist, she has worked in the Carolina newsrooms of NBC News Nightside, WBTV, WFAE and FOX Charlotte. She has received writing grants from the N.C. Arts Council and the regional Arts & Science Council. She resides in Charlotte.

T. BROOKS SHEPARD is a Grammy-nominated jazz producer and music writer whose work has appeared in *Cigar Aficionado, The Boston Globe,* and *American Visions* magazine. He produced a number of Top Ten jazz albums including *Closer to the Source* with Dizzy Gillespie and Stevie Wonder.

JERRY SHINN, a former editorial page editor and associate editor at *The Charlotte Observer,* is author of several books, including *Loonis! Celebrating a Lyrical Life* and *A Great Public Compassion: The Story of Charlotte Memorial Hospital and Carolinas Medical Center.* The Charlotte native is married with two children and two grandchildren.

BLAND SIMPSON, Professor of English at UNC Chapel Hill, is a longtime member of the Tony Award-winning Red Clay Ramblers. He collaborated on the musicals *King Mackerel* and *Kudzu* and authored *Into the Sound Country* and *The Inner Islands.* Simpson received the 2005 North Carolina Award in Fine Arts.

JONATHAN SINGER started as a copywriter at CBS, New York. As a creative director he has won numerous awards for editorial and design. In 1998, he collaborated with Grammy-winner Cissy Houston on her autobiography, *How Sweet the Sound* (Doubleday). He lives in Charlotte where he continues as a ghostwriter.

CLYDE SMITH, PHD, authors *ProHipHop,* a hip-hop marketing and business news blog. Dr. Smith began graduate studies in 1992, following a ten-year career in the performing arts, culminating in a PhD in Cultural Studies in Education from Ohio State University in 2000. He currently resides in Raleigh.

ED SOUTHERN is the author of *The Jamestown Adventure, Parlous Angels* and a forthcoming book on the American Revolution in the Carolinas. He is the executive director of the North Carolina Writers' Network and lives in Charlotte.

SAM STEPHENSON, a native of Washington, N.C., is the director of the Jazz Loft Project at the Center for Documentary Studies at Duke University. He is the author of *Dream Street: W. Eugene Smith's Pittsburgh Project* (W.W. Norton, 2001) and is working on a biography of Smith for Farrar, Straus and Giroux.

STEVE STOECKEL is a writer, musician, electronics technician and amateur tango instructor residing in Charlotte with his wife, two cats and six thousand honeybees. He's best known for his work with N.C. band The Spongetones.

LORI K. TATE is a freelance writer and North Carolina native who lives in Cornelius, N.C., with her husband, John, and their tabby cat, Azalea. She writes for a variety of magazines in the state and relishes any opportunity to write about music and the performing arts.

TOMMY TOMLINSON is a local columnist for the *Charlotte Observer.* He was a finalist for the Pulitzer Prize in commentary in 2005. In 2004, *The Week Magazine* named him the best local columnist in America. He lives in Charlotte with his wife, Alix Felsing, and a hound dog named Fred.

MEG FREEMAN WHALEN teaches music history at Queens University of Charlotte. The former arts editor for *Charlotte* magazine, she is now the public relations manager for the Charlotte Symphony.

KEVIN WINCHESTER lives in Waxhaw, N.C., and holds an MFA in Creative Writing from Queens University of Charlotte. His writing has appeared in *Tin House, Gulf Coast, StorySouth, Southern Hum* and the anthology *Everything But the Baby.* Currently, he is Visiting Lecturer in the English Department at Wingate University.

REV. BILLY C. WIRTZ is a musician, columnist and host of a syndicated radio show. He is also a former special ed teacher and pro wrestling manager. He collects vintage cowboy boots and has a mayonnaise phobia. A South Carolina native, he currently lives in Cocoa Beach, Florida.

Index

Index of Song and Album Titles

NOVELLO FESTIVAL PRESS

Novello Festival Press, under the auspices of the Public Library of Charlotte and Mecklenburg County and through the publication of books of literary excellence, enhances the awareness of the literary arts, helps discover and nurture new literary talent, celebrates the rich diversity of the human experience, and expands the opportunities for writers and readers from within our community and its surrounding geographic region.

THE PUBLIC LIBRARY OF CHARLOTTE AND MECKLENBURG COUNTY

For more than a century, the Public Library of Charlotte and Mecklenburg County has provided essential community service and outreach to the citizens of the Charlotte area. Today, it is one of the premier libraries in the country—named "Library of the Year" and "Library of the Future" in the 1990s—with 24 branches, 1.6 million volumes, 20,000 videos and DVDs, 9,000 maps and 8,000 compact discs. The Library also sponsors a number of community-based programs, from the award-winning Novello Festival of Reading, a celebration that accentuates the fun of reading and learning, to branch programs for young people and adults.